WINESKIN

WINESKIN
FREAKIN' JESUS IN THE '60S AND '70S

A MEMOIR

MICHAEL HICKS

FOREWORD BY STEVEN L. PECK

SIGNATURE BOOKS | 2022 | SALT LAKE CITY

Cover design by Haden Hamblin.

FIRST EDITION | 2022

LIBRARY OF CONGRESS CONTROL NUMBER: 2022945766

Paperback ISBN: 978-1-56085-453-1
Ebook ISBN: 978-1-56085-428-9

CONTENTS

FOREWORD

I can't recall when I first met Michael Hicks. I must have run into him years ago at some event or another in my career at BYU. However, I do remember my first encounter with him as a person whom I had to get to know better. One day, as he was cleaning off some of his office shelves, he called to ask if I wanted his copy of the two-volume set of Alfred Russel Wallace's autobiography, *My Life*. As the co-discoverer of the theory of evolution by natural selection with Darwin, Wallace was a hero of mine, so much so that I had visited his insect collection at the British Museum, had a sizable collection of biographies about him, and nearly all of his published works. Despite this fascination, I only had a photocopy of his then out-of-print autobiography. Of course, the first question that came into my mind was, Why did Michael Hicks have a copy of this work? My second question was, How soon could I pick it up?

I had never been to Michael's office. I knew of his work, of course. I found his published poetry fantastic. I was familiar with his historical work in Latter-day Saint music, like his history of the Mormon Tabernacle Choir. There was also a brilliant collection of his singing and lectures on YouTube. But it was not until I walked into his office that I realized here was a kindred spirit—a philosopher of assemblages of meaning. The office was alive with colors from shelves of books, vinyl LPs, signed concert posters, stacks of CDs, awards, signed copies of art and photographs, book covers, his own delightful artwork (and that of his mother, whom you will meet in this book). It was not cluttered, but a carefully curated space alive with representations of the multiple contexts condensed from his life. Clearly, an exemplar of someone adept at pulling the marrow from life, as Thoreau recommended. I knew I was looking at the iceberg-tip of a creative, artistic, and curious mind. There was a bold aesthetic joy to the place. A rare genius with multiple interests. No wonder he had the autobiography of Alfred Russel Wallace.

Hicks served as Professor of Music in the division of Composition and Theory in the School of Music at Brigham Young University since 1985. Beside his training hundreds of students—many of them to become professorial colleagues—the breadth of his creative works and scholarship is startling. Michael has had performances of his chamber music around the country and is widely known as a musicologist, composer, and performer. To the Latter-day Saint audience, he will be immediately known for the vital work in the history of music in the church—including his recent Signature Books release, *Spencer Kimball's Record Collection: Essays on Mormon Music*, which is delightful. But don't try to pigeonhole him. He's also written a book on '60s rock and academic papers on everything from John Cage to animals' love of music. He has published a stunning list of scholarly work in the field's top journals. But wait. He's also a poet —his psalms are some of my favorite reasons to follow him on Facebook (or whatever it's called these days).

But these are not the reasons to read this book, although they should set your sights on the excellence and clarity of the writing you are about to read. You should read this book because he has lived a wildly exciting and almost unbelievable and surprising life. Or maybe I should say fantastical life because if I tried to write these events in a novel, you would say that I've gone too far and have not portrayed a realistic enough character even for the magical realism I write. I can rarely say of a biography, "I could not put it down." I could not put this one down. Michael Hicks's life story is marvelously compelling. Every life plays out in a sequence of accidents, misdirection, choices, chance meetings, opportunities granted and denied, and the pull of the Tao into places unexpected and uncanny. But here? Get ready. There are many surprises ahead.

I can't think of a better way to announce his book than selectively quoting Nephi 1:1 of his own playful version of the Book of Mormon: "Why write this book? ... I've gone through a lot of crap and that always makes for good reading [and] along the way God's put his thumb on the scales for me over and over. So, thinking that by now I know something of both his favor and caprice—sometimes the same thing—I decided it's time to write". (*The Street-Legal Version of Mormon's Book*).

And, oh, my, are we blessed he did.

Steven L. Peck
BYU Associate Professor of Biology and recipient
of the 2021 Smith-Pettit Foundation Award for
Outstanding Contribution to Mormon Letters

ACKNOWLEDGMENTS

A third of the people I want to acknowledge for helping me write this didn't want me to write this. Another third of them divide into four groups: people who wonder why I didn't mention them, people who wonder why I did, people whose names I changed, and people whose names I didn't. The reasons for doing any of those things I take full responsibility for.

The last third, the people I *will* acknowledge, are: Ron Barney, Darius Gray, and Curt Bench, who urged me to tell all this stuff about myself, thinking it might give consolation to readers whose path was, like mine, not the "beaten" one. Monica Grant, who reminded me of stuff from the Wineskin days proper (or improper). Brian Harker, who counselled me about proportion and tone. Jeremy Grimshaw, who has always patted the back of my prose and/or bravery. Gary Bergera and Ron Priddis, who reached out their hands on behalf of Signature Books, hoping I'd fill those hands with pages worth reading. And Steven Peck, for writing a foreword that serves as a fitting "advance epilogue."

Last of all, the clientele likely to be the most embarrassed and yet, I hope, heartened, by these reminiscences: my wife, Pam, our four children, their children, et al. The LDS Church published so many "faith promoting stories" under that rubric in the nineteenth century. This is a latter-day one of those. Readers may differ about whether mine's a faith worth promoting, but I'd stack it up against other contestants any day of the Millennium.

Nor do people put new wine into old wineskins; otherwise the wineskins burst, and the wine pours out and the wineskins are ruined; but they put new wine into fresh wineskins, and both are preserved.

—Matthew 9:17 (New American Standard Bible)

PREFACE

Jesus is not a crime. You might think so for all the crimes committed with his name on the case files. But, as we used to sing in the early '70s at our Christian coffee house called The Wineskin: "He's done so much for me, I cannot tell it all." He has. And I can't. In a universe whose moorings keep shifting, whose pylons keep getting knocked out, I can't get over Jesus and the hurtling, chrome-plated ride my life has been with him as the backseat driver in my head. Or—sorry to have mixed my metaphors there—the helmsman. I think of a postcard my mom had taped to her refrigerator: a painting of a stolid, unruffled, robed and bearded Jesus at the oar of a midnight ship, waves jutting around it like giant shark fins. His moonlit face, the image of what we all secretly craved in high school, looked blank in the best way: blankness as peace. I still feel that peace from him, although, as you can see, I don't capitalize his pronoun anymore. Because, to get back to where I started, I've appointed myself the lead detective on his still-suspicious role in my life and the life of so many friends. He's the man at the oar, yes, but also, everlastingly, a "person of interest." So I'm on the case. What follows are the facts as best I can glue them together.

1. GENESIS

I slept in a crib until I was almost 4. I'd climb into it, then Mom would swing up the side and fasten it. One night I woke up and, through the shadows of the room, saw the closet door slide open and a man-sized creature stand up in it, slowly walk to the crib and crouch beside it with his head down so I couldn't see it. When I leaned to look down through the bars, he lifted his head, grabbed the bars and shook them, roaring at me, his eyes glowing. I covered my head with the blanket, happy that the bars were there to protect me.

That's my earliest memory. Meeting the devil.

It might have been one of my half-brothers pulling a trick on me. Maybe even a stunt by my dad, who, it turned out, wasn't actually my dad. But whoever it was, I never forgot that night. It's the reason I slept with a blanket over my head, kept a light on in the hallway, and left the bedroom door open until I was in junior high.

When I was nineteen, I recounted the event to my first Mormon Sunday school teacher. She said it meant the devil knew I was one of God's "young lions" and he was enraged I'd finally come to Earth. A comforting thought, enthralling, even, to a middle-class loner nerd like me. Also a nice line in the script for grooming me to join her living-room-sized D-list polygamy cult.

But I'm getting ahead of myself. Forgive me. Sometimes it's like I'm flooring it in a motorboat, staring back over my shoulder at the wake.

If anyone should have been a target of the devil, it was my mom, Marilyn. She grew up in Santa Paula, California, second daughter of a schoolteacher-turned-banker and a petite, frizzy-haired water-colorist. For a few years you could see the two of them with their neighbors in the cover photo of Santa Paula Presbyterian's weekly bulletin. Lyall Dustin Webster was a deacon at the church and, like his newspaper editor dad, a Tom Dewey conservative in politics but gum-chewing witticist about everything else. Gladys Viola Armstrong Webster, a standard-bearer in the Ventura School of Artists, trained her two daughters, June and Marilyn, in horticulture and natural-food nutrition. If you wonder who was buying all those Adelle Davis books in the 1930s–40s, look no further than Gladys's shelves. There you'd find the dietary canon of the Webster family—Lyall, Gladys, June, and Marilyn, with their two cats, Pete and Repeat, running underfoot and hunting birds in the orange grove down the road.

By the time World War II ended, Marilyn's head brimmed with sermons and Bible verses she'd learned in church and at her parents' hearth. With high school diploma in hand she headed for college to study art, though not Gladys's naturalist landscape brand of it. Marilyn wanted to draw and paint for fashion magazines, travel posters, and road maps. By 1950, right after graduating in art at San Jose State, she landed a job with the largest American map company, Gousha, headquartered not far from campus.

She started attending the adobe and red-tile-roofed First Baptist Church in downtown San Jose where she met a young divorcé, a skinny railroad switchman with three sons who all lived with their mom. Neil Hicks was not only muscly, with a sun-beaten face, but a "good Christian man," who kept his membership card current by attending church each week. The beams in his and her smiles at their wedding in June 1951 nearly shorted the camera's light meter.

Two months into their marriage, Neil's first wife dropped the boys off at the newlyweds' one-bedroom apartment and renounced her charge of them. Marilyn became an instant hands-on stepmother of three young boys. She quickly learned why they should not have been in Neil's house. The shouting and screaming at the boys provoked more than one police call from neighbors. Marilyn's idyll of a quiet pairing with good-Christian-man Neil got torn down almost overnight.

She thought having a child of their own might settle Neil down. But he'd had a vasectomy after the third of his boys was born. In 1955 he tried to get it reversed, but the fix failed. So he and Marilyn went to Dr. Lewis Michelson, an OBGYN at Stanford Medical School who'd done "donor insemination" since the mid-1940s. He set one up for her at his San Francisco sperm bank. She miscarried.

He set up a second one, and, *voilà*, I came to exist. Marilyn and Neil—Mom and Dad—chose the name Michael Dustin Hicks, the first name probably the most popular that year in the USA and the middle name the same as her dad's, he being a descendant of the infamous Indian-butcher Hannah Dustin. As for the last name, babies produced from donor insemination still lived in legal limbo. So it was as if I were pre-adopted, but off the books, born a Gemini, but living a double life before it even started.

Raising another woman's sons alongside her own, Mom tried to be the heartbeat of Jesus in our home. That heart pounded most loudly in her art. Both our house and First Baptist were well-stocked with Mom's imagery. She did other art, of course, including drawings of California missions for Gousha—themselves a bankshot off her overtly religious art. But what lingers most in my memory are drawings she did of Nativity scenes for church bulletins, the huge banner of Jesus' crucifixion and resurrection that hung in the Easter services each year at the San Jose Civic Auditorium, her huge pastel knockoff of Sallman's portrait of Christ that hung in the chapel, her two pastels of Jesus that hung in our living room—another Sallman copy and one of the Gethsemane prayer—and her drawings of First Baptist's exterior, which appeared on everything from an LP of the church's choirs to the church directory to a trivet the church mass-produced and used for birthday gifts. Unlike the blue-collar he-men she preferred, her Jesuses were always soft and, except for the beard, androgenous. We lived in the afterclap of the American 1950s and this Soft Jesus was standard issue.

If Mom was Jesus' heartbeat, Dad was Jesus' whip. He could be tender and solicitous. But the sword of Damocles always hung from those traits. Something buried in his Kansas childhood under bootlegger parents mingled with Solomon's alleged wisdom: "Blows that wound cleanse away evil" and beatings "make clean the innermost parts." He used quotes like that to justify naked-butt belt-whipping and similar degradations. Two of my half-brothers were the chief targets. Mom shielded me from him as best she could.

Dad took me to church each week with Mom, often with a transistor radio in his pocket, the earplug wired up to his right ear to listen to pro games of baseball and football. But he had two side-religions

3

With Mom in 1960.

that I remember best. One was Freemasonry, which he subscribed to for pragmatic reasons: by being a member of that secret society he could get special treatment from fellow Masons. The other was a one-man faith system he called "finesse." Let me explain that.

He sometimes took me to the railroad yard and let me ride in the engines or sit in the shanty while he and his co-workers played pinochle. One day I asked him how he was able to get paid for playing pinochle. He asked me back, "Do you know what finesse is?" I said no. He said, "The woman over in that building who makes the assignments looks at all the things that need to be done—this car needs to go on that track, that car needs to be hooked onto a car on that other track, and so on. She decides that all these things add up

One of Mom's large pastel drawings of Jesus that presided
in our house before she and Dad split up in 1965.

to a full day of work. My job is to see how I can do all those things
in the least number of moves, so that I can spend the rest of my shift
playing pinochle. And that's finesse." That was how he wanted to
live—to get everything done in the least number of moves. Which
could mean simple and efficient or, just as easily, cruel and deceptive.

When I was two years old, I became a celebrity at First Baptist
because of my talon-like memory: Mom took me to the pulpit to
recite John 3:16, the scriptural amulet of Protestants everywhere.
I can't remember when I didn't know that verse. And my earliest
memories of other scriptures come from John, too. One night I had
jumped out of my crib and run to Mom's bedside for fear the devil
might be hiding in my closet again and she read to me, "Peace I leave
with you, my peace I give unto you," etc., from John 14. I also recall
having to memorize John 1:1–5 for a gold star in Sunday school,
though the connection with Jesus ("The Word") in those verses was
pretty abstract. I memorized them fine, but that was probably when

I first realized that this religion was wrapped in mysteries I had no spare attention span to solve.

You see, unlike my mom, I had no feel for "the Lord" beyond that title's attachment to Sundays, holidays, and the stock nightly prayer: "Now I lay me down to sleep / I pray the Lord my soul to keep / And if I die before I wake / I pray the Lord my soul to take." That was the routine for Baptist kids: pray and go to sleep but confess that you might never wake up. So Jesus was the vault you hid in till death came and opened the door and hauled you away to heaven—your soul, at least. Whatever that was.

My earliest two encounters with death involved hamsters and an uncle I'd never met. For two weeks I tended two hamsters Dad had bought me, fed them, enjoyed their tiny fingernails scuttering in my hand. But one night we decided to move their cage out of the kitchen onto the back porch. It must have been too cold for them, because when I went to feed them in the morning, both were dead, hard as rocks. I was dumbstruck and grieved for almost as long as I'd owned them. Then Dad's brother George died. I went with my parents to a funeral home in Los Gatos where George's body was lying in an ornate, polished open box made of dark wood. I'd never seen him before in my life and was shocked to see him in a box, face-painted and stiff as a mannequin—although Mom assured me he wasn't really there: George was in heaven, despite the evidence before me.

That funeral home was lit about the same as First Baptist's creaking dark wood chapel, whose services I recall only in shards. The first Sunday of each month we had "communion," which offered doughy pellets as "bread" and tiny cups of unfermented grape juice as "wine." I looked forward to that wine eagerly, because we never got grape juice at home, just orange and tomato. Meanwhile, when the pastor droned through his sermons, I'd stare at the inside covers of the hymnbook, with all the different kinds of "amens" you could sing. I never got to hear the choir sing the sevenfold amen, which I couldn't decipher in my head but seemed like the gold standard.

I did love going to Sunday school, though, because they always gave out candy, had flannelboard stories, and spent the rest of the time singing and memorizing scriptures, both of which I was good at. The Top Three songs were "Jesus Loves Me," "Jesus Loves the

A First Baptist directory with Mom's cover illustration of the church.

Little Children," and "Fairest Lord Jesus." So Jesus for the win. We also got to learn the "Romans Road," assorted verses snipped from the Book of Romans that charted Paul's how-and-why-to-get saved spiel, beginning with Romans 3:23. (Look it up; I don't need to.) With sugar, melody, and memorization, Sunday school was like a parallel universe—although that was a concept you'd never hear about in Sunday school.

Whether the Big Meeting in the vast chapel or the little meetings in kids' classrooms, most of what I was supposed to remember *at* church I've forgotten. I mostly remember scenes *after* church. Like the time I peed in the backseat ash tray because Mom and Dad were talking to friends and I couldn't hold it any longer. Or staring every week out the backseat window of our Impala at the 88-Cent Store marquee, wishing I could go inside. Or looking up at the mammoth

"Jesus Saves" neon signage on First Baptist's steeple, which lit up at night like a vagrant lighthouse.

One after-church memory is more fleshed out, probably because it involved food. Mom and Dad often took me to Smorgy's restaurant when church ended, usually without my teenage half-brothers. I was indifferent to smorgasbord food except fried chicken, which they had crates of and I gobbled up like a hog at the trough. When the meal was over and Dad paid the cashier, I got to pick from a trunkful of Made-in-Japan trinkets next to the cash register. That made going to Smorgy's like walking into a giant box of Cracker Jack. And when we walked out, the carpet in the shopping center was dotted with stepped-on pieces of popcorn from the machine at Sears, which I peeled up and shoved in my mouth when my folks weren't looking.

There was church at church and there was church on TV. To be honest, I felt more divinity in the God that descended into our home on invisible airwaves. TV church came in two brands, the home brand and the scary brand. I found myself drawn to the scary brand—the Oral Roberts grab-'em-by-the-scalp healing type. I watched with boyish dread the close-ups of desperate people commanded in a southern drawl to "Heal! In Jesus' name!" I mimicked it as if I were in a play when no one was looking. But I knew it didn't suit our home brand, either in format or camerawork. The home brand was Billy Graham revival meetings: singing by the statuesque choir, pep-talks by slicked-up second-string deacons, charisma-soaked Graham preaching statesmanlike threats of damnation, and those in the audience, now feeling duly threatened by God, walking up to the altar to "accept Jesus into their hearts as their personal Savior." These Billy Graham stadium events were dismally formulaic. They lacked Roberts' energy and incandescent hijinks. Nevertheless, watching Graham revivals helped school me in how to go up to the altar myself. Which I did one Sunday during the end-of-meeting altar call at First Baptist. Dad pushed me into the aisle, and I officially accepted Jesus into my heart. With him now officially installed, I was ready for baptism.

The baptistry at First Baptist sat above the choir seats on the stand, so the congregation could see the baptizee's head before it got dunked. After donning a white robe, I walked down the few steps into the water. I was relieved that it was so much warmer than I'd expected, almost like a kettle on a low simmer. The pastor, Dr. Clarence Sands, put a handkerchief over my mouth and nose, then laid me back in the water "in the name of the Father, and of the Son, and of the Holy Ghost."

When it was over, we went to Smorgy's then returned home to what had become my imaginary forest: dark green curtains lining the living room, with a lit black and white TV illuminating the Hicks campsite. By its light I built houses, then forts, then mansions, out of worn-out playing cards from the discard pile of Dad's Southern Pacific pinochle games. I watched *Captain Kangaroo* every morning and westerns at night—*Gunsmoke*, *Wyatt Earp*, *Wagon Train*, *Bat Masterson*, and *Cheyenne*. The only one I didn't like was Dad's favorite, *Bonanza*. It was about a dad and his three or four sons, depending on the season.

In 1961 I turned five. Mom decided not to send me to kindergarten but to Alameda Day School, a pre-school on her route to Gousha, which had just rehired her. Alameda's director, Caroline, thought I and two others, Todd and David, were smarter than the other students. So a few minutes after post-lunch nap time began, she'd sometimes spirit us away to art galleries, dinosaur bone exhibits, the Rosicrucian Egyptian Museum, and one-of-a-kind events like the downtown open-air showing of John Glenn's space capsule on its twenty-stop world tour. After waiting in line, we walked up the stairs of its scaffold, and all I could think was how puny this bucket was, a tenth the size it was in my mind. How could anyone stand to be in it for more than five minutes? I got a chill. I had never understood claustrophobia before, despite my longtime crib caging.

I had my first crush at Alameda: Cathy. "Crush" was more literal than you'd think. Our playground had a small corral filled with wooden orange crates. I goaded Todd and David into pulling the crates out of the corral, letting me climb into it, then piling them back on top of me. My grand plan was to cry out from under the crates to get Cathy to swoon with pity and help lift the crates off me. I assumed she'd buy the idea that I'd been trapped there by accident, that the crates had somehow fallen on me.

When Todd and David begged Cathy to help rescue me, she laughed and walked off with her mini-entourage. My pals dutifully dug me out, though not before getting yelled at by Caroline for their apparent *Lord of the Flies* savagery. They protested that I'd *made* them pile crates onto me. I confirmed that. It was my one George Washington moment. "I cannot tell a lie: I begged them to pile the orange crates on me in the corral." God must have loved my honesty.

I learned something else at pre-school about crushes: that your mom could be in one, too. One day when she picked me up at Alameda, a man was sitting in the front passenger seat beside her. I got in the back seat and they kept talking, his hand on her headrest, stroking the back of her hair. She told me this was her friend from work. After a few minutes he got out and walked to his car parked up the block. We drove home and I knew this was some other kind of TV show.

By fall of 1962 I was six and ready for first grade. There was only one hitch: Dad had already taught me how to read. When I was going to Alameda, he trained me at night in phonics. I picked it up quickly, although I refused to accept that the "PH" in "PHONO" on the entertainment console was pronounced like an "F." Once I got good at reading, I studied volume after volume of our *Golden Book Encyclopedia*, along with fantasy books like *Doris and the Trolls* and even Christian self-help snoozers like Pat Boone's *Twixt Twelve and Twenty*. I was now getting a crush on the printed word, which Dad also had, at least in the form of crossword puzzles, anagrams, and obscure definitions. I browsed through the Webster's dictionary a lot, too, partly because my Mom was a Webster, supposedly related to Noah Webster, and partly because of Oakland TV personality "Mayor Art." Every weekday afternoon he signed off his kids show by saying, "I'll be seeing you …" upon which the chorus of kids on the set yelled "Subsequently!" From the first time I heard that, words of four or more syllables were my new prey, ready to be read and, whenever possible, used in a sentence.

The first week of first grade we learned the spelling of words for colors, using Crayola crayons to fill in pictures of ducks and flowers and chairs and balls. As the second week began, I asked the teacher when we were going to start *reading*. She sent me to her boss who had me reading out of different grade-level readers and, when I could read the word "mountain" in the "difficult words" section in the back of the fourth-grade reader, she decided I needed to skip to second grade. I got excited because my next-door friend, Robbie—a Catholic, Dad always reminded us—was in that second-grade class. I'd only seen him on the playground during recess. My heart beat noticeably faster as I walked into his classroom and we grinned at each other. Reunited. The problem was that I knew nothing about arithmetic. I was an academic mutt, a mix-breed of prodigy and dummy. I won spelling bees but barely passed math. Oh, and I couldn't print letters, either, just read them.

For all three terms of the school year, our second-grade teacher, Miss Kadri, gave me C's in handwriting, physical education, art, and music. I got B's in science and health. My only A's were in reading, language, spelling, and history. On the progress report she gave Mom at year's end she wrote that my reading *aloud* needed work. Also, "Lately he is trying to put 'fancy' curves on letters. This must be discouraged." Worst of all, "He does not concentrate as he should. Fails to complete all his work." Overall, though, "He has made a good adjustment" to being thrown from the horsey pasture of first grade into the lion's den of second.

What bothered me more than Miss Kadri's critiques, though, was that the other boys in my class had an extra year of growth on me. And sports were the state religion of grade school. In that I was something of a heretic playing a saint. I wanted so bad to compete, but I was skinny and uncoordinated. Mike Whitney gave me the nickname "Fishy" because he said I handled the ball in foursquare like a fish. (I still don't know what that means.) I was good at playing army, though. I had a war surplus helmet and knew all the lingo from the TV show *Combat*, which I'd bark out like Vic Morrow. My barking-soldier shtick was part of the tough-guy persona I hoped would allure my second crush: Jan Emery, a beautiful, smart blonde in our class. But there was yet another Michael, a year older, who had a crush on her, too. One day, as Jan and we two Michaels stood in line for an assembly, he started playing with the back of her hair. She liked it and I thought, "Oh, yeah, I saw this show."

❀

Third grade with Miss Charter, my grades got stirred around like chunks in a stew. I got C's in handwriting, science, health, physical education, art, and music; B's in history, reading, language, and spelling. Yet, somehow, I got really good at arithmetic and I went from C's to A's. I remember Charter's class, though, mainly because I sat behind Ed, who had a knack for double entendre, innuendo, and wordplay. Every time he thought something sounded potentially dirty, gory, or taboo, he'd turn his head around and grin. I grinned back and sometimes cracked a joke in his ear. But Ed became my third-grade Judas when he dared me to spell "fuck" on the spelling toy we had in the cabinet. I did, showed it to him, and he ratted me out to Miss Charter. She sent me to the school psychologist who grilled me about why I would do such a thing. I wanted to tell him that (a) it was just a word and (b) no word was a foreigner to my lexicon. Besides, it wasn't taking the Lord's name in vain, about which I'd been warned since before my John 3:16 pulpit stunt.

A few weeks later, I compounded my crime by writing what I thought were the words to *Louie, Louie* for a girl who begged me to do that. My lyrics not only included "fuck" but "boner." Miss Charter caught me handing the slip of paper to the girl, which led to my second trip to the school psychologist. I was seven years old and already a repeat offender for cuss words.

Sending me to the psychologist would have made more sense for other reasons. I had developed an obsession with weirdness. Start with my fascination with Oral Roberts. Or my crate stunt with Cathy. Or befriending Ed at all. And obviously, the devil in the closet. But those only scratched the surface.

There was my monster obsession. At 3:30 every Tuesday and Thursday afternoon, Channel 7 played a monster-based B-movie on its afternoon show called *Chillers from Science Fiction*. I watched, even studied, *Invasion of the Saucer Men, Kronos, Them, Man with X-Ray Eyes, Reptilicus, Attack of the 50-Foot Woman* … I could go on and on. They're soldered into my brain. None of the classics, mind you. No *Frankenstein*. Just *Son of Frankenstein* and *House of Frankenstein* and *Abbott and Costello Meet Frankenstein*. Deep-limbic-system kitschy horror for free at 3:30 in the afternoon. And even then I knew that my monster fetish and First Baptist weren't that far apart. Every

12

An avid fan of monster movies, I got my friends Robby and Skippy to tear up bedsheets and wrap me like a mummy for my seventh birthday.

Sunday we pretended to drink blood, like vampires. Or celebrated a man who rose from the grave, like a zombie. Or even had the doctrine of being transformed into a "new creature," which werewolves did with every full moon. Not to mention that word "creature" itself.

My imagination was also pricked by *The Twilight Zone*. That series initiated me into so much I thought I needed to know of the universe, but always its most terrifying dimensions. Indeed, *dimensions* were what many of the episodes in the series dwelt on: people living in one scale of size, not knowing that they were actually much larger or smaller than some other kind of people above or below them. There was also the big "reveal" at the end of each episode, which was all I knew or needed of revelation. Like church, it was terror and inspiration at once. It took me years to get over the *Twilight Zone*, especially that haunting fear that intelligent life in the universe

13

was not at human scale, but had a range of scales, maybe an infinite range. Where God was in that spectrum, I had no clue.

My devotion to *Chillers from Science Fiction* and *Twilight Zone* were symptoms of an even larger breach in my brain, some might say. I had a crush on the scurrilous, the uncouth, the cheap, the grisly. I collected monster cards I got in packs of bubble gum. I bought or "found" every copy of *Famous Monsters of Filmland* and *Castle of Frankenstein* I could lay my hands on. By the end of my stint with Miss Kadri, I'd started climbing into paper recycle bins, office dumpsters, even neighbors' garbage cans looking for bizarre leftovers, from thrown-out *National Enquirers* to *Playboys* to *Mad* to cheesy half-size mags about celebs and politicos, 7-inch records, and anything that reeked of World War II or Korea. I had this burning instinct to archive the offscouring of suburbia, store it under the bed or in the corner of the closet, next to my scary friend.

And then there was magic. I watched the *Magic World of Alakazam* on TV religiously and, after some begging, Dad took me to the Ali Kamar Magic Shop in downtown San Jose, a few doors down from the Fox theater where I went as many Saturdays as I could. The man and woman who ran Ali Kamar demonstrated lots of tricks they had for sale. I was spellbound. Dad bought me some; I practiced and clumsily tried them out on family and friends. Card tricks, too, which I learned from books, although I spent ten times more hours building those houses of cards on the living room floor than practicing my card magic. I even tried some escape artistry, getting half-brothers to tie me up and then allow me to escape. That turned out not to be in my skill set. Or, let's say, tying me up too tight was in *their* skill sets.

One artifact of my weirdness in those days was my cursive letter to Santa, December 2, 1964:

Dear Santa,
I would like a Strombecker Road Racing Set. This would be my choice for Christmas. If I had one I would do this with it: First I'd go to the library. I would look for a book called Methods of Shrinking Heads Among Savages. Then I'd shrink myself. After that I would get in the car, drive through the hall and tear up the house.
Yours Truly,
Mike Hicks

I was assigned to write that letter to Santa by my fourth-grade teacher, Miss Gallagher, who wrote in response: "Be sure you don't just shrink your head by accident or you'll really be in trouble!" You see, she and I had a thing for each other. She got me. That *simpatico* between us was the fuel for the torch I carried for Miss Gallagher most of the year. And I already loved the name "Gallagher" from the Disney *Wonderful World of Color* series called, yes, *Gallagher*. My report cards from her spilled over with A's.

But the two incidents I remember most from her class were a spelling bee and one more trip to the school psychologist.

In our fourth-grade spelling bee that spring we got down to the final two contestants, which, as usual, included me. My female nemesis was powerful and the class was oooing and ahhing as we battled it out. When she stumbled on her last word it was my turn. Miss Gallagher turned to me and said, "For the win: your word is 'Czechoslovakia.'" The class giggled and oooed again. But, you see, the world map had been down in front of the room for most of the term. I had stared at it every day for months and that country's name was so *weird* I'd imprinted my memory with it. So, even though the map was now rolled up, without skipping a beat, I said, "c-z-e-c-h-o-s-l-o-v-a-k-i-a, Czechoslovakia." I won and the class cheered.

Within a few weeks, the intercom speaker came on and the tin voice of the front office secretary said, "Mike Hicks, please come to the psychologist's office." The class oooed again, though at a much lower pitch, almost growling. They knew my checkered past. I marched off to the psych's office where he gave me this weird test. I had to deduce things—what's missing from this picture, what's the shortest path from this to that, what should be the next number in this sequence, weird puzzly stuff that seemed pulled straight out of the tool chest in my skull. A couple of weeks later my parents got a letter that said I needed to transfer in the fall to a school across town where they'd made up a program for "gifted" children.

Unfortunately, to switch my schools was one of the few things Mom and Dad could agree on. Because Mom was about to switch homes, leaving Dad pining in that green-curtained living room as he handwrote short letters that both adored and denounced her.

2. EXODUS

One morning in August 1965, a month before I started fifth grade, Mom told me to pack my things. She was taking me to live with her in an apartment a few blocks away. She didn't say why. I later found a letter written right before the move in which Dad promised he'd gotten rid of the gun and shells and that there'd be "no future escapades like that" or of the "despair" that the gun incident, whatever that was, had caused. He almost chirped about how much his "counseling" with Pastor Sands was helping. "I offer you a home of a completely different physical nature," he wrote, especially now that his two older sons had moved out and the third was on his way to Vietnam.

But Mom had had enough.

In more letters, Dad took another tack. *Divorce*, he insisted, "has but one meaning. This being self before God or purely God second. I'm guilty of putting God second, but only to you." He couldn't sleep because he knew she was violating God's will by leaving. "God means for you to be here," "you owe God the position you hold as a wife and mother," and so forth, honing his hard-edged pledges to change for her. In note after herky-jerky note, he invoked "God" more times than I ever heard him do when we all lived together.

And what was she doing to her son by depriving him of a father? "What goes on in those sharp wits of his? Remember his mind is far ahead of his years." She'd pay for wrecking me. "I cannot understand how you, the most unselfish person I have ever known, have suddenly become so different, so changed, so unwilling to wait and try our life. I know what a broken home is, what it means to lose everything dear yet, when I think of revenge, as it is only human to do, I remember Pastor's statement. 'Let God do it. He knows better how.'"

With her eternal harm to me as the subtext, he wrote Mom

17

awkward, rhyming poems. One long one, "The Parting," ended with these lines:

A son grown up without a dad
one day will question you,
And dad will tell his now grown son
Unwanted, love so true.

But then the wounds, from damage done
One day will heal up fine.
And in your heart a hurt should live,
Those broken vows of thine.

So go your way, so have your fun.
Regret you may endure
From running from the one kind man
Whose love for you was pure.

Yet God, in all, will see your deed.
His watchful eye will know
Your very heart, this unkind deed
of love you won't bestow.

Tucked into his mild threats of divine retribution were demands that she pray harder about returning. Because it was God's will for her to come back, he was sure of it.

She was just as sure it wasn't. God had "led" her out of that home. But now she was wringing her hands about Jesus' declaration that marrying after divorce was de facto adultery. She talked with her sister about it, Pastor Sands, too, and, of course, her parents.

In October 1965, within the week after she filed for divorce, Mom got separate letters from her parents. Lyall's, as usual, was a formal, typed-out letter. In seven paragraphs he laid out the case for post-marital mercy. Jesus' statement on divorce and remarriage should *not* be given a "strict literal construction," which "is inconsistent with his whole teaching, including the matter of forgiveness, doing unto others as you'd have them do to you, etc. In other words, would God himself be less forgiving than He would expect humans to be, and so condemn to unhappiness for the remainder of their lives two people who, having made an unfortunate marriage seek to make a new start in an effort to find happiness with someone else? I can't think so." He offered block quotes from William Barclay on law, principle, and reason with respect to scripture. He then cautioned against haste in remarriage, given the necessity of finding the *right* man. He closed with a mini-manifesto, typical of his small-craft advisories about morality: "Well, dear, I can't solve your problems for you, but at least I have tried to help you get away from looking at the matter through the narrow angle that some clerics seem to feel duty bound to limit themselves to. After all, the Bible says that Jesus said many more things, so many, in fact, that the world could not contain the books if they had all been written down. I'm sure he would have shown as much kindness and love in considering your case, for example, as he showed in all His dealings with those who came to him sincerely for help and healing."

On the other hand, Gladys, as she always did, handwrote a honey-sweet, matter-of-fact letter. It referred Mom to the United Presbyterian Constitution, as well as Romans 7:22–24 and 8:1–11. Jesus had no *law* against divorce, she said, only a *principle*. It's all grace, she said, not law. "But if we want to do the will of God as you do, but find it is impossible to make a Christian home where love does not bind two people together, then He will forgive, give us another chance, I know according to his word." She went on to quote these hymn lyrics:

> There's a wideness in God's mercy
> Like the wideness of the sea
> There's a kindness in His justice
> That is more than Liberty
>
> For the love of God is broader
> Than the measure of men's minds
> And the heart of the Eternal
> Is most wonderfully kind

God would *never*, she wrote, "condemn you to a life of loneliness or misery, because of mistaken judgment."

Mom's sister, June—herself divorced for a few years—also weighed in. Gladys's solution to everything, she said, was to "pray pray pray" and in the case of loneliness pray "that the 'right one' will just magically drop down on your doorstep." But, she said, while June and Mom had been raised on a healthy diet of food, they had, in some regards, a bad "psychological diet." June had arrived at a blunt conclusion: "To hell with it!" As for dating after divorce, June said, "Quit worrying so much about being a good girl or a bad girl—go out and *live* a little."

With all these letters flying up and down the west coast, I did the most logical thing: I became a stamp collector. I clipped stamps from envelopes, bought some from advertisers in the back of comic books, and asked neighbors if they had any, especially from other countries—like my friend Joe Szczesney (pronounced "sez-nee"), the spelling of whose name only I could remember. Learning of my new hobby, Gladys wrote Mom, "Does Mike want canceled stamps or unused ones? I have quite a lot of used stamps, different kinds + some foreign. Let me know, if he does, I'll send them to him. I'm glad the 'monster fad' has gone into discard where it belonged." As it turned out, the stamp "fad" faded after a couple years, while the monster fad remained. But my "collecting" of anything weird was baked in.

My greatest disappointment in my parents' parting was how humdrum the stated reason was. I'd watched a lot of *Divorce Court* on TV while my parents were auditioning for the real thing. "Mental cruelty" was the reason for almost every TV divorce. When my parents' final decree came through, it was for that same boilerplate "mental cruelty." Whatever happened to creativity? Poetic license? They both believed the other had committed adultery, they later told me. But they settled for the most nondescript of reasons to secede from marriage.

Whether or not Mom was a good wife, she was not a good Baptist. Six months before she even filed for divorce, she made a clean break from our old church and started taking me to Peninsula Bible Church on Middlefield Road in Palo Alto. Called "PBC" by its adherents, this church attracted her because it was hip, young, and trendily non-denominational, full of scrubbed, upwardly mobile, tech-savvy, artsy, generic Christians who orbited around Pastor Ray Stedman's ideal of "Body Life"—the title of his second book, which became a handbook for this church's Epistles-of-Paul-drenched Christianity. PBC's vibe was non-hierarchical, its chatter unstodgy,

Mom and I dressed for Peninsula Bible Church, 1966.

its dress casual, its chapel well lit, and its sermons Bible-intensive expository. Close reading of God's word, but only through the lenses of modern adult human relationships.

To me, at first, it was just another church, different from First Baptist mostly for its better lighting, breezier decor, cushioned pews, and architecture that Stedman's wife, Elaine, called "early Safeway." An imposing inscription from 1 Corinthians 6:19–20 ran across the front of the chapel in huge capital letters. Sitting in the pews with Mom, I read it over and over: "YE ARE NOT YOUR OWN" on the left side and "YE ARE BOUGHT WITH A PRICE" on the right. Though the signs struck me as an unnerving invitation to Christian slavery, Sister Stedman assured the world that "the hippie movement felt right at home" at PBC.

Pastor Stedman's sermons didn't connect with me at nine years old any better than Pastor Sands's had at First Baptist. So I did my best to fake illness when I could and stay home in bed watching cartoons, especially my favorite, *Beany and Cecil*. When I went to PBC, the meetings did feel fresher, less buttoned down than at First Baptist. But contrary to my earlier practice, I always ditched Sunday school at PBC. Right after the big meeting with Stedman at the pulpit, I'd head to our car with a friend or two to read comic books or *Mad* magazines I'd scored from recycle bins and kept in a worn suitcase behind the front seat. Most weeks we got busted because there was a man assigned to prowl the parking lot for stray kids. Mom was in singles classes scouting new good Christian men to audition for her defiance of Jesus' anti-remarriage dictum. Getting caught in the back seat with a trunkful of comic books was the price I was paying for that. Like the sign said, I was not my own.

Meanwhile, down the Peninsula, some developers had built new mega-theaters, indoor colosseums with the futuristic brand name "Century 21." My first visit to one was to see *The Greatest Story Ever Told*. Mom insisted I go, thinking this Technicolor retelling of the Gospels would be the honey that got me to drink the medicine of the real thing. Her ruse worked. I felt the thrall of this kitschy biblical epic. It had the same faux-ancient-world trapping as gladiator films, which I also loved, but with the glacial pacing and half-frozen acting of a parade of B-list players. Telly Savalas as Pilate? Ernest Borgnine as a centurion? Sal Mineo as Uriah? It was like an epic made of cameos and that was weird enough to appeal to me. I was so taken with it that, for only the second time in my life, I stayed in the theater and watched the whole movie straight through again. The first time was with the Beatles movie *Help*, a few months earlier. This Jesus movie, though, was four-and-a-half-hours long. When John Lennon said at the time that the Beatles were bigger than Jesus, I got it. But for me, in sheer movie screen immersion, he was dead wrong.

Greatest Story or not, though, my knowledge of Christian doctrine sagged badly. When I saw an ad for the 1964 movie *491*, it explained that Jesus said we should be forgiven "seventy times seven" times. So, the movie speculated, what about the 491st time? I started trying to count my sins, because I was already sure I might have crossed that numeric forgiveness threshold. I maintained a private neurosis about that for three years, till I reassured myself that the number Jesus gave

(a) wasn't his personal number, just one he'd given Peter as a bench-mark, and (b) the number was really symbolic of "a lot," not a fixed integer. Sidebar: I also liked sinning more often the older I got.

You see, I'd never felt Jesus in my heart, at my side, on my shoulder, or anywhere around me. I'd chosen to have a "personal relationship" with him when I walked to the altar call to get baptized. But I never even talked to him in my head, let alone listened to any voice in there that bespoke a "relationship." And while my mom racked up her list of friends at church, I felt lonelier at PBC than I did at home, at school, or even with the TV.

I wasn't supposed to know my IQ score but I tricked it out of my dad. Let's just stipulate here that it was preternaturally high. How was I using that IQ? Weirdly. Like in summer 1966 when, as a newly minted ten-year-old, I'd call people up and pretend I was Wayne Fontana of the Mindbenders and tell them they'd been chosen at random to hear a live performance of "A Groovy Kind of Love" over the phone. Then I'd play the 45 on the record player. The hearers would either hang up or start getting giddy or even crying about their good fortune. That was my thing. Pranks, insults, minor deviancies. But I was certified as "gifted." So, for a year and a half, every weekday, I got bussed from our side of San Jose across town to Bohnett Elementary, now retooled for kids in my IQ range. The good news: that gifted group included Jan Emery. The bad news: I was over her.

The bus rides to Bohnett were nerdy and disjointed. Kids who mostly didn't know each other, but were supersmart, got picked up from all around the city and its suburbs to go to the same school. We befriended one another quickly, though, because we all had *exile from our actual friends* in common. I remember little about my stint at Bohnett. Which is paradoxical, since memory was one of the things that made me so "gifted."

I remember that we had two main teachers that first year. One was a suave, wavy-haired charmer in his early thirties. The other was a tough, brainy fifty-something woman with hair dyed red-dish brown to cover the grey. The man teacher conducted classes in the way we were used to—except that he was a man, which I'd never had for a teacher. The woman teacher, who seemed to be the man's adjunct assistant, always had us doing broad-themed projects with partners, building things and presenting them in class. It was a brand of California joint creativity that yielded about what arbitrary collaborations usually do.

But three things about Bohnett stick with me. One was being trapped in a scholastic cage of guinea pigs slogging through the new SMSG program, the so-called "New Math." I remember lots of calculations with different number bases than our supposedly out-moded "Base 10" system. We'd have to convert from one base system to another, a skill that only made sense to me when our county became Silicon Valley.

Second, I started taking Spanish. I got quite good at it, although the Latino population at this school was essential *nada*, so I didn't get to practice the language on native speakers till high school. Still, I had a parroting skill that made me sound authentic to less gifted gringos. I got good enough at vocal mimicking that I fantasized about becoming an impressionist like Frank Gorshin or Rich Little.

The third Bohnett thing that sticks with me was when, during the glee club rehearsal of "You Gotta Have Heart," one of the most popular girls in the school sat crying through the whole song, and I wanted so much to know what was wrong, but I felt too spazzy and poor to talk to girls like her. Every now and then I still sing that song to myself and remember Miss Popularity sobbing through it and hoping the pain went away—or didn't. It reminds me, too, that people who have it all might have things you'll never hear about.

Maybe Mom was an older, more weathered version of that girl. After *Peyton Place* debuted on ABC in the fall of '64, wherever she went, people asked her, "Did anyone ever tell you you look like Dorothy Malone?"—the shapely, thick-browed blonde who starred in the show. When Mom would get asked that in front of Dad, I could never tell if it made him cocky, as in "Yeah, and *she's mine!*" or angry, as in, "Yeah—and she's *mine.*" She, of course, loved it, as in "Yeah, maybe I can do better." She was sunlamp-tanned and narrow-waisted, her bleach blonde hair teased up and hairsprayed. She hardly looked like a woman who had a deviant-but-gifted eight-year-old son.

Now, with me having reached the age of ten, she had two rivals for her attention, neither of whom was the guy in the car with her that day at Alameda. One of these rivals, Stan, had lived across the street from our home with Dad. His wife often babysat me. Once Mom had moved us out to our apartment a few blocks away, Stan told Mom that he and his wife were divorcing and now he and Mom could start dating. He plied me with gifts to make me an advocate for him with Mom. A charming guy, however lumbering, a paint salesman who I learned later on—from him—had orgies, made his own porn, mostly from black and white glossy snapshots, loved commercial girl-on-girl erotica, and lied about pretty much everything else, including getting a divorce from his wife. But despite Mom's college degree and white-collar upbringing, she still felt drawn to blue collar guys like Dad. Stan had a white-collar job, but his mind's collar was so blue it was almost black. And no Jesus talk from Stan, not that I ever heard. "Mr. Personality," Mom later said of him, "but no character."

As time wore on, it became clearer that Stan was swimming in a pond of delusions. When he was dating Mom, he claimed he had women stalking him and even that the actress Elke Sommer—who allegedly had had sex with him at his paint store—was one of them. He also claimed mafioso types were hunting him down. Or something. The stories shifted like flags in a storm. June commented about his tales in a letter to Mom at the time:

> Stan's situation sounds like something out of the cheapest pulp magazine ever printed. I can hardly believe what I read and it's hard to imagine that a human can't go anywhere to get away from all that, isn't it. But, if one has a job, one can't up and leave—he'd be followed too. Does Stan's boss know the situation? Or has he a boss? If he has a boss, couldn't the boss hide sometime and take hidden pictures as evidence? … The women after Stan must be deranged completely or, as you said, on dope or LSD or something. The police must not be trying very hard or pretty inept not to have been able to do something more drastic by now. Down here [San Diego] they round up whole gangs of dope peddlers every so often. Seems to me that a little concentrated surveillance of Stan's home and a few hidden cameras would get them all the evidence they need—and how about tracing a few of the phone calls he gets. I don't think they're trying very hard. Maybe a few of the police even envy him or aren't taking it all seriously enough.

Mom later summed it up: Stan was "a chronic liar."

Stan's rival, Bruce, was the gallant, would-be shining armor type, a divorcé in the PBC singles group, owner of a small surplus business named—I kid you not—"Miscellaneous Sales Company." The business consisted mainly of him buying government discards at auction for cheap, then reselling them for everything from scrap (gold screws) to functional equipment (parachutes). Far more educated than Stan, he was also moody, hyper-religious, and obsessed with the correctness of his Maine upbringing. To me, he had one big advantage over Stan: he'd hired me to work at his warehouse for 75 cents an hour—minus what I bought from him, like the clicking boxes from parking meters, which I sold to friends at a small profit as pretend bombs they could scare people with. During lunch hours Bruce played shuffleboard with me at his condo nearby, where he also got me hooked on shortbread cookies and introduced me to stereo. He had a large Ampex reel-to-reel tape deck attached to a Fisher receiver and waist-high speakers, through which he played me stereo demonstration tapes. Hearing the sound of a train or an ocean liner slowly moving across the room became my new religion—a bona fide miracle. I couldn't believe it, but there it was.

Bruce also knew how to show me and Mom a good time after PBC each Sunday. No mere visit to a smorgasbord with a box of free trinkets. Bruce took us to the San Jose Flea Market. All afternoon he and Mom would visit booths together, letting Bruce do his virtuoso dickering, as I roamed around on my own, rummaging through tables full of war memorabilia, piles of comic books, and boxes full of everything from plastic army men to custom stick-shift knobs. The flea market fit both Bruce's and my temperament, his for the bargains and mine for the rambunctious exoticism of the place. The center of it for me was a huge book mall with every book priced at a nickel. The first one I bought was the novel *Gallagher*, for obvious reasons. The second was Aimee Semple MacPherson's *This Is That*, sermons and memoirs of a charismatic woman preacher from Los Angeles. I could tell it was rare, with alluring pictures from a bygone era of churchery. I actually read most of that one—especially after I myself became an oddball preacher type in my own right and, along the way, got hooked on charismatic female demigods.

After Mom's divorce from Dad became final in August 1966, I had to weigh in on Mom's two suitors every week. I thought Bruce the obvious winner. But Mom still had an inexplicable thing for dangerous, possibly psychotic Stan. So I put my thumb on the scale for Bruce whenever I could. Soon Mom went to a fortune teller to help her decide. Bruce wanted the soothsayer's name so he could pay her to forecast his potential success. Bruce even asked Mom's sister to write him a *letter of recommendation* to give Mom. This all should have been a red flag. But it wasn't.

In mid-December, Mom left me at home for the weekend, with our landlady, Mrs. Figliomeni, agreeing to check in on me every few hours. All Mom told me was that she was taking a trip to Reno with Bruce for a gambling and entertainment romp. When they got home, they were Mr. and Mrs. Bruce Gray and we started packing up to move, first to his apartment with the Ampex and then, within a few weeks, to a new house on Casita Way in Los Altos.

This newish pale green rambler in a cul-de-sac was the official domicile of the new Mike *Gray*. Bruce said he was going to adopt me and the name "Hicks" had always been a splinter in my psyche. I'd walk into Sunday school class at First Baptist and the kids would start hiccupping. Besides that, "hicks" were ignorant country folks, one notch above (or below) "hillbillies." By contrast, "Gray" sounded almost aristocratic. For two and a half years, 1967–69, I was Mike Gray on every grade roll, every return address, and in the ears of anyone I met.

But "Gray" or not, making friends in the money-drenched domain of Los Altos had its potholes. I was about to stroll into the last half of sixth grade and discover that the protected safe house of "gifted" had been demolished.

My first day of school at Portola Elementary, some boys invited me to one of their houses after school. I arrived, and a slant-grinned runt named Darren walked up to me. He had a long shock of blond hair sliding down the side of a face that was as close to a weasel's as I've ever seen on a human head.

"I call you out," he said.

"What?"

"I call you out."

"I'm not hip to that phrase," I said, in my typically un-hip attempt at sounding hip.

Darren turned to the others, laughed, and told them I didn't know what it meant to be called out. Then he explained to me that that meant a person was challenging you to fight. The winner would confirm or rearrange the order of who could "pound" (beat up) whom at the school. Darren detailed who was where in the order as of now: Joey at the top—improbable, I thought, because he was the shortest guy in the room, even shorter than Darren—then Ricky, the token Latino, then … I don't remember who, but Darren was somewhere in the mid-range, which is where I'd have to start.

I told him I didn't want to fight him because I wasn't mad at him. Which made me a chicken. Which put me on a different list.

Darren—apparently the Aaron of this Mosaic gang—explained that who could pound who had a lot to do with (a) who you got to make out with and (b) who you could go steady with by giving her a "Christopher."

"What's a Christopher?" I asked.

More laughter. Darren showed me one that hadn't been given to a girl yet: a small round, silver-red St. Christopher medal. In Catholicism Christopher was the patron saint of travelers. The medallion was a talisman to protect its wearer in his or her travels. For Portola sixth-graders, it was a medal one conferred on a girl to seal her fidelity to a boy. Now, I swear this group didn't have a Catholic in the bunch, except maybe Joey, who was Italian, and definitely Ricky, who was, by the way, not only bigger and more muscular than the rest of us, but also a year older—this was his second shot at sixth grade.

It was as if mom had adopted me out to another planet, one as alien as any I'd seen on *Chillers from Science Fiction* but with Catholic medals. I spent the next three months desperately writing letters to old friends in San Jose, hoping for replies that rarely came, and even phoning some of them long distance, which got me in hot water with Bruce when the bills from Bell Telephone arrived in the mail. I had yet to accept myself as an exile to the craziest kid culture of the upper-middle class of the San Francisco Peninsula. I only blended in, sort of, because a few girls thought I was cute. But I didn't see myself that way at all. I was skinny as a fence post and wouldn't pound anyone. Yes, I was the tallest kid in almost any room, but I was a year younger than the other guys. Thus I started entering cultural puberty before my real one.

The first step into the funhouse of real puberty came when Joyce invited me to her thirteenth birthday party. We all sat in a circle and played spin the bottle. The rule was: two spins that matched up the same two people and the pair of them had to go into the living room, where the Bee Gees' *Rare, Precious, and Beautiful* was playing, and make out. I spun onto Joyce once, then she spun onto me right after that. So we went into the living room and sat on the couch. My brain bolted when she said, "I can't believe I got my birthday wish." A girl had a crush on *me*. We made out for I don't know how long, then, emboldened like a superhero who'd just discovered his powers, I left the living room and started talking with another girl, who, as it turned out, also had a crush on me. I talked myself into instant crushes on both girls and disappeared into a walk-in liquor cabinet with the second one. We made out for longer than Joyce and I had. A faux-torrid love triangle ensued for a few months. One afternoon Joyce took me to her pink plush bedroom, laid down with me, and placed my hands on her sweater-covered breasts, such as they were. It was an act I was too young to get either the sense or the magic of.

What did I have to show for all this sixth-grade romance? I could mentally compare one's kisses with the other's for wetness, tenderness, etc. And two girls fit my Gemini nature. But, while I was used to having crushes since Cathy at Alameda, the ritualization of kissery in these upscale neighborhoods felt bizarre.

Adding to the scariness of the place, a few boys started sniffing glue in the orchard next to campus before and after school. Cheap, no pusher needed, they kept the glue tubes in Baggies in their jacket pockets. I was invited to join in, but it just seemed to make stupid guys stupider. And I was on a mild anti-drug crusade, anyway, including an oral presentation in social studies class that warned about marijuana, LSD, and two hallucinogenic fads at the time: smoking the dried scrapings of banana peels and smoking dried hydrangea leaves. So, I didn't sniff glue or drop acid or smoke … anything.

Not yet, anyway.

Seventh grade began in fall '67, and I moved to Egan Junior High, four blocks farther than Portola from Casita Way. At the age of eleven, I had already flirted with the god Eros. I had rejected the pleasures of chemical euphoria. But over the summer, I acquired three non-drug addictions: autographs, shoplifting, and music. One was to connect me to pop culture idols. The next one was to blend cunning and liberty. The last one was for bliss.

Bruce tried to bond with me as his putative son, but now that we lived in the same house, we weren't clicking much. He was still all Maine and I was all California. He bought a family dog, a schnauzer he named Martin. But that toy-sized hoppity creature was not what I considered a real dog. (We'd had a Labrador when we lived with Dad.) Besides, I already had pets: a small suitcase with a glass pane in it covered with snails I'd plucked from the lawn and fed on grass clippings.

In attempts to bond with me, Bruce took two approaches. One was to give me a small reel-to-reel tape recorder made by the Craig company—because that was what *Consumer Reports*, Bruce's second bible, had rated the best value. I used it ravenously, taping, replaying, and memorizing TV bits from the young George Carlin, the Smothers Brothers, and *Laugh-In*, as well as songs KFRC played on my clock radio. The one I remember replaying the most was the Beatles' "Strawberry Fields Forever," the last forty seconds of which suited my sci-fi longings. Bruce helped satisfy those longings by giving me some of his Book-of-the-Month-Club choices, all of which I used for sci-fi anthologies. The story I read and scared myself to death with, over and over, was Philip K. Dick's "The Father-Thing." You might know it: a son discovers that his father has been replaced by an alien replica.

The second approach Bruce took with me was actually a life-altering gift: a plump paperback called *1001 Things You Can Get for Free*. That became *my* new bible, the best section of which explained how to write to movie and TV stars and get signed photos. I loved movies and TV and wanted whatever totems I could get from my favorites. So, using the book's tips, I started writing. I got a good harvest. *Preprinted* stuff from the Monkees (which made me hate them a little), a real hand-signed 5x7 from *Star Trek* star Leonard Nimoy, an 8x10 inscribed to me "Be Happy" from James Coburn, signed photos from Charlton Heston and Joey Bishop (both secretary-signed, I found out later), and even a beautiful 8x10 of Elizabeth Taylor and Richard Burton, inscribed in fine-tip markers, one black, the other blue. I sent a card to *Peanuts* artist Charles Schulz, which he inscribed and sent back to me, although, because my handwriting was so hard to read—those fancy curlicues Miss Kadri had warned Mom about—he signed it to "M. Mitzi Gray." I now had the core of a collection that I started supplementing with in-person signatures, from the Olympic runner Jim Ryun to master pianist—and *Peanuts* theme composer—Vince Guaraldi. In March 1968, Mom and Bruce took me to see Jack Benny at the Circle Star Theatre in San Carlos. I went to the stage door after every set, got shooed away by body-guards each time Benny came off the stage, until, when the show ended, some honcho's wife, having watched my dogged pursuit and even struck up a few conversations with me, yelled at the bodyguards and ushered me herself into Benny's dressing room, where he signed my program amid a crowd of photographers and reporters. That was my final initiation into the art of autograph-hounding.

Between (a) Dad's training me to lie about my age for better deals and (b) Bruce's nifty instruction book, I was now an apprentice at getting things free. Which brings me to Kepler's Books. In the B-list rich-kid maelstrom of the sixties south of San Francisco, Kepler's was the Mike Gray sanctuary. The biggest store in Village Corner— the covered open-air mall on the intersection of El Camino and San Antonio—Kepler's had long magazine stands spread at the feet of its exterior front windows, all crowded with mass market staples like *Life* and *Look* but also more exotic literary confections, from *Eye* to *Ramparts* to *Poetry* to *Evergreen Review* to *Berkeley Barb* to *Los Angeles Free Press* to, in time, a new paper from San Francisco, *Rolling Stone*. I picked up, leafed through, and walked away with three or more of these a week for two years.

Inside the incense-and-patchouli scented store stood tall shelves set at odd angles to divide the space into alcoves for various topics, from science fiction to political satire to erotica to black literature to abstract art to the occult to Maoist tracts to cartooning, and on and on. Prowling the Kepler's inventory became my intellectual sequel to the trips to Smorgy's I'd been raised on—except that here they didn't give away prizes, I just took them.

My cousin Tom came to visit and taught me the basics of stealing books: wear a big coat, cut the bottoms out of the pockets so you could slide books into the lining of the coat, walk into the store, pick a book (or books), insert, adjust, walk out. I ended up stealing books from all the sections I just mentioned and more. I made it a personal challenge to see how many I could take or how big the books could be. I credit the proprietors—who knew my face and ambling figure well, nodded at me, and smiled every time I went in and left without buying anything—for not having me arrested. But this was a "free" everything time in the world. Free speech. Free love. You could take any object or phenomenon, stick the word "free" in front of it and that was a new thing. I stole Abbie Hoffman's book *Revolution for the Hell of It*, published under the pseudonym "Free," partly because it seemed an insult to him—and the whole era—not to.

In the Sears shopping center kitty-corner from Kepler's were two inventories of records with which I could hone my craft and fuel my inner musical engine. One was Hal's Records, with full bins of every genre. It stood next to a giant Co-Op store with a separate drugstore attached to the main building. The drugstore had two bins of LPs standing waist high in front of you as you walked in the main door from the sidewalk. My technique for both Hal's and Co-Op Drugs was simple: I walked in with a small armful of LPs and walked out with one or two more than I came in with—after slipping the shrinkwrap off the new ones when no one was looking. I had a perfect excuse for walking in with records: our art teacher at Egan had a policy of letting us listen to whatever records we'd bring to her classes, which were just us sitting around doing our own drawings or paintings. You know: "free."

I still went to church at PBC, that was the law in our house. But my real church was the psychic cathedral of the Haight-Ashbury district in San Francisco. I went to the Haight with Mom and Bruce twice in 1967 as if patronizing a freak show, just when the word "freak" was becoming sanctified. I bought posters, including one that said "Haight-Ashbury Loves You" with a gang of hippies strewn around the letters. And I believed it—who else would love a freak like me? The soundtrack for this cathedral was *psychedelic* music, which ran the gamut from "Purple Haze" to "Hair" to "In-a-Gadda-da-Vida" to "The Rain, the Park, and Other Things." No matter whether superficial pop or underground rock, it was all part of some oceanic experience we were having, one that didn't require surfboard skill or bravery, just right-brain surrender. I was already halfway there, my head crammed with *Twilight Zone, The Outer Limits,* Ripley's *Believe It or Not,* and Frank Edwards's *Stranger than Science* books. Psychedelic music was the crown.

However esoteric and eclectic I tried to be with the music I listened to, the Beatles were always the lodestar. The first week of June 1967 my next-door neighbor Brian invited me to his house to listen to the Beatles' latest, which he'd just bought: *Sgt. Pepper's Lonely Hearts Club Band.* We sat in silence through the first side, our brains sweating, trying to absorb and sort through these imponderably fresh songs and sounds that ranged from garage rock to Victorian tropes to hypnotic induction. Then Brian turned the record over and we listened, just as mesmerized, to the second side, which ended with the apotheosis of weirdness. Who got revelation like that in a church? A new sort of religion snuck into the life of everyone I knew through that album.

So, as we rounded the year toward Christmas, I begged Mom for the Beatles' next album, *Magical Mystery Tour.* Magic and mystery—I felt I was born and bred to be tourist in those two domains. I kept looking for a gift-wrapped flat 12-inch square under the tree. It never showed up, just a giant box that I figured was another coat like the one whose pocket linings I'd been cutting. On Christmas I opened it. Tucked into balled up newspapers, there it was. Shrink-wrapped gold.

I was thrilled. Mom grinned and hugged me. But Bruce wasn't even there when I opened the box, stayed away from Mom and me both on Christmas that year, preferring to work all day at his warehouse. He was already practicing not speaking to his family, who'd both disappointed him by not living up to—something. He did talk to Martin the schnauzer a lot, though, railing about how defective

Mom and I were. I kept playing "All You Need Is Love," seeking refuge in the promise of that line.

When he wasn't talking to Martin about us, he was sometimes yelling at Mom from his office across the hall from my bedroom after I'd gone to bed. She was a bad parent, he'd shout. I needed more corporal punishment, which he was happy to provide—no one ever hand-spanked me but him. (Dad only whipped me with a belt.) The rage in Bruce's voice as his muscled arm plunged toward my rump I can still hear, the bruising still feel. On the plus side, his shout-fests started me closing the door to my bedroom for the first time since meeting the devil.

My paltry vengeance was stealing stuff from the middle drawer of Bruce's dresser, where he had a line of open cases of Smith Brothers cough drops and assorted gum flavors—all *Trident Sugarless* except for my favorite, *Black Jack*. In time, I was stealing other stuff from him, though those bonus thefts were harder to conceal, since I couldn't swallow them—war memorabilia and first day covers, mostly, along with some Filipino coins and currency. I don't recall all the thefts, but I considered them payback for his cruelty, puny trophies for my archive of revenge. He never caught me. But it didn't matter much. Because even by that Christmas with him, Mom was planning to leave Bruce.

Six months earlier she'd written him a letter complaining that they already couldn't talk to each other "in a spirit of love and understanding" and were living "miles apart" in the same house. She attacked his "inability to accept the fact that Mike is part of me" and would be part of their family as long as it stayed together. If things didn't change, she said, they'd need to "jointly agree to go our separate ways." Bruce demanded perfection, and a kind of demented perfection at that. No one could meet it. Even the way I buttered my corn on the cob sent him into a gritted-teeth rage. (I spread a pat of butter on the cob as I turned it and he demanded that one lay the pat of butter on the cob and let it melt. As shown in TV commercials. And, apparently, the state of Maine.) She and Bruce, she wrote, weren't ready to "join the ranks of the happily married." If they couldn't join, "let's not waste each other's time any longer."

In other words: all you need is love.

During the Mike Gray years, I insisted on holding a *Mad* magazine in any group photos with Bruce's family.

By April 1968, Mom had started sleeping on a cot in the den. She was there alone when Bruce, using the excuse of telling her that Bobby Kennedy had been shot, burst in and, to put it nicely, forced himself on her. Within a month of that, he filed for divorce, saying she had not turned out to be the kind of wife he expected. His rationale included a claim that she was having an affair with Stan. He said he'd seen Stan's car pass by the house a few times, circling the cul de sac like a shark. Mom insisted she'd had zero contact with Stan during her marriage to Bruce and cross complained against Bruce for—here we go again—mental cruelty. Once papers were filed, Bruce not only kept up his silent treatment but refused to visit Mom in the hospital—or even take me to visit her—after she was in a small car crash. He even put his name in newspaper personals ads to get dates. Sometimes women would call the house, Mom would answer, they'd ask who she was, she said, "His wife," and the phone clicked.

In May 1968, with the tethers to Mike Gray-ness unraveling, I had my first big religious event: an outdoor festival of idolatry called the Northern California Folk Rock Festival. Since before I became Mike Gray, I'd longed to see the Doors, a group named after Aldous Huxley's *The Doors of Perception*, which chronicled mesca-line's quasi-religious effects on consciousness. In that same vein, the Doors urged us in the first track of their first album to "Break on through to the other side," a side I knew had to be out there, wherever or whatever it might be. Now the group was going to appear at the Santa Clara County Fairgrounds, where I'd eaten many a strawberry shortcake and petted many a lamb when I was little. The whole festival lasted two days, Saturday and Sunday, the 18th and 19th, eleven acts each day, 10:30 a.m. to 5:30 p.m. Big open field, no chairs, catch-as-catch-can open seating. I and two friends—Larry and Hokey—arrived at the gate early enough on Sunday to be able to sprint toward the stage when the gate swung open. The stage had a wire fence about six feet in front of it to let press photographers and band members loiter and swagger freely, insulated from us rabble. We got within six feet of that fence and sat cross-legged, faces tilted up at the stage, tens of thousands of people behind us.

Although we were there for the Doors, we had to sit through almost six hours of other groups first. I was steeled for boredom. But instead I got a spaceship to a new world, with all these artists I hardly knew fulfilling deep cravings I hardly knew I had: Taj Mahal, Electric Flag, Country Joe and the Fish, Ashish Khan, and, maybe most of all, The Youngbloods, who capped their set with "Get Together," the new hymn of the Bay Area. It proclaimed the triumph of love over fear—i.e., "the way we die"—and praised "the one who left us here," who will "return for us at last." Jesus? Who knew, who cared? We all belted its pseudo-Christian chorus by heart:

Come on people now
Smile on your brother
Everybody get together
Got to love one another right now

When they finished, the crowd wouldn't stop clapping and yell-ing for an encore. Lead singer Jesse Colin Young asked for requests. The crowd, as one, yelled "Get Together!" Jesse said, "Are you sure?"

"Yeah!" He kept trying to switch us to another song, but we were relentless. So the group started up on "Get Together" one more time, to an avalanche of cheers.

As the Doors set up, and we waited for lead singer Jim Morrison to hit the stage, the clouds above us thickened. When he walked up to the microphone, he started yelling "Make it wet!" It started to rain. We shuddered, sure he had supernatural powers, just like Jesus—or maybe the Antichrist, whom I thought I knew all about from my days at First Baptist. The group ran through their short canon of classics as the rain clicked on and off. Morrison, hair freshly cut short—by himself—and clad in snakeskin pants, surprisingly be-witched us more than entranced us, not just for his seeming power to summon a storm, but for that drug-soaked psychosis we'd read about, including his collapsing on the stage, screaming "fuck" into the microphone, and acting as if he were in a padded cell, not on a stage. Schtick, taunting, insanity? I loved it through every speck of terror.

All afternoon I'd chatted it up with an Asian-American girl of maybe sixteen, Jerri. She was a real photographer with a Nikon camera and multiple lenses in tow while I was taking what shots I could with my new early birthday gift, a Polaroid Swinger cam-era that took only tiny black and whites. Jerri and I instantly felt a brotherly-sisterly "get together" love for each other. She invited me to come up to San Francisco and spend a day with her in the Haight, not far from where she lived. As the festival ended, I knew I'd had a religious experience, maybe my first. It was my own Wood-stock, fifteen months before there was such a thing. I went home with ringing ears, a soul full of indelible memories, a cache of one-of-a-kind instantly developed photos, and a ticket to the Haight with a flower girl.

An even more profound musical revelation opened to me a few weeks later. That July the film *2001: A Space Odyssey* began its 87-week run at the Century 21 theaters. I went the first week. I'd heard it would be weird. Mission accomplished. Special effects beyond anything ever seen. A psychedelic light show near the end, followed by a surreal sequence whose possible meaning(s) haunted our imaginations for weeks. But it was the soundtrack by György Ligeti that chilled me. Waves and webs of sonorities, churning like a petri dish of microorganisms, tight clusters of pitch, no beat, just floating, but still magmatic. I couldn't get over it.

Neither the festival nor the Ligeti helped me in my seventh-grade music class, though. The teacher, Mr. McDowell, wrote on my report card: "four assignments not handed in." Regarding classroom citizenship, he wrote in all caps one word: "TALKATIVE." Debasement and bragging rights at the same time.

Jerri and I exchanged letters for a few months. And I did spend that day busing around San Francisco with her and walking through the Haight. She took a great shot of me flashing a peace sign under the famous street signs that intersected Haight and Ashbury. She sent me an 8x10, which I treasured. I never saw her again.

I had just turned twelve years old.

Mom got the old piano in her divorce decree and moved it into the house on Casita Way. I learned you could make anything sound classic and spooky and rich and dreamy by just playing either single notes as a melody—I became an expert, I thought, at "Love Is Blue"—or, even better, making up pretend-symphonic textures on the black keys only, when keeping the sustain pedal pressed down firmly. I even figured out some harmonies and could play all three chords of a 12-bar blues progression on the white keys. When fall semester of 8th grade started at Egan, I talked three buddies into skipping music class and breaking into a mysterious locked room in an adjoining building where we'd heard that musical instruments were stored. A friend hoisted me onto his shoulders to the high open slant window, I slithered in, dropped to the floor, and opened the door from the inside. My friends came in. The room had a blonde upright piano, a drum set, and cabinets full of musical instruments—a string bass, a flute, tambourines, and other handheld percussion instruments, from woodblocks to a glockenspiel. Along with them was a Wollensak reel-to-reel tape recorder with one reel on it—maybe blank, maybe with something else on it, we didn't care. Because of my daily Craig experience, I knew how to run the machine. We started playing and recording what we could, eking out some blues, making up lyrics as we went, repeatedly playing "Pistol Packin' Papa" and "Mother's Lament," the last track on Cream's *Disraeli Gears* album (part of the latest psych canon). After about a half-hour, Mr. MacDowell burst into the room, shouted at us to put the instruments away and come back to music class. We got no punishment for our transgression beyond having to watch the teacher sit at his desk and sob as we listened blankly to Tchaikovsky. But this instrument-room event, along with the folk-rock festival and Ligeti's mystery music, was my initiation into my life's next phase: guerilla music-making and do-it-yourself recording.

At the end of the semester, I went to Dad's for Christmas and he gave me a guitar he'd bought at a pawn shop in Oakland. He liked to brag that he'd almost gotten shot for it. He'd taken the guitar down from the rack without asking the pawnbroker, who pointed a pistol at Dad and told him to put the instrument down. Dad said he'd buy it and handed the pawnbroker a ten-dollar bill. It was an awful guitar, with steel strings set so high above the fretboard that my left-hand fingertips got hard callouses within the first two weeks of trying to play it. Along with the guitar came an *Alfred's Guitar Method* book that started by teaching me how to play "Jingle Bells" and "Hot Cross Buns" on the high E-string. I'd never heard of "Hot Cross Buns." And who needs a book to figure out "Jingle Bells"?

Fortunately, my oldest half-brother, Dave, had Christmas gifted me the new Richie Havens album called *1983*. When I got bored with the Alfred's book, which took about seven minutes at a pop, I'd put the Havens LP on and strum made-up chords to it, pluck out odd melodies as simple as those Alfred one-string tunes. I thought I'd been ushered into the back door to folk-rock heaven. Dad's crusty mom, visiting for the holiday, sat on the couch and said to me, over and over, "You'll never learn to play that thing." I snatched up the gauntlet to prove her wrong.

I quickly became a Laura Weber addict. I watched her every week, on channel 9, got her songbook *Folk Guitar Playing*, learned a full palette of chords, the calypso strum for "Sloop John B," the 12-bar blues progression, and folk songs ranging from "O Susanna" to "Greensleeves." She made it easy to kiss Alfred's book goodbye. Soon I was playing by ear and could sail through a few of my favorite radio songs.

As if to celebrate, I stole a bottle of glow-in-the-dark paint from Accent Arts at the Sears shopping center and used it to paint stars and free-form psychedelic shapes on a couple dozen pieces of typing paper. I taped them to the ceiling of my bedroom, left the lights on to get the paint luminously charged, turned the lights off, and stared up at them as I fell asleep at night. With Mom and Bruce no longer speaking, I could enjoy my own fake universe in peace.

Jesus, I'd heard at PBC, said that "the gates of hell shall not prevail against you." At first that made no sense to me. The gates weren't going to unhinge and come charging at you. It only made sense if he meant those gates couldn't stop you from getting *into* hell. Because a detour through hell is sometimes the only road to heaven. And that's what 1969 would become for me.

3. GRAY DAYS FOR GRAY

Whenever I walked by Egan's principal, Mr. Shonack, he'd grin and say, "It's a gray day for Gray!" which he thought was funny and I did not. The reason he said it was the reason I hated hearing it: his office was the sequel to my grammar school's psychologist's office.

The first time I got sent to Shonack's office, it was for having porn in my locker. Not anything pictorial like *Playboy*, mind you, just the Victorian classic *My Secret Life* and Henry Miller's *Sexus*. I had no desire to read them, really, just to show them off as trophies of my thievery and as pocket-mines of salaciousness, the kind of stuff third-grade Ed would have snickered at. My taste in literature was a far cry from that. Once fed by Bruce's sci-fi Book of the Month picks and the smorgasbord of titles at Kepler's, it had now been shaped by our social studies teacher, Mr. Gonella. He was our guru in eighth grade, a short, trim, broad-grinned charmer with charisma dripping off him like sweat, who took us through civil rights classics like *Black Like Me* and *Manchild in the Promised Land*. I was so enthralled by them that I went on to read *The Autobiography of Malcolm X*, Dick Gregory's *Nigger* and *The Shadow That Scares Me,* and Eldridge Cleaver's *Soul On Ice*, then gave an oral report in Gonella's class on the Black experience in America. I also wrote naive anti-war poems for Gonella with stanzas like: "Bombs are bad / They make us sad / They hit your head / And make you dead." He raved about that one, said it was deep and honest and penetrating. Even then, I thought he was being more kind than wise. But his classes were pitch-perfect indoctrination in the premises of '60s political counterculture on the West Coast.

The second summons to Shonack's office was for bringing a switchblade to school. The cousin who'd taught me the slit-pocket shoplifting technique had taken me along with him on a trip to

Tijuana. While there I bought only novelties and contraband: *Horseshit* brand cigarettes, mini-bottles of whiskey, firecrackers, and a switchblade. After the hazing I'd gotten my first week at Portola, I wanted to rebrand at least a piece of myself as a tough guy. Switchblades had a gang imprimatur on them, at least as far as I could tell from *West Side Story* and the odd TV show. So, although I wouldn't know the first thing about brandishing it, I brought my switchblade to school to show it off. Someone saw it, reported it, and—next stop, Shonackville. He took the knife away and, because switchblades were illegal in California, turned it in to the police. He said.

The third time Shonack summoned me to his office, I got formally suspended from school for a day. I'd brought one of those mini-bottles of whiskey to school and showed it to select friends, some of whom I let take a sip with me. Again, someone tattled, so Shonack searched my locker and busted me. Not only was alcohol distribution suspension-worthy, this was my third strike.

That suspension led to my ultimate vengeance on both the Mike Gray pretense and the devil's intrusion into my childhood closet. I lifted a bayonet from my stepfather's Korean war collection and stabbed my bedroom closet door, over and over, then taped a sign to my hallway door jam: a page of binder paper lettered in laundry marker with the words "Everybody hates me, so I hate everybody." The bayonet and signage were my answer to both Bruce's speak-no-more shunning and Satan's cribside roaring. The sign got Mom all weepy. But Bruce only saw the dozen-ish slanted holes in the closet door. As usual, he wrestled me onto on his lap and spanked me like a toddler. And that was that. Mom helped me pack and we moved to an apartment in the next town over, Mountain View.

It was a newish two-story townhouse with carports and a swimming pool. You walked through the front door into a small, tan-carpeted living room where we'd put the TV against the right front wall and a gold paisley couch across from it. The first half-flight of stairs led to a bookcase, then reversed to a short hall with doors both to Mom's bedroom and mine on the right. We each had our own balcony facing in opposite directions. She never went onto hers, I spent hours on mine, which overlooked the parking lot of the apartment complex next door.

My room was stuffed. A pair of bunk beds stood on the right. I slept on the bottom one, with my transistor FM radio leaning between the bed and the wall, its antenna sticking up next to my head at night. At the room's far end was a closet with sliding wooden doors. In front of them was an easy chair I never sat in, just used it to lean my huge library of records against. In the corner, a dresser from the 1850s that Mom and Bruce had bought at a farmhouse in Michigan held a few of my clothes that didn't need hangers. A big mirror jutted up from it. To its left was another dresser, a cheap caramel-colored one I'd had since my crib days. I used it for more clothes, books, comic books, magazines, and assorted souvenirs. On every available inch of wall were posters, handbills, bumper stickers, brochures, and some of my own art. Freed at last from the Casita Way emotional dungeon, I was primed for revival.

As if coronating my newly resurrected life, they held another festival, a sequel: the 2nd Annual Northern California Folk Rock Festival. A friend and I went to the afternoon concert of the first day. We sprinted like gazelles through the gates to grab the best seats in the open-seating arena. We made it to the front row of the E-section (a whopping $6.50 a ticket) and I took three rolls of pictures at the edge of the stage, with artists like Canned Heat, People (featuring Larry Norman), Country Joe and the Fish, Elvin Bishop, Santana, and even Doc Watson. Chuck Berry missed his set, but I tracked him down behind the stage and got him to sign my program—given my autograph addiction, this was even better than hearing him play. The next week I took my rolls of film to be developed and when I went to pick up the prints two days later the photo shop said they'd lost all the rolls. So they gave me fresh rolls as "replacements" and no doubt sold my negatives to some collector. I kept asking myself "WWJD?"—what would Jerri do?

With the festival under my belt, I felt ready for my own onstage debut. During the last week of school each year, Egan held a talent show. My friend Hokey and I signed up. For the solo competition, I walked with my guitar onto the outdoor stage in the center of campus, dressed in jeans, a khaki shirt, and floppy migrant worker's hat, and played a two-song set of Phil Ochs songs that I learned from a protest songbook I stole from Kepler's. The first one, "There But For

After Mom's split with Bruce, I grew my hair
out and played guitar incessantly.

Fortune," had great lyrics, and I could play the chords, but I'd never actually heard the song and couldn't read the notes on the page. So I made up the tune. Then I launched into Ochs's "Draft Dodger Rag," which I'd heard on underground FM radio and could do a decent job on. I got big applause from the students and polite applause from their parents. In the group competition, Hokey came up with me. I was dressed the same and Hokey, carrying a ukulele, wore an Uncle Sam hat and beard. We did Country Joe's "I Feel Like I'm Fixing to Die" and then the old spoof on Christian commerce called "Plastic Jesus." The version we sang started with a chorus that went:

I don't care if it rains or freezes
Long as I got my plastic Jesus
Sittin' on the dashboard of my car

Ridin' on the radio
He keeps me everywhere I go
And with my plastic Jesus I'll go far

The parents seemed a little more stunned by these songs, while the hip kids—and Mr. Gonella—went half-wild. We closed the show and waited for the results.

I didn't expect to place in the solo category, given the genuinely accomplished pianists and baton twirlers. But Hokey and I had to at least place in the group section, since there were three awards and just three acts to consider. We watched through the picture window in the science classroom where the judges were scoring. After just a few minutes of haggling, one of them went to the board and erased my and Hokey's names. Only two awards were given. We'd been disqualified. Mr. Shonack told us later that day that some parents were so offended by what we'd done, especially "Plastic Jesus," they had to cut us from the competition.

It was official: I was counterculture. And the Establishment was counter Me. It was my real graduation from junior high.

That was the week I quit shoplifting. Theft had become like an extra limb for me, but it wasn't the Sermon on the Mount that got me to cut it off. It was semi-amazing grace and Jill, a rich, skinny, snooty, and just-pretty-enough-to-be-ultra-popular redhead at Egan.

Wednesday I had brought my usual stash of records to school along with a sports jacket for a class picture they were taking. Wanting to celebrate school's end, after the final bell I went to the Co-Op with my records in tow, along with the bonus jacket, and a resolve to walk into the supermarket and fill my pockets with candy to accompany my usual bonus record or two. I snatched a couple of boxes of Tomoe Ame—my favorite Japanese treat—some Red Vines, a box of Boston Baked Beans, and a bag of Sugar Babies. As I walked out the front door, a short man in a suit, looking for all the world like a wirier Mr. Gonella, darted up from the bench outside the glass double-door. I was inches taller than he was, so, even though my front pockets were full of unopened candy, he couldn't see it. He asked me about the records, I gave him my usual explanation. His voice stiffened, but I had grit and, though shaky, held my own. He checked the records and saw that none of them was sealed. He asked about the extra jacket I was carrying, and I offered to let him search it, because I knew enough not to put contraband in an obvious receptacle. He went through every pocket. Clean. Then he asked if I often walked around stores without buying anything.

"Sometimes. It's a free country." He didn't have a good follow-up to that, so he just warned me. I rode off with a pile of records, including two new ones, and pockets stuffed with candy.

The next day, Jill was telling her friends at school how she was shoplifting sheets at Co-Op the day before and got caught by this short detective. I told her the same detective targeted me, and suddenly Jill and I bonded. I'd outfoxed the man who arrested her. Jill had hardly spoken to me before and now we were pals.

But here's the amazing grace part. I got spooked enough by faux-Gonella and Jill's looming court date that I quit going to Co-Op for good. Still, I tried one more shoplifting run at Hal's. I went in with a friend and slipped the Mothers of Invention's album titled *Absolutely Free* into the pile I'd carried into the store. The clerk came out of the back and asked me about the records under my arm. I explained my art class's open-turntable policy.

"We can listen to whatever we want to."

"Even Frank Zappa?" he asked.

"Sure."

It was clear: this clerk knew exactly what I was up to. And he knew that I knew that he knew. But he didn't say anything more, just eyed me as my friend and I walked out as casually as we could. I never stole a record after that. I even bought a few from Hal's in coming months.

Meanwhile, my flirtation with Eros resumed. Joyce and I had drifted apart, although she'd started wearing a surplus army jacket just like mine. I saw her hanging out more with junior high jocks and even high school freshmen. But on the night before the last day of school, Joyce and I, two other guys, and a newer girl, Madeline, pulled a huge prank that some would call a "happening": we threw cans of paint on the exterior walls of half the campus, then filled the drinking fountains with more paint. Afterwards, Joyce, Madeline, and I, now partners in crime, went to spend the night in two sleeping bags in the ravine behind Joyce's house—Joyce and I in one, Madeline in the other.

I actually prayed it would turn out otherwise.

Madeline was blonde, beautiful, and British, alluring as a lynx in a crowd of alleycats. I hardly knew her, but during that last week she asked to write in my yearbook. She took a pen and wrote this on a blank space near the back: "I know something I can never tell you but I can never forget." I showed it to my friends, who all said she must have a crush on me because what else could that inscription mean? So I hoped we could make out that last night of school behind Joyce's house when Joyce wasn't looking, though I didn't know how.

We stayed up all night talking, Joyce cuddling and kissing me in our sleeping bag. About 5:00 in the morning, Joyce got dozey, and I quietly coaxed Madeline into telling me what she meant by her inscription. And she did.

A few nights earlier, some friends and I were partying in the back of the camper at my friend Bob's. That was the night we tried smoking catnip, all of us wanting a cheap thrill with no legal consequence. The result? Worse than dubious: no high whatsoever but throat burns worse than any chili powder. When we needed to pee, some of us just went to the hedge between Bob's driveway and the one next door. When I did, Madeline was sitting on the other side of the hedge—it was her house and she liked to sit outside looking at the stars. So the secret about me that she'd never forget was that I'd baptized her in urine.

The sun rose and Joyce's mom called out the back door to see if she and Madeline wanted breakfast. Joyce told me to get out of there, and I sneaked off through the bushes. I'd decided to cut graduation—I'd already walked across that stage, khaki-clad and guitar-toting—and now trudged home from the enclaves of the upper middle class to the denizens of Mountain View. My hope level had gone from 10 to 0 in one night, my last night in Los Altos till the '70s.

The Egan yearbook did get it right about me, though. Amid the class pictures, it noted the things for which each graduating senior would be known. Mike Gray, it said, would be known for "his

seemingly endless collection of books, records, and tapes." If the '60s
killed me, at least I had the right epitaph.

In summer '69—my second summer at Dad's house in Oakland—I mostly remember getting drunk on my stepmother Lillian's
overstock of vodka and Gallo wine, playing late-night penny-ante
five-card draw with Dad and his friends, and getting belt-whipped
on my bare butt and back by Dad in the garage after he'd dragged me
out from the crawl space under the house—along with other abuses,
which I, of all people, find too delicate to mention. I hitchhiked
a couple times from his house to Berkeley, where I visited record
stores, Moe's Books, and the Print Mint, the virtual conveyor belt
of the San Francisco psychedelic Baroque. I bought all the Fillmore
and Family Dog postcards I could afford to flesh out my collection.
I have no idea where I got the money.

I grew obsessed with the flamboyantly reimagined lettering of
Wes Wilson. At home I tried to duplicate it, making my own faux
posters for pretend events. This phase didn't last long because Wes
had a fluency and discipline I couldn't ape convincingly—at least not
at the age of thirteen. Two other artists in the Gray/Hicks pantheon
daunted me the same: Mort Drucker of *Mad* magazine, whose fastidious but seemingly spontaneous caricatures have never met their
match, and Frank Frazetta, the modern Rembrandt of fantasy, horror, and mystery. I knew I'd never come close to Frank in technique
or imagination. I tried a few drawings in his style, but as with Wilson and Drucker, gave up.

The two Bay Area artists who captivated me and yet seemed *possible* to imitate were Rick Griffin and Robert Crumb. I fixated first
on Griffin, with his fastidious cross-hatching, flying eyeballs, eclectic
symbol juxtapositions, and pseudo-Victorian lettering styles (see the
masthead for *Rolling Stone*). Mom helped my Griffin mimicking by
giving me quill pens, India ink bottles, and eventually a Rapidograph
pen, which, with my clumsy, unsubtle hands I kept breaking. It was a
long time before I realized I'd already fawned over Griffin's work on
the pages of *Surfer* magazine a few years earlier. My brothers got the
magazine and, other than what we called "surfskates" (later known
as "skateboards"), I had no appetite for the real thing. Or even the

ocean itself, for that matter. I'd taken a few tosses in the waves and preferred dry ground. But Griffin's Murphy comics in *Surfer* had apparently bankshot their way to my psych art fawning.

If Griffin was my Matisse, Robert (or just "R.") Crumb was my Picasso, although a supremely vulgar funny-paper version. I learned his work from *Zap Comix*, copies of which I'd get at Kepler's and a couple more visits to the Haight. The ferocity of Crumb's caricatures of sexual deviancy was my kind of eccentric. I knew nothing about genitalia except my own and the other boys' I'd seen in the showers at Egan. So Crumb's splashy versions of private parts and sex acts didn't impress me so much as shock me. I had no mental warehouse of actual erotic experience to put it in context. But I knew the comic book foundations and joists of his art better than most kids. Mom had always made sure I observed the technique of drawing carefully. So I mingled the old styles I knew from DC Comics and Looneytunes with Crumb's archeological reconstructions of them. I slavishly redrew and made-up comics in pencil and ink at the Formica-topped dinner table and on a portable drawing board I hustled around with me from the living room to the kitchen that adjoined it.

In the midst of trying to draw like Griffin and Crumb, I made my first attempt at writing rock criticism. When the group Traffic's *Last Exit* LP came out, I heard that *Rolling Stone* paid twenty bucks apiece for record reviews. Not realizing that that's what they probably paid their *regular writers*—not semi-literate juvenile hacks like me—I wrote a gushy review of *Last Exit*, saving my beatific praise for the song "Medicated Goo." I folded up the binder paper with my handwritten blue ball-point review on it and mailed it to *Rolling Stone*. I never heard back.

Rolling Stone and all the other counterculture magazines and newspapers I read in the '60s often talked about marijuana ("pot" or "grass" or "weed"), amphetamines ("speed"), and LSD ("acid"), not to mention non-LSD psychedelics like psilocybin, magic mushroom, mescaline, and even the banana peels and hydrangea leaves I'd mentioned in my sixth-grade oral report. Almost everyone I knew was talking about those things, too, although only the "bad" boys were really using them or, at least, lying more convincingly than

My pseudo-underground comics character Norton the Yippie in a
strip I drew for the Mountain View High School *Eagle* (1970).

others about using them. Besides the glue-sniffers, some of us were
trying vague, untested but rumored "highs" not only from catnip, but
from No-Doz, which I took a huge batch of (once) and phenobar-
bital, a few pills of which I stole from Dad and downed during an
unsupervised visit with him (once). My friends and I all knew about
heroin, opium, and morphine, too, but so far they were off our to-do
(or to-lie-about) lists. Those were for Vietnam vets. They'd earned it.

The only vet I knew was my youngest half-brother Larry, who
lived with my oldest, Dave, in San Jose. In mid-August Mom
dropped me off to stay the weekend with them. Dave and I decided
to head up to the Bill Graham's Fillmore West, where the headliner
was the Chicago Transit Authority, a huge, blaring big-band group
who were one album away from changing their name to just "Chicago" and becoming superstars. As we sat cross-legged on the floor
of the huge auditorium, I got handed a joint (a weed cigarette) by
the stranger to my left, took a puff (a "toke"), then passed it to the
right. Soon the guy on my left passed me a half-empty bottle of Ripple wine, which I polished off. You hardly needed to inhale a joint or
drink cheap wine to get high at the Fillmore, though. The air swirled
with weed smoke, which thickened every minute for hours. I was so,
as we'd say, "ripped" by the end of the concert that I thought I was

actually a college-age, draft-dodging hippie, stumbling around when I got up to use the men's room and wandering my way back—no easy feat, given the state of my brain, the gauzy air, and the random cross-legged floor seating. I'd officially graduated from Billy Graham to Bill Graham.

After the concert Dave drove me back to his place in San Jose, where I left the apartment to "get some fresh air" and come back to my senses. But for a half-hour I roamed through the rows of parked cars under carports, stealing every high-end stickshift knob I could get my hands on. Selling those at the flea market—as I'd seen people do when Bruce took us there—was how I and a few friends planned to make more money than we were getting from allowances or birthday cards. Fifty cents a knob, a buck for a classy one, of which I found a trophy example that night.

My *best* friend at the time, though, wasn't a thief. His name, like my veteran half-brother's, was Larry. Like me, this Larry was thirteen. But he looked five years older and could even grow a decent beard. We bonded partly over our non-athleticism, both of us losers on most playing fields. The difference was, he was too big to mess with. So he was sort of like my unwitting bodyguard who even got high school senior girls to, let's say, "party" with him and then would then tell the wide-eyed me all about it. He even gave me a button that summed up our feelings about Christianity. It read: "No Easter this year. They found the body."

Larry lived in a room attached to his divorcee mom's garage. I hung out there with him after school and most nights. The decor under its low-hanging ceiling included lawn chairs, a space heater, and a table draped with an Indian tapestry from Cost Plus Imports. Most of the time he kept only black lights on, which made the fluorescent paint on some of his posters glow. The place reeked of patchouli oil and the sandalwood incense he burned incessantly. We listened a lot to Quicksilver Messenger Service, the Paul Butterfield Blues Band, Pink Floyd, and Ravi Shankar on his half-decent stereo system, with two-foot-high speakers sitting on cinder blocks against the wall perpendicular from the door.

Why am I telling you all this? First, as Thomas More says in *A*

51

Man for All Seasons, "I show you the times." But more important, to lay down tracks for my first miracle.

The morning after the Fillmore West concert and stick-shift knob haul, I walked out of Dave's San Jose apartment, tapped out and grizzly-eyed, and there stood my friend Larry. I nearly fell over for shock, since he lived twenty-plus miles up the peninsula from where Dave did. Now we were face to face in San Jose. It turned out that two blocks from Dave's place Larry's dad had an apartment next to some duplexes he owned and rented out. Larry was staying with his dad for the weekend—*his* visitation—and he said he wanted to show me something.

He walked me to the back of one of the duplexes where there was a plot of about twenty marijuana plants, as carefully tended as any flower or vegetable garden. Larry had already decided to fetch some coffee cans from dumpsters, steal three of the plants, and stash them in the cans. Was I up to helping him? What could the gardeners do—call the police? So we made sure the coast was clear, dug up three, stuffed them in the cans, and temporarily planted them out of sight behind the juniper bushes in front of Dave and Larry's apartment. The next night I revealed the planting to Dave, who was driving me home the following morning. He was justly angry at what we'd done—he could have been cut from law school if he got caught—and drove me back home with the pot plants on the backseat floor, a light towel covering them. When I got home, I put them under a sunlamp in the heating room off my balcony at our townhouse. The sunlamp ran all day, every day, because Larry and I had heard that the cannabis resin in the leaves ran thickest the more sun the plants got. This setup would make them super-potent.

As the plants grew, Larry and I learned how to roll joints with Zig Zag rolling paper, a brand we picked because the Zig Zag logo, with its grinning bearded pirate appeared on a well-known poster for a dance at the Avalon Ballroom. Larry could roll joints by hand, but I preferred a little cigarette roller I'd stolen. I came to pride myself, as did Larry, on rolling a perfect joint—not too fat, not too thin, and not too loose (you couldn't really roll one too tight). Licking the ultra-thin paper's glue edge without wrecking the whole thing was the hardest part. Nobody I knew ever got good at that. But we wanted to be ready to roll joints when we had enough weed from our plants to sell. While waiting for them to be ready to harvest, we filled our practice joints with oregano—another promised pleasure-generator that just burned our throats when we tried smoking it.

After a few weeks of tending our plants and practicing oregano joint-rolling, I cut off some leaves and gave them to Larry to dry and grind up for us to smoke. I hoped this would be "good stuff" and knew pothead Larry would be the best judge of that. A couple of days later the leaves were crispy, and we met in Larry's room, rolled some joints with them, lit up, and smoked them—the first weed I'd had since my night at the Fillmore. But while that Fillmore night had been blissful, now, within minutes of my first toke of our home-grown stash, I literally went out of my mind. Everything around me seemed to flatten like a movie screen, Larry's face got wobbly, and my hearing distorted, crunching up every word we spoke. I closed my eyes while golden lightning shapes shot around in my brain. I heard more and more layers in the music on the turntable—weed did that to all music—but I still got scared as a whipped puppy both for what was happening in the moment and the thought I might never come out of this. I don't know how to describe the next couple of hours. But, even then, I thought Larry had salted the weed with LSD, which he'd used a few times already and wanted me to try.

I didn't tell Larry, but I didn't want any more weed, ever. When-ever I smelled it, I got sick to my stomach, my hands shook, and I started to freak out like I had that night. But I was still committed to doing the things you had to do to be hip. So I kept growing the plants in the heater room off my balcony.

If we were going to sell any weed and make good money, we needed more plants, because it takes a lot of leaves to make even one ounce of the stuff. Larry gave me some seeds that had settled in the one-ounce "lids" (plastic bags of weed) he was *buying* on the side be-fore we started selling. He asked me to grow them into new plants. I read up on the subject and learned it was best to germinate the seeds before planting them. So I laid seeds in rows on a wet paper towel, folded the towel over, and stuck it under my mattress. Each morning I'd check to see what might have sprouted. After a week I had a few seeds that seemed good candidates for planting. They went into two more dirt-filled coffee cans under the sunlamp, where they grew quickly.

One day, when I was watering them and adjusting the sunlamp, I saw something that made my heart start pounding fast and hard. Through the six-inch space between the heater and the exterior wall, I spotted a doorknob for a door on the balcony of the adjacent townhouse. I suddenly realized we and the next-door neighbor shared the heater room. If anyone from that townhouse ever opened the heating room door, they'd see the light from my sunlamp and the leaves of the plants beneath it. Within twenty minutes I tore down the whole setup, stashing the sunlamp in my closet, uprooting the plants, cutting the leaves up and bagging them, dumping the dirt from the coffee cans into the garbage can, sweeping the heating room floor, and doing my best to make it look like nothing had ever been there but the heater.

Not more than an hour after I finished, someone knocked at the front door. Mom opened it and there stood the landlord, a dour, brown-haired thirty-something German immigrant evangelical Christian who'd always made snide remarks to Mom about me and my friends, especially Larry. He stood at the door with a heater filter under his arm and said he'd come to change ours. When he said it, he stared at me as if I were a moose he was about to shoot. It was clear he knew what he'd find next to the heater and was ready to call the cops on me when he did. I grinned and offered to take him up to the heater myself. I did, opened the door, and he turned his head and stared icily at me. As they say, the jig was up—not my jig, though, his jig. He thought he'd nailed me, but the space was clean as a whistle and all the evidence that would have sent me to juvenile hall was gone.

I thought at the time and have believed it ever since: this might be the greatest sleight-of-hand God ever did for me. Had I not seen that doorknob at that instant, Michael Hicks might never have survived the drug-busting criminal justice system of the day. My first miracle. A revelation.

Still, the Friday night before my first fall semester of high school was set to start, I got roughed up by a cop and spent half a night in jail. Why? Remember stick-shift knobs? Two friends and I had amassed a heavy box of them to take to the flea market. We had other stuff, too, including stolen records that I didn't want anymore, all stacked high in the living room of the townhouse, where we were having a sleepover before heading to San Jose the next morning. Mom was out late with, no kidding, Stan. We three guys got bored and thought we'd get more inventory from the cars in the apartment parking lot over our back fence. We opened car doors that were unlocked and got a few knobs. With big pockets in my black leather shirt, I'd volunteered to be the bag man. The first car I myself broke into belonged to a juvenile public defender who saw me from the balcony of the second-floor apartment where he was having drinks with a lady friend. He came running down and confronted us three. Since my friends had no knobs in their pockets and I had them all in mine, he threw me up against the back of his car, pinned my arms back, threatened to kill me if I didn't admit to more thefts than the one I owned up to. I told him this was the first time I'd done this and most of the knobs weren't my haul. But I was the guy with all the evidence. So he sent me and my friends up the stairs to his lady friend's apartment then called the Mountain View Police.

I'd left the rear sliding-glass door of our townhouse open, its floor-length curtains rippling in the night breeze. If the cops had gone to the townhouse, we'd all have been busted for months' worth of theft. But they didn't. They just took us in two separate cars to the police station and called our parents. My two friends' parents came right away to pick them up. They were cited only for trespassing, since there was no evidence of theft.

My mom, though, couldn't be reached. So the cops put me, a thirteen-year-old, in a single-occupancy cell. Hours wore on and just past midnight the police opened the cell door and started questioning me about Mom. Why was she leaving us kids alone? Where would she be? Who was she with? And how much did she drink?

"A glass of wine at dinner now and then."

"How often is 'now and then'?"

That sort of thing, on and on. When she showed up around 2:00 in the morning, they questioned her about her whereabouts that night. She gave them a piece of her mind, and they grumblingly sent me home with her. She muttered some slow, low-voiced admonition in the car as she drove back to the townhouse. I don't remember anything specific about what she said. But I pled guilty to petty burglary and they assigned me a probation officer.

So here I was, a gangly long-haired kid a year younger than his classmates, starting high school in a new town with a probation officer on his tail. Hell or purgatory, not sure which. I salved my wounds with the stolen records in my bedroom and one more visit to the Santa Clara County Fairgrounds, where on September 26 Santana was headlining. I needed some ear-splitting rock to envelop me before a drizzly California winter set in. I took my two partners in crime with me.

I'd seen Santana before. We always considered them a local group. But they'd just played Woodstock in July and their first album had come out on Columbia in August. On this night, the moderate-size crowd sat on the floor of the fairgrounds hall and watched Taj Mahal first, then Elvin Bishop, both of whom I'd seen before, too. When Bishop's set ended and Santana took the stage, streams of Hell's Angels, as if on cue, poured into the hall, and walked up to the foot of the stage, standing in front of all the people who'd sat through the opening acts. After a few songs, Santana started up on "Soul Sacrifice," and we decided to leave because we couldn't see, even standing up, and the atmosphere was more and more menacing. On the way out I stepped in front of one Angel "mama," and she said, "If you get in front of me, I swear I'll kill you." I thought of how that was the second "kill you" threat I'd gotten in a month, once from an off-hours public defender and now from an open-vested arm-tatooed biker girl. The line between sinner and saint was thinner than one strand of my hair.

I wasn't ready to face my new high school, so I cut all my classes for weeks at a pop. Some of the time I stole bikes and rode from our Mountain View apartment to Los Altos High to hang out with my old Egan friends, swap stories and trade guitar licks. But alliances always realign from junior to "real" high school. And I was a cross-district emigrant to boot. I started to feel like a barnacle on old friends'

lives. So I stayed home more and more, occasionally meeting with my probation officer, who threatened to arrest me again for truancy.

At home each day I did four things. One was watch game shows and reruns of sitcoms on TV as I lay on the gold-flowered couch in our puny living room. The second thing: drawing pen-and-ink comics, fancy lettering, portraits, you name it. The third thing was figuring out how to play more songs on the guitar, from "Proud Mary" to "Suite Judy Blue Eyes," neither of which I played better than to earn minor league bragging rights with no one in particular.

The fourth thing—the best thing I did in high school while not *at* high school—was to put my old portable record player on top of the piano for hours at a time, teaching myself the chords of my favorite songs, and basically constructing my own system of music theory at the keyboard. What was I playing? Mostly the blues, but in different keys. Some Beatles, too, from whom I learned chromatic alterations and chord substitutions. The Rolling Stones' *Beggar's Banquet* album, the only one of theirs I owned. And, from memory, a few hymns I liked—"Trust and Obey," "Great Is Thy Faithfulness," and "How Great Thou Art" being my three favorites, all learned at First Baptist, then reprised at PBC. The words of the hymns meant nothing to me, but the music meant everything.

When Mom got home from work, I'd show her things I'd drawn or songs I'd worked up on guitar or piano. Maybe that's why she didn't explode when she got a call from the school saying that I hadn't been attending for the previous three weeks. They'd sent a letter earlier, but I got to it before she got home from work and I tore it up. Now *my* jig was up.

I started attending Algebra pretty regularly because I was good at it and the teacher liked me. (He also enjoyed calling my mom and chatting about my progress, even flirting a bit with faux Dorothy Malone.) I only attended Earth Science a handful of times, but took all the tests and, implausibly, passed the class with a D-, partly because, I sensed, the teacher would do anything to avoid having me in the class again. As I gradually faded back into Mountain View High, I hung out for hours a day in the art room, drew there instead of at home. It was like junior high but with no music, just chatter.

I sold some cartoons. People even commissioned a few from me—
Old West characters and hippies, which were sort of the same thing.

Mom only railed at me for cutting school once: the National
Moratorium to End the Vietnam War. It was raining. I put on that
big-pocket black leather shirt I'd been busted in, but no shoes. I
stole a Stingray bike down the block and pedaled it in heavy rain
from Rengstorff in Mountain View to University Avenue in Palo
Alto, where I went into the moratorium office and volunteered to
sell black "Stop the Killing" armbands on the sidewalk for a couple
of hours. Then thousands of us marched down University Avenue. I
rode home on the same bike and ditched it in some junipers near our
townhouse. I didn't tell my mom about any of this, of course. But a
friend of hers saw me in the march on TV and phoned her up. Mom
scolded me but I never felt sorry, except for the purloined bike.

I soon quit stealing bikes in favor of hitchhiking. It seemed easy
as pie: stick your thumb out on the side of the road and sooner or
later, mostly later, someone would pull over, you'd get in and ride
with them as far as you and they were headed in the same direction.
Looking back, I can't believe anyone ever did this. But the world
turned on a different axis then. I hitched from Mountain View south
to San Jose and back many times, and locally all the time, whether
from Mountain View to Palo Alto, or vice versa, or up and down the
El Camino, just to see where I'd end up. Hitching went smoothly
most of the time. Once, near Foothill College, on Highway 280, the
driver, a guy, put his hand on my leg and kept it there till he dropped
me off. Another time Larry and I were hitching to San Francisco
and the driver was smoking a joint, which he shared with the two of
us. Larry sucked on it a few times. I turned it down. But the smoke
in the tight-windowed car got me stoned anyway.

I stopped hitching when Larry did. One afternoon he got picked
up on his way to San Jose and taken at knifepoint by the driver to a
motel where he had to give oral sex to the guy repeatedly that night
and the next day. The guy then kicked him out and drove away after threats to kill Larry if he went to the cops, which a high school
freshman weed-dealer wasn't likely to do anyway. So Larry was done
and I was, too.

Now, as the '60s were ending, I was thirteen years old and had already *given up* drugs, theft, and hitchhiking. Oh, and a stepfather. And I even started to distance myself from my friend Larry.

Why? Mostly over sex, which I'd had none of but he bragged about lots of. In reply to his bragging, I started lying about this girlfriend I said I had "balled" a few times. He wanted to know every detail of the balling and I wasn't very good at making those up, even with the Crumb comics in my head. So I was pretty sure he was on to me. He said he wanted to meet her, and I kept lying about how busy she was. Still, the girl I was fantasizing about to Larry was clear as day in my mind's eye. I'd seen her a lot at the bus stop and daydreamed about her high hemline swishing on her tanned thighs as she walked up the bus stairs. But she wouldn't have known me from a weed in a coffee can.

After realizing that *Zap Comix* weren't the best source, I studied sex from books I'd stolen or peeked at on Mom's bookshelf. She'd bought a paperback copy of David Reuben's 1969 bestseller *Everything You Always Wanted to Know About Sex* (*But Were Afraid to Ask)*. I got a few tidbits from it, but I was more interested in the less clinical and more phantasmagorical version of sex in the Victorian porn I'd stolen, Henry Miller's books, the Kama Sutra, and, of course, *Playboy*, boxes of which I'd dug through in Bruce's garage. Although Mom had Reuben's book and others of that ilk, she was pretty prudish, at least when she was touting her enlistment in Jesus' army of the saved. But she painted and drew nudes all the time, including a fetching rear-view oil painting she gave Bruce for their bathroom then took back when they split. And she always went to "adults only" movies with Stan. Yet when I got a paperback of the novelized version of *The Graduate* from a recycle bin, she saw it in my room and, without saying a word, locked it up behind the glass door in the hutch.

If truth be told, I wasn't interested in the sex themes of *The Graduate* so much as the fact that the movie's star had suddenly redeemed my middle name. For years, when people asked me what my middle name was and I said "Dustin," they'd say, "Oh, like 'Dusty.' Maybe I should start calling you 'Dusty.'" And they'd have a cheap laugh and never look at me the same. Then, one day in the fall of '69, a girl at Mountain View High asked me what my middle name was.

"Dustin," I said.

Her eyes widened. "Like Dustin Hoffman?"

I thought for a second, then said, "Yeah." In that one moment, something changed in my vision of myself. It was as if I'd been born again, a notion whose religious resonance I knew nothing of.

Which was about to change.

4. SECOND EXODUS

In 1969 the Christian singer-songwriter John Fischer released his first album, *The Cold Cathedral*. His flight from deep-freeze Christianity led him to PBC, where, early in 1970, they held an evening service spotlighting him. Mom urged me to go, and, reluctantly, I did. Looking like an outtake from Peter, Paul, and Mary, he played guitar and sang and talked, and I fell halfway into a trance. I'd grown up with folk music on our radio and record player. The Kingston Trio had been background music when I was a toddler. Simon and Garfunkel had landed neo-folk classics like "Homeward Bound" in my ears. The Youngbloods had bequeathed the world their version of "Get Together." I'd studied "folk guitar" with Laura Weber on TV. And the Beatles had just discovered and recorded a nasal troubadour named James Taylor, whose "Something in the Way She Moves" I often heard on the radio by my bed. Fischer channeled and blended all these influences and sang even more nasally than Taylor—his voice sounded as it were already on the radio. But his lyrics were what made me catch my breath. They were plainspoken sermons that went down to the bone, as rock had always done for me, but playfully, almost gleefully, and with no trace of melancholy.

I went home and called Larry to describe the experience I'd just had. Not interested. One more wedge between us.

And then, suddenly, I got roped into reading the Bible. One of Mom's best friends, Margie, had two daughters, one my age, one three years older. Early in 1970, the older one went on a beach trip with friends, bodysurfed into the waves, and vanished. Coast Guard searches failed, and within a few weeks Margie and friends held a memorial service at PBC. Because of her friendship with Mom, Margie asked that her scripturally illiterate and part-time criminal son read 1 Peter 1:3–9 from the *Good News for Modern Man* translation at the service. I wanted to be prepared, so I practiced and practiced. The words blossomed fresh in my brain every time I read them. It seemed like it was a letter sent to the darkest alleys I'd been wandering through for most of my life. These words jolted me: "it may now be necessary for you to be sad for a while because of the many kinds of trials you suffer." Then the scripture talked about being tried like gold and how you should "rejoice with a great and glorious joy, which words cannot express, because you are obtaining the purpose of your faith." This actually sounded like *good news*. I'd been sad for so long and never thought I'd be jubilant.

Mom's friends said I read the passage beautifully at the service. All I knew was that it felt beautiful, despite the underlying horror of the occasion. And even before the service, I'd started reading the rest of *Good News for Modern Man*. At First Baptist we kids had memorized a few scriptures—like John 3:16—in King James language. But Mom had clung to the Revised Standard Version as her Good Book of choice since the 1950s. Then, about the time Mom started taking me to PBC, she started reading the breezy paraphrase of New Testament epistles called *Living Letters*. I never picked up the book, although it sat on her nightstand all the time. But I did get a strong dose of it through another book that was a pop Christian hit in 1967, *How to Be a Christian Without Being Religious*, an explication of the *Living Letters* version of the Book of Romans, but with cartoon illustrations throughout. Mom recommended it to me and I finally read it alongside *Good News* in 1970. *Good News* resembled *How to Be a Christian* in its light vernacular diction and cartoonish illustrations. But unlike *Living Letters*, *Good News* was a real translation from the ancient texts, I was told, not a modern paraphrase of the English texts. As a vernacular collector, I always wanted fun wedded to authenticity.

Soon I'd read my way from 1 Peter to Revelation, with its visions of many-eyed, many-headed beasts. Creatures like that had been in my sights since I was in grade school, from *Chillers from Science Fiction* to Rick Griffin's psychedelic poster art. But now this. I called Larry and read passages to him excitedly. Again, not interested. He invited me to try some heroin with him, and I knew our roads had irrevocably diverged. I thought his had a dead end and mine led to bona fide adventure.

John Fischer announced at church that he wanted to start a Christian garage band with PBC teens. He held a Sunday night audition in his modest, fluorescent-lit office at the church, to which I brought my pawn shop guitar and played a creditable version of Davey Graham's "Anji." I was in. We started rehearsing in the drummer's garage, spending most of our time on Crosby, Stills, Nash, and Young's "Wooden Ships," which John said was about modern young people's quest to flee the world as it is. That was John's youth-minister approach to the gospel. He'd started his latest Sunday school class by holding up a copy of King Crimson's new album and talking about how "21st Century Schizoid Man" was about alienation from true spirituality. On another Sunday, he unpacked Simon and Garfunkel's "Bridge Over Troubled Water," explaining how we should hear its lyrics in the voice of Christ. We should understand Jesus' shifting relationship to each of us through the lyrics' successive stages from first verse to last.

No more comic books in the parking lot for me.

But we didn't just interpret secular songs through a Christian lens back then. From April 1969 through February 1970, gospel songs flew through the airwaves around us. Not just songs about spiritual hunger, but ones that name-checked Jesus. The Top Four hits of that ilk from April 1969 through February 1970 were "Oh Happy Day," "Spirit in the Sky," "Put Your Hand in the Hand," and "Fire and Rain." The first of these was black church choir singing about that day "when Jesus washed my sins away." It was a huge radio hit that everybody knew and even spontaneously sang in the halls at Mountain View High. "Spirit in the Sky" was an oddball guitar boogie, à la Canned Heat's "On the Road Again," with a young Jew named Norman Greenbaum singing in a sharply contradictory non-bluesy way about how when we die, we're going up to the spirit in the title. The second verse made it explicit: you "gotta have a friend in Jesus," it said. It was infectious and, with Christmas in the air, it became a sort of rock-skewed carol. In February the Canadian band Ocean issued a record that urged listeners to put their "hand in the hand of the man who stilled the waters ... the man from Galilee."

But that same month one more song blasted all the others away in this new Jesus-pop canon: James Taylor's "Fire and Rain." The song's second verse implored, "Won't you look down upon me, Jesus? You gotta help me make a stand." That record made Jesus more hip than anything else in or on the air. Every alienated soul among us sang it without a trace of irony. When we got the album *Sweet Baby James* that contained it, we heard a kind of sequel in the song "Country Road." Taylor sang, "Sail on home to Jesus, won't you good girls and boys?" We were ready to take him up on the invitation, however out of context his offer might be. So, all these songs were like messy angels swarming around John Fischer's catalogue in our ears.

After three jokey, clunky rehearsals of our garage band, John decided we weren't all that committed to Jesus. So he sat us down for the entire rehearsal time and read us scriptures from *Good News*. I don't remember which verses, but, again, they got to me. I felt, as they say in churchier circles, "convicted." I don't think the band rehearsed after that.

John came to my apartment after school one day to do more of this scripture reading and "heart to heart" talking. (I think Mom put him up to this.) He knew about my troubles with the law and truancy and all the "gray days for Gray" I'd had. He could tell I'd been "prepared" for the next step in my path. Seeing some of my artwork, he asked if I'd draw up a prospective cover for his next album. Under the spell of Rick Griffin, I laboriously drew in India ink a scene from the Book of Revelation, with a seven-eyed Lamb of God in a triumphant stance. John accepted it graciously, but it was too disturbing for his purposes.

A few weeks after completing the album cover, I was at Dad's house in Oakland for my Easter visitation. It was late, March 27, 1970, the Friday night before the holiday proper. Dad and his wife, a few of their friends, and I were playing five-card draw for hours on end at the dining table. Midnight came and went. Feeling spent and anxious—as usual with Dad and his entourage—I went into my bedroom. But I couldn't sleep. Come 2:00 a.m. I was still lying awake in the dark. So I decided to talk to Jesus. I started crying, pleaded for rest, pledged to live better, and asked him to come into my heart—again. A tide of warmth washed over me. It was momentary, but for me, it felt like the opening of a door latch into a new way of life. I was born again, again. I slept like a baby till late in the morning. The devil couldn't touch me.

I didn't know what to do next except that I needed to read more about it. Beyond the frisky imagery of the Book of Revelation and the head-patting bromides of Paul the Apostle's letters, literacy of a new sort drove me. Books, books, books, with a side order of tracts and pamphlets. My mom and PBC had already shown me that there were three kinds of Jesus books a Christian had to face. One—my favorite—was the *pop* kind. *Good News* and *How to Be a Christian* were two. But the pop Jesus book I came to like best was H. S. Vigeveno's *Jesus the Revolutionary*. The Jesus some of us wanted to envision, then embrace, was at heart a hippie radical. The pictures had always implied it, the flowing-haired, bearded Jesus whose pictures had hung in our house and First Baptist. But the new images circulating were even edgier: the Soft Jesus I'd been raised on was now Hard Jesus. The Son of Man now = the Son of Manliness. Besides looking like that, Jesus fought the "establishment," that vague nemesis of the counterculture. So *Jesus the Revolutionary* co-opted, then flipped, Abbie Hoffman: this was revolution for the heaven of it.

Then there were the *heady* books. One was C. S. Lewis's *Mere Christianity*, which PBC types took to like high-bred ducks to a royal pond. I was too much a vernacular guy for that one. I wanted my religion folky and a little street-tough. Whatever ideas Lewis purveyed, he sounded like a professor, not a stump preacher, which was the only kind that made me spiritually salivate. An even more hifalutin book was Francis Schaeffer's *Escape from Reason*, which Fischer made the textbook for one of his youth Sunday school classes. Lewis I could eat in small bites. Schaeffer I couldn't get past my soul's lips. I was pretty literate, but still just shy of fourteen. I needed splashy showmen—or shamans—who were the pulpit equivalent of Jim Morrison.

A third book category was the *dark* type. I've thought of different adjectives—*questioning*, *skeptical*, *oppositional*, etc.—but the truth is that we saw these books as bursting from the wrong side of the war between Christ and Satan. They had the library mark of the beast. The two that eventually strained or stained half the friendships I had in high school were *The Last Temptation of Christ* and *The Passover Plot*. The first was a novelized dip into the earthlier, hidden motives and ruminations of Jesus. It was a cult hit in high school, and, although I hadn't read a word of it, I shunned it on the advice of my born-again-before-me comrades. The newer book, *The Passover Plot*, was not overt fiction but a scholarly speculative argument that Jesus and his friends had staged his death and resurrection. It was a conspiracy theory built to counter the divine conspiracy theory we all had been raised with, the one about the "World" vs. Jesus. We Jesus Freaks, as we were starting to be called, disliked both *Last Temptation* and *Passover Plot* because they portrayed Jesus as more man than God. And that was threatening. Our increasingly fervent fanaticism only worked on the basis of Jesus as, to borrow a phrase from the Catholics, *very God*.

Pop, heady, and dark. Those were the Jesus book stacks I was strolling through in my first year of high school. More than any of its competitors, though, the New Testament keep drawing me in. In April 1970 I graduated from *Good News for Modern Man* to the *New American Standard Version* of the New Testament, the scripture of choice for John and the legions of Jesus Freaks now attending PBC. It felt slightly more legit than *Good News for Modern Man*, but it didn't lather my spirit the way *Good News* did. So I switched back and forth. I didn't tell my new brothers and sisters that, though, since they seemed more and more fixated on the less breezy newcomer on the Bible block. But I was willing to trade a translational rigor for more fun.

By the final weeks of freshman year at Mountain View High three things had happened. First, I was playing guitar and leading songs like "Oh Happy Day" daily on the lawn beside the library. I'd mutated from would-be hippie gangster to a vaguely pious disciple with shoulder-length hair, an army surplus jacket, and denim bellbottoms. Second, I started arguing about God with Helen in the art room. Helen was a curly-haired brunette Jehovah's Witness with unrivaled pencil technique, which she devoted to photo-realistic animal portraits on paper that she taped to one of the long Formica-topped tables. She always had a copy of the green hardback *New World Translation of the Holy Scriptures*—the official J.W.

Bible—on the table beside her. I was trying to keep up with her prodigious artistic talent, badly, as we debated God, Jesus, salvation, etc., nonstop. She had her doctrines down cold—from Jesus not being God to transfusions being a sin—and I was a neophyte flailing for Christian orthodoxy as I conceived of it. She was as resolute as granite, so I called our debates a draw—no pun—over and over. No doubt she thought otherwise. But I officially had Jesus in my heart and she didn't even believe in that. So a draw. Still, her quick mind with a thousand scriptures at the ready honed my own thought to a razor-sharp edge.

The third thing was meeting Diana. She'd eavesdropped on my head-butting with Helen and put her own more learned and seasoned thoughts into the mix now and then. After some days of this, she thought I was worth enticing to a Bible study group at her and her mom Alice's place. I started going to it each week. Great discussions, new friendships, and a well-schooled pastor who visited the group now and then: William Pickthorn, Stanford-trained Assemblies of God minister, Bible scholar, and champion of historic "charismatic," gifts-of-the-Spirit style religion. I didn't know anything about that from PBC, let alone First Baptist. But I got indoctrinated, first by precept—Alice had a wall rack of tracts on assorted topics, like fasting, healing, the Second Coming, and even exorcism—and second by example: when we prayed at Alice's Bible studies, I could hear lots of ecstatic, unintelligible, half-whispered murmuring.

Alice and Diana's group had its own ministry, too. Every Sunday afternoon they'd visit three or four women's wards at Agnews State Hospital to sing and chat with heavily drugged patients in varying states of madness. The group could use another guitarist and singer. I eagerly signed up. I found my first visit and every visit thereafter a mix of terror and transcendence. Terror because, since my friend Larry's maybe-LSD stunt, I worried every day that I might be verging on insanity myself. I had waves of anxiety and depression—typical high school ailments—of course. But I also had a fear of psychosis, a fear that I quietly suffered behind the mask of Jesus freakiness. I worried every Sunday why these women we visited were in Agnews and I wasn't. Would I end up there with random teenagers visiting me out of pity?

But our half-hour-per-ward visits were also my ad hoc therapy. Because patients in these wards often had not had visitors for years, sometimes decades, according to their visitor sign-in cards. From the realms of their psychotropically medicated haze they welcomed us the way schoolkids welcome the Good Humor man. Love, joy, and even a trickle of peace ran through every visit. We'd each sit down with one or two women at a time and converse about their lives, the world, and … let's just say that if there was something the Enlight-enment called the New World, every Sunday was a different, one-off New World. The older women (most of them) often had page boy haircuts and heavy rouge and believed they were living in anything from the 1920s through the 1950s, but rarely any year beyond. And every woman, young or old, lived in her own cosmos of beliefs and visions and serpentine craziness that we entered with acceptance and goodwill.

And then there was the singing. We'd have patients join in on Christian classics like "In the Garden," "Old Rugged Cross," "What a Friend We Have in Jesus," "Bringing in the Sheaves," and "How Great Thou Art." We'd sometimes get requests and tried to oblige. "Praise the Lord and Pass the Ammunition" was a favorite. We didn't really know that one, but we were in the Kingdom of the Mad, so melodic precision and harmonic niceties hardly mattered. Jim, the other guitarist, would fake it with me, the two of us eyeing each other's left hands and either imitating each other or compromising. It was like dropping in on *One Flew Over the Cuckoo's Nest* but for women, with guitars and Jesus as the medicine.

We did this for almost two years.

Summer 1970 I went to PBC's Camp Koinonia, with John Fischer and youth minister cohort Ron Ritchie presiding. The camp flowed easily in the "Body Life" vein with a tinge of rock festi-val communalism added in. The coinage of our common lingo at camp—and for the next couple years—included a smattering of Greek terms. "Agape" (pronounced "ah-gah-pay") was the highest form of love. "Maranatha"—a common greeting—meant Jesus was coming. "Parousia": Jesus coming again, again. We had Jesus fish symbols everywhere, on decals and candlesticks and kitschy wood sculptures, because the Greek word for "fish" was an acronym of the name and titles of Jesus. Suddenly, I was everyone's "brother." The family vibe touched and rattled me at the same time. I loved "family" as an idea but hated how it had played out in my life till then. I was even more unnerved by the woods, log cabins, and sleeping beside strangers, dorm style. I was used to being safeguarded in my own walls, in my own bed, surrounded by my purloined books and records, my transistor radio leaning against the wall. Yet the Christian camp's foreignness was my ticket to a slim, blissful ride. So I loved Camp Koinonia and couldn't wait to get home.

As we left camp, we signed one another's *New American Standard* New Testaments as if they were yearbooks. Girls I'd met for the first time at Koinonia left inscriptions like these:

Mike — in JC I love you! You're on my prayer list, remember that I'm prayin' for you every day. Mike, you also gotta remember our deal, a prayer for me in return can <u>always</u> be loved!

"To believe in God is to get <u>high on love</u> enough to look down on your loneliness and forget it forever." WOW heavy! Loving you — I care

Guys were more formal:

To a dear brother in Christ and love whom I pray the Lord may give you his wisdom and the innocence and open heart of a little child. May the Lord's Spirit give you peace.

That fall I got deeper into my Bible-hefting, gospel-singing, Ag-news-visiting study group. And new things were afoot. One was that I got rebaptized in Alice's apartment-complex pool. Pickthorn did the honors for me and other group members. No white robe this time, just jeans and an old plaid shirt. Another new thing was that I started meeting with the group for early morning prayer—6:00 a.m. at Alice's place, all of us kneeling and one-by-one lifting up our voices with an out-loud prayer or, scarier than that, tongues and prophecy. We'd been studying 1 Corinthians 12–14 and Acts 2, the core texts of the "Charismatic Movement" that I was just realizing I was part of. The old-school vernacular term for this was "Pentecostalism." That was, to my mind, Oral Roberts-ville, an outpost of what Greil Marcus called "Old Weird America." But the Charismatic Movement was part of the New Weird America—my America. Over-the-top, improvisatory, spirit-filled artifacts of gritty human experience were all I ever craved. Now I had it. Larry had a fluorescent psychedelic poster with a black cat on it and the words "The Kingdom of God Is Within You" blazing from its surface. That's where we lived, hippies or Jesus Freaks. The mailing address was the same.

The "prophesying" that I took up with my friends was to hesitantly but loudly proclaim in the voice of God—Father or Son, it didn't matter. "The Lord" covered them both. I, and others who did this, typically declared to the group that the Lord was with us, that he wanted to bless us more, that he had "a work" for us to do, etc. Sometimes there was an exhortation, some ornamented version of "do more" or "be better," but always on the premise that the reward was more blessings. As often as not, these God-utterances were "interpretations" of speaking in tongues. And tongues were the initiation into full-blooded Jesus-freakery.

I could only speak in tongues, my friends said, after I'd received the "Baptism of the Holy Spirit." It was a phrase borrowed from Jesus then repurposed by nineteenth-century evangelists like Charles Finney, whose autobiography I'd recently checked off on my "to read" list. The baptism of the Holy Spirit was what one sought after the mere "baptism of water," which I'd already had twice. It was the sudden "indwelling" of God. Just as we talked about accepting Jesus into one's heart, this was accepting the Holy Spirit as Jesus' roommate there. At our Bible study sessions at Alice's house, people often mentioned the experience. The night I asked to receive it, everyone there, about seven men and women, laid their hands on me as I sat in what they called the "prayer chair." I would only know for sure that I'd received this spiritual baptism if I spoke in tongues. As they kept their hands on my head—now steeply bowed from the weight of those hands—they all spoke in tongues, now softer, now louder, interrupting their jubilant nonsense with "Baptize him, Lord," "Hallelujah," "Thank you, Jesus," or just "Jesus, Jesus," repeated over and over, usually whispered, but forcefully, as if it were the plural of "cheese." But I couldn't speak in tongues, didn't know how to start. Alice said I was just too "timid."

That night, though, one of the girls, Annie, drove me home. She was pretty, older, smart, and chic, and worked a desk job at IVC. I lay in the back of her van not saying anything but feeling flushed with what I knew was the Spirit. She told me to keep praying when I got home and then to just "let your tongue go." But, when we reached my house, she took me by the hand and, awkwardly, like a stuttering first grader, I started to speak in tongues.

It was not a torrent of syllables. It was more a dribble of phonemes. Like a flooded engine it kept getting stuck, then revving up and restarting. Annie spoke at the same time as I did and kept squeezing my hand as though milking it. Her tongues-speech was smooth, slick, and confident. She'd done it for years. If I was a leaky spigot, she was the Jordan River—although I thought my spiraling syllables were more colorful. My tongues-speech was like a studio remix of other languages, snippets of Spanish, French, German, Hebrew, Russian, sliced and spliced into a new language. Annie's was more uniform, direct and plain.

How did I do it? Well, I didn't know it before then, but I'd prepared. I'd not only taken Spanish classes since sixth grade at Bohnett, but now I was a sophomore in high school taking French and German as well. I tried to take Latin, too, but no one else wanted to, so the only Latin teacher on campus had to turn me down. So I started studying it and other languages on my own from library books. I also bought pocket-sized manuals on Hebrew and Greek, the biblical languages, which I craved to learn. I bought up Living Language record sets in Italian and Russian from the local St. Vincent de Paul store.

In a backhanded way, speaking in tongues seemed a natural fit. Most of the tongues-speaking I heard, though, didn't sound bona fide. It babbled and shuddered. The languages that I studied didn't. Every church or conference or revival we went to, people spoke in tongues. Much of it sounded grotesque—a kind of spasm where syllables got squeezed out by God like paste from a tube. The speakers convulsed as they held their hands up, shaking, crying, and if "the Spirit" was strong, collapsed on the floor. They blubbered from the top of their speaking range down to the bottom. Evangelists often interjected it between English sentences as they held the arms of folks on whom they were about to lay hands, letting each person fall back on the floor, quivering—an Aimee Semple MacPherson-style

71

move they called being "slain in the spirit." Now and then a church friend would brag about how someone heard them speaking in tongues and identified it as some African dialect or, in one case, "Ancient French" (Annie told me that one). But most tongues sounded like "she bought a Honda" or something like that. Maybe divine, but not from a God I'd want to spend too much time with.

When *I* was doing it, though, I could feel the syllables form in my mouth as a divine confection of all the languages I'd studied. It was like scat singing, but without the melody, a loose improvisation from the huge cache of phonemes stored in my self-educated tongue. I remember lots of the words—I said them for years—words like "puriaki" and "kantistima." If I worried that other people's tongues sounded too little like real languages, I worried that mine sounded too much like a mere kaleidoscope of languages I'd studied. But the spirit burned in me so strong that I learned to snuff out worry. About this, at least. The antidote to teenage anxiety? For me it was speaking in tongues.

We all sang in tongues, too, most often at the end of a song, where we called it "singing in the spirit." We'd hit the last chord and then keep singing in pentatonic scales (think the black keys on the piano), soaring ditties with ad hoc lyrics that mimicked our prayers, all checkered with tongues. The pentatonic scales kept the music from clashing—there was no real dissonance. These singing spells would last five minutes or maybe ten, maybe more—hard to say, since we were trying to stay outside time in an inadvertent rehearsal for eternity. Heaven help us if we let a clock on the wall stunt our praise.

Via our tongues-speaking, "interpretation," and lots of post-prayer-meeting brainstorming, we decided the next step for us was to open a coffeehouse. Since Alice ran an eponymous employment agency—Alice Allen Associates—she had her ears on the local small business scene. A couple of blocks from the Brass Rail bar and strip club in Sunnyvale, there was an oblong cinder block building with side-by-side store fronts. One was a neighborhood grocer, the other was vacant. We all thought the vacant space would make a great "drop-in center," the common name for any place where teenagers hung out for conversation. If we had a place like that, especially one that served coffee and donuts, we could lure grocer patrons and curious adolescents like me into the front door and talk to them about Jesus. Even get them to accept Jesus into their hearts, if we were lucky. Alice and guitar Jim got money together for a down payment.

I quit PBC and started attending Pickthorn's Assemblies of God church in Palo Alto. It was fully decked out with vintage Pentecostalism—boisterous hymns, tongues, healings, and revivals. What I remember most about his church, though, was an evening service in which the guest speaker was a friend of Annie's, a guy from San Jose named Larry Norman. I'd seen him in concert twice before, at the two folk rock festivals, when he was in a rock group called People. Now he'd just released a dazzling solo LP on Capitol called *Upon This Rock.* I bought it and played it again and again on my little record player, learned every lyric and chord progression. It came on the heels of John Fischer's latest, *Have You Seen Jesus My Lord,* but swerved harder toward the rock and blues that steamed in my blood. Now, standing at the front of our chapel with thick, shoulder-length platinum blonde hair framing an incandescent face, Brother Norman spoke softly about his faith in Jesus. Then he pulled his steel-string guitar from the case and, after a half-whispered verbal introduction, strummed a single power chord and soulfully blared out "Forget Your Hexagram," a stark warning to occultists that "the rules were set down long ago, when the spikes went in the wood." The congregation shifted in their seats, less at the message than at the messenger's style, which would have been raucous even for PBC. This church was pretty staid, despite the miraculous flamboyance of its origins. But that night, especially when Norman floated into his mellower songs, I went to post-John Fischer heaven.

I learned the lay of this new musical Jesusland at another festival in a field in San Jose—but my first overtly religious one. I don't remember any of the groups who played that afternoon except Love Song, rising stars in the day, whose "Front Seat, Back Seat" sounded like a tamped down Grateful Dead tune. The festival introduced the song to me, and, for months after that, I sang it to myself whenever I could, cheating on the lyrics, since I had no source except what I and some friends remembered from that day.

I was sittin' in the front seat
Tryin' really hard to be the driver
Thinkin' I was makin' real good time
But always windin' up the late arriver
But now I been tryin' out the back seat
And I find it is a very great relief
Now I'm ridin' in the back seat
And I'm leavin' all the drivin' to the Chief

What bothered me about the event was the acrid alfalfa smell of marijuana drifting through the crowd starting minutes before the first group played and lasting until the final electric guitar chord rang through the field. I hated weed since the Larry/LSD debacle and thought—just as George Harrison did about meditation and LSD—that we were past that, that Jesus was the new, improved euphoria of choice. To me, the weed smell dropped a profane bomb into this sacred fest.

Our Bible-study group soon migrated from Pickthorn's Assembly of God church to the down-home rural-suburban Calvary Gospel Temple in Santa Clara. I don't recall why, other than that Alice quarreled with Pickthorn, who was never radical enough for her. Calvary Gospel was more rough-hewn, free-form and noisy, like a black church but with pinker faces. Our group joined en masse and became the new "it" group there. We were, except for Alice, younger, but still full of the old-time fire that Pentecostal types drank instead of cocktails. We were utterly, almost militantly, devout, religiously self-contained and resistant to any authority but charisma, which Calvary Gospel's pastor, Hugh Rounds, had gallon-loads of. He was jolly, a recovered drunk, "saved by grace," as he always reminded his congregation, who preached with simple, vibrant southern color. Sunday meetings included lots of ad hoc speaking in tongues, something almost anathema in Pickthorn's church. The most eloquent and frequent practitioner of tongues at Calvary Gospel was John Hole (pronounced "hula"), whose thick Norwegian accent and multi-lingual skills flavored his gift as he stood up and spoke out like a foreign preacher executing a coup on the meeting. After each strange tongues outburst, we'd sit in awkward silence till someone interpreted. Each message from Deity was like the kind we got in our prayer meetings: you're righteous, praise me, repent, love me, I'll protect you, etc., with short biblical phrases strewn throughout. Then more awkward silence till Pastor Rounds resumed or we sang again.

Sunday nights a couple dozen Calvary Gospel members recorded a half-hour radio show called *Camp Meeting Time*. Our group almost doubled the size of the ad hoc choir for that program, which sang songs like those we sang at Agnews, as well as the show's title theme "There's a Meeting Tonight (Meeting at the Old Campground)." Pastor Rounds jaunted around the pulpit strumming a four-string banjo as we sang, keeping it on his shoulder when he gave mini-sermons between songs. Beyond "Jesus," I don't remember a single word he said at the pulpit or on the radio. But I soaked up his style, especially how to use a microphone, when to get in tight, when to back off, and when to modulate one's voice. His techniques were pretty standard in the pulpit world. They were new to me, though. I studied them, quietly, under his tutelage-by-example and used them for the rest of my life. (I even spoke a little on the *Camp Meeting Time* show one night, transcriptions of which are blissfully inaccessible.)

Sometimes Pastor Rounds brought in visiting pastors for revival services. That was when things got wildest at church—louder speaking in tongues, whole-body shaking, dancing in the aisles, and getting "slain in the Spirit." One of Rounds's favorite guests was Emanuele Cannistraci (pronounced "can-a-stracey"), a short, smart, blustery Italian American who, it turned out, was about to take over the temple.

That November a new concept album came out, riding on the wave of those earlier Jesusy hits. *Jesus Christ Superstar* told the story of Jesus through his death—no resurrection, the linchpin of Christians—with the same humanistic tinge as *Last Temptation of Christ*. Jesus wasn't God, just maybe a god, manufactured from adulation. One of my schoolmates, Nancy, sang the album's radio hit "I Don't Know How to Love Him" in a school talent show, convincingly. It was a great love song, usable by the hosts of the smitten around the world, with or (mostly) without Jesus. But I hated the trappings of it. To true Jesus Freaks it was blasphemy.

At that same talent show, I sang two John Fischer songs: "Salvation Song" and "Light," which seemed to harmonize with all the

The linoleum block image of Jesus I made for Christmas cards in 1970.

Jesus/God songs on the airwaves, including the latest by George Harrison, "My Sweet Lord." My two-song segment in the show was the born-again sequel to my Egan talent show debut. When this show ended, I got little response except from my fellow disciples at Mountain View, among whom I was becoming a bit of a leader. As if to ice the cake of my notoriety, I sanded down the face of the pawn-shop guitar Dad had bought me, stained it chocolate brown, and painted a huge red cross on it with "Jesus" painted in green on the crossbar.

5. NEW WINESKINS

Come spring 1971, I wrote to Mom's parents, surveying my new life:

> I have felt in these past few months that the Lord was leading me into languages (esp. Hebrew) and the study of linguistics, and He seems to be blessing my studies. I also have a very good Arab friend (he just came from Cairo) who is teaching me the Arabic language. In exchange, I am teaching him U.S. history. He also has given me much insight into Arab-Russian-Israeli relations that helps in the study of Biblical prophecy.
>
> Back to our coffeehouse: We (some Christian friends & I) got it a couple of months ago & we've been working on it to get it open. The name of it is "The Wineskin" (see Matthew 9) & the Lord is blessing tremendously. (We worked on it yesterday for 13 hours straight till almost 1 o'clock AM.) People have donated furniture, money, wall-to-wall carpeting, lamps, electrical service, and most importantly, themselves and their service. Pray for us.

We'd been toying with the term "wineskin" for months. Jesus had taught his disciples not to put new wine into old wineskins but only into new wineskins. We decided the Holy Spirit was the new wine and we were the new, i.e., young and pliable, wineskins ready to be filled. So why not name our new venture "Wineskin"? After we cleaned the building out, painted the cinder-block walls pastel yellow, dragged thrift-store couches and easy chairs into the faux-living room near the front, we were ready to host visitors on Thursday, Friday, and Saturday nights. Other than friends we invited, almost no one came.

It didn't matter much. However badly decorated, it was our suburban temple-in-miniature. We knew we were enriching the city of Sunnyvale, pouring goodwill from our wineskin into the neighborhood. During open hours, guests or no guests, Jim and I played guitars and led the singing of gospel songs with a little improvised harmony. Most of the songs were from our Agnews playbook. But we also sang newer novelties like "I Was There When It Happened" and three original songs I wrote during the Wineskin's early months. The first one was a barnburner called "Arise," about Jesus healing the man at the pool of Bethesda. Its upbeat country gospel chorus went:

> He said, "Arise, take up thy bed and walk"
> And then He made the lame man whole
> He said, "Arise, take up thy bed and walk"
> And then He saved his lowly soul

The second was a slow-walking solo whose lyrics I adapted from the Book of Revelation, where Jesus tells the narrator (in the song's chorus)

> I am he that died for you
> And, behold, I live evermore
> I'm the Alpha and Omega
> The Bright and Morning Star.

The third, my favorite, was "A Song in My Heart," a John Fischer-ish pop-gospel song with lines like this:

> My soul was lost in darkness
> Living in this world of sin
> Then I cried, "Please help me Jesus"
> I opened the door and he walked in
> And now I know that he's my friend

Then the chorus:

> He put a song in my heart
> You know I'm gonna sing it
> He gave me a brand new start
> And now I'll let my voice ring it
> He's the one who set me free.

Between songs, we sipped from our coffee mugs, chatted about the Bible, and listened to cassettes of favorite preachers expounding doctrine. We always had a coffeemaker going and the pungent aroma filled our noses. While I don't remember serving much of the brew, except to ourselves, I do remember that we always had free donuts to give away, day-olds that we got free from a local market

Talking about Jesus between songs during the Wineskin years.

through some friend of Alice's. Every open hour, we served and ate these plump, half-smashed, chewy glazed ones. We always had more than we could wolf down. It was years after my Wineskin days before I could eat another donut—the saturation level was a mile high.

"Wineskin" was an odd name for a coffee house, of course, because most people who heard it assumed we were a bar. But we decided that the misunderstanding was good, because we wanted people who were looking for bars so we could save them. With the Brass Rail in plain view nearby, we had a few alcohol-friendly locals who'd drop in from time to time. The most frequent was a short, chubby, retired Italian transplant named Joe, who loved to sing a solo version of "Amapola" to me outside the coffee house because he thought I looked like a girl. Which I did, sort of, thick blond locks draped on my shoulders, Larry Norman-style, but my hips narrow as a speed-freak fashion model's. I always had to insist to Joe that

I was a guy. Every time I thought I'd convinced him, he still sang "Amapola" to me and then made a joke about how it was written by a polar bear.

All that year I built my life into a cabin with three rooms: my education—which only marginally included classes at Mountain View High—my personal campus ministry, and, as we now called ourselves, the Wineskin group. The woman I lived with? Not so much. Mom had her own life, proofreading Silicon Valley tech manuals, dating prospective boyfriends, and wallowing in Parents Without Partners, a group I thought benign, almost noble, but which she later described to me as a sexual "cesspool." If that was true, I can't fault PWP for congealing into that. This was the era of "free love," in which multi-partner sexual "exploration" was *de rigeur*. I stayed out of all that. I never even went on a date in high school. I had girl friends, a fair number, but no girlfriends. I lived in a mystic-puritanical world of disembodiment and tight filtering of high school social life as normatively enacted. I know it existed, like the mountain ranges of Santa Clara Valley, on the horizon. But it was miles away from my head, even though I went to high school every day.

Don't get me wrong. While I wouldn't cross the hallway to see a football game, I still had crushes, as I'd had since Cathy at Alameda, and fantasies to boot, either about girls I knew or, more often, media images—the cover to Nancy Sinatra's *Boots* album comes to mind. But I was both too afraid and too pious to delve into the ordinary boy-girl scene. Nerd without skills, cute guy without guts, I was just wired differently. How many of my friends, for instance, had a long, handwritten prayer list in their bedroom that they went through, name by name, for an hour or so every night, speaking to God about their needs, pleading their cases, and thanking heaven for them? And then serving communion to himself? And then getting up for a 6:00 a.m. prayer meeting every weekday morning, where he'd speak in tongues and, on a good day, speak the word of the Almighty?

Because I started each day so early and was up late each night at the Wineskin, I usually took a nap in my bathrobe on my bunkbed after school. One Friday afternoon, the door knocked. I answered it and there stood Stan in his sport coat and slacks, carrying a black briefcase. He said he had a date with Mom but didn't have time to go home and could he shower at our place? I said yes, then went back to my room. After his shower, he knocked on my door. I opened it, and, with just a towel around his waist, he told me he needed to show me something, walked into Mom's bedroom, opened his briefcase, and dumped out piles of black-and-white snapshots he'd taken of women's genitalia at "parties" he'd been to, a couple of girl-on-girl porn magazines, and an oblong white vibrator. He kept putting different pictures in my face, switched on the vibrator, and pushed it up under the hem of my bathrobe. I backed away, he laughed, then opened his towel on Mom's bed, laid back on it, spread magazines and photos all around the bed, and—I'll leave to your imagination what he spent the next couple minutes doing till he was done. He switched off the vibrator, cleaned himself up, put the porn back in his briefcase, got dressed, and greeted Mom at the door when she arrived home. After she freshened up, she left with him for yet another X-rated movie.

I kept quiet about this till Sunday morning, when Mom told me he was picking her up for lunch. I told her what he'd done two days earlier, insisting that, on Christian grounds, she had to stop seeing him. Incredulous at first, she seemed less and less surprised, knowing the backwaters of his past. When she came home from lunch, she said she had told him what I'd said, he denied it, and she compromised by telling him not to come to our place when he knew she wasn't there. But she didn't break up with him. Which was how Mom broke up with me.

I don't remember subjects at high school. I remember a few assigned books, like Hinton's *The Outsiders* (which I hated) and Hawthorne's *The Scarlet Letter* (which I counted a notch on my literacy belt, like Deuteronomy). I remember a few jarring moments that lingered with me for days, even years. One was seeing *Cosmic Zoom*, the Canadian film short that gradually zooms out from a boy rowing a boat until you see the earth, then the solar system, then galaxies, then reverses and goes back to cells, molecules, atoms, and sub-atomic particles. I was shaken. It was the scale and proportion schtick of the *Twilight Zone*, but now made "real." My whole sense of human existence never quite recovered, which seemed to be the point. Another neurosis trigger was when a history teacher told us how, if an atomic bomb hit, we'd be instantly vaporized, with no warning or indeed no point in "ducking and covering," as we'd been taught to do since we were toddlers. So, not only was I a speck in infinity, I was an utterly transitory speck. Between Stan and the indifferent cosmos, it's no wonder I kept fleeing into the arms of Jesus.

By then, my reputation as a semi-haloed high school Jesus freak was pretty solid. One day on the rainy corner of campus, I ran into a wide-eyed teenage guy with curly brown locks leaning against a fire hydrant. We introduced each other and I started talking to him about Jesus, my usual conversation starter in those days. He smiled a lot, nodded, seemed like an eager prospective "win," whom I was just about to ask if he might receive Jesus into his heart as his personal Savior. All of a sudden, he asked, "Are you Michael the Archangel?" Stunned, I told him no, suddenly surmising that his brain was as soaked in hallucinogens as mine and my Wineskin friends' were in the Lord. The magical mystery tours that we both cruised through differed only in their brands. Those days in the Bay Area you never knew—at least, at first—who cherished LSD or Buddhism or Carlos Castaneda's "Yaqui Way of Knowledge" or Satanism or, yes, Jesus. I think we all had to find a reality that didn't include Nixon or Vietnam. Because those were the reality on the news every night.

As I began my junior year, our Wineskin group launched a new, all-consuming venture: a halfway house for drug addicts and alcoholics. Alice had this project at the top of her checklist of personal redemption. Like Pastor Rounds, she was an alcoholic who'd quit drinking through Jesus—and A.A.—and now wanted to augment her ministry by getting state referrals to what would be a Jesus-oriented live-in facility a few blocks from the coffeehouse. At fifteen, I didn't understand the finances or logistics of the house as a business. But I was at the Wineskin House, as we called it, almost every evening for the next fifteen months.

We didn't use the front door because it opened onto what was now a three-bed bedroom for male clients. Most nights no more than two of its beds were occupied. Beyond that room were more bedrooms, including Alice's, a kitchen with an adjoining dining room, two bathrooms, and a large family room where we had prayer meetings, singing, and more "rap sessions." Between an easy chair and a couch was a fireplace and a small bookshelf filled mostly with religious books. Walter R. Martin's anthology of putdowns, *Kingdom of the Cults*, dominated the shelf, at least in my mind. I smiled just leafing through it, because Martin clearly was rassling with orthodoxy in a tiny ring for which only he owned the ropes. I read from it all the time, partly to understand my Jehovah's Witness and Mormon friends at Mountain View High, but mostly because it had weird, mind-blowing teasers. And for me that was a menu of desserts. The menu of other books—pop, heady, or dark—couldn't hold a candle to this one.

As for "treatment" for our live-in clients, I don't recall anything that wasn't based on the most quoted scripture amongst us back then, II Thessalonians 3:10: "if anyone is not willing to work, then he is not to eat, either." Work to eat. That was most of the treatment. Daily chores as salvation. Among those, the kitchen-strip-and-repaint was our descent into the maelstrom. Late into the night, stripping the beige walls, brushing paint remover onto them, then sticking our broad scraping knives into the multicolored layers of paint and sliding the blades straight up the surface. The paint curled and plopped onto the plastic sheets we'd spread on the floor. It was as if we were skinning the walls the way old settlers skinned the bison whose bones were buried deep underfoot. But now we were our own prey: every breath, our own lungs were being skinned from the inside. It was like Filipino pilgrims flogging themselves with bundled bamboo sticks to bloody their backs and catch Jesus' attention, except it was happening inside our own chests. For hours, night after night, we slid our scrapers up the walls, each stroke trying to reveal the original tint of the walls. Which we eventually did. It was canary yellow.

Beyond this project and daily cleaning, we ate together—usually sloppy joes, grilled cheese, and tuna casseroles for lunch and dinner, with cereal, scrambled eggs, and those day-old donuts dominating the breakfast menu. At night we kept the coffeehouse open. I was usually there, guitar in hand. I can't say if the coffeehouse became an extension of the halfway house or vice versa. Both were long, unbroken scenes of religious stasis or ritualized blue-collar worship. But they were one ministry in our minds, two chambers of the same heart.

I remember only a few of the residents at the Wineskin House. Three in particular: Brad, Joseph, and Fred. Brad was our only acid head. Curly reddish-brown locks flipping over his temples, with a scraggly beard and broad smile, he'd supposedly blown his mind on LSD. That was all I heard about his background. His foreground was a chipper, boyish, unpredictable, mostly jovial resident, who complied with our own Jesus-grade insanity. After living with us for a few weeks, he got a foot smell problem that radiated through the house like a fireplace with the flue shut. We made him bathe and bathe, use different soaps, and, finally, submit to an exorcism. Yes, the Demon of Odor—whom we apparently had not enough faith to drive out of Brad. I don't recall how or why the smell left him, if it actually did before Brad moved away. But his departure blew out a beautifully unkempt flame in the place.

Joseph was Brad's opposite. A late-middle-aged, wiry professional gardener with high energy, a quick wit, but a face beneath his bald pate that always looked worried. What tales from his past drove him to the bottle I didn't know. But he was supremely polite and took a gangly teen like me under his wing, at least, when it came to gardening. His greatest legacy in my life, I suppose, was a love for the coleus plant, its broad leaves, with purple centers and frilly gray edges. He loved coleus for its hardiness and ease of care. After a couple of months with us, Joseph graduated back to a solo life. A couple months later, he was back, his face looking more worried than ever.

Fred was my first Indian. We didn't use the term "Native American" back then, and I don't think Fred would have appreciated it. He was an Indian and proud to say so. Black-haired, though balding, handsome as a pedigreed pup, Fred almost always spoke sotto voce through semi-clenched teeth. You could get a grunting laugh out of him with the right quip. But profound hurt always seemed submerged under his placid surface. My claim to fame with Fred? I taught him how to play guitar, with Hank Williams—my latest musical crush—our only repertoire. At the drop of a hat, we'd sit down together and I'd strum and sing "Cold, Cold Heart" or "I'm So Lonesome I Could Cry" or—befitting our Wineskin trappings—"I Saw the Light," as Fred awkwardly, stutteringly tried to finger the chords and strum in time with me. If anyone wondered whether Fred loved to drink: he did. I know because he sometimes went astray with a beer or two that we could all smell and which he always denied.

During that year and a half, I learned so many things about alcoholics. I can't distill those things well into words. You learn them like you learn the faces of relatives, not verbally but holistically. Let me just toss these few thoughts on the table. An alcoholic develops his own pendulum that swings from self-medication to tearful recrimination and back. Before the pendulum reverses direction comes a pause, an interval of lying through glazed eyes and slushy speech. I saw men on that pendulum so many times: the steely resolve and discipline, then the moment you smell some secretly procured alcohol on their breath, the confrontation, the adamant denial, until, within hours to days to weeks, all the emotional blocks they've stacked up tumble down. Tears, contorted face, blame for their upbringing or whoever cheated on them or wronged them, then a resolve to never succumb to the bottle again. I choke up remembering it, not so much because of the sorrow that pours through me when I recall the cost alcohol has exacted on the world, but when I think of what sensitive, sweet-hearted people all the alcoholic men I knew tended to be. They could play me and all of us Wineskinners sometimes, make us feel like we'd been had by the most manipulative guy in the county. But the better I knew them, the more profoundly I felt their inner hurt. The bottle was their hospital, its contents the only medicine that smothered the voices screaming in their heads. I loved being with them and hated being with them. And, at some level, I sensed that I was them.

As we settled into the Wineskin House routines, I kept up my Mountain View High ministry. Prayer meetings on the lawn and "witnessing" (talking about Jesus) whenever and to whomever I could. Some called me a "Bible-thumper," partly because I carried my *New American Standard* or *Good News* around with me and read aloud from them to others when they'd let me. A local newspaper mused about all this:

Savior Alive, Well For These Pupils

"Tell 'em Jesus Christ is alive and well," a very religious Mike Hicks said Friday.

Sitting on the slightly damp front lawn at Mountain View High during a breezy afternoon, Mike and six companion Christians were getting it on for their Savior.

A bit of silent prayer every morning before school and a once-a-week gathering after school, usually on Thursdays, is their regimen.

Mike, a bright-eyed Junior, and some 15 others have organized Mountain View High into the latest Peninsula school to come under the influence of what mocking students like to refer to as Jesus Freaks.

"If I have to be called a freak," Mike retaliated, "I'd rather be a freak for Jesus."

Hicks helped get the Students for Christ movement going at the beginning of the semester, spreading the word one day that there would be an after-hours prayer meeting.

Some two dozen pupils showed up and the idea had a following.

The students began praying together every other day and now it's every morning, heads bowed reverently in the comfort of the social studies resource center which faces the front of the school.

A violation of the church school separation laws, you say.

Not the way the kids see it. Their administration advisors say they can pray all they want on the school grounds as long as it is either before school or after.

There's a committed corps of about 15 students, but some come, some go.

Ed Pidcock, an 11th grader who joined Mike and his friends Friday afternoon, has been praying at school for about a week.

"I met Mike at church last weekend," he said. "He told me about the students for Christ at Mountain View High. So I showed up."

"We're not unique," Hicks said. "There are groups like us all over, at Palo Alto High, Gunn, Wilcox in Santa Clara, Awalt, even some junior highs.

"We pray every day because being a good Christian means praying not just on Sunday, but every day."

Although there was nothing ecumenical in our outlook, a few of us Jesus Freaks at Mountain View once visited the large adobe Catholic church across Castro Street from campus. We knelt on the kneelers behind the pews, whispering our usual "Jeeeeeesus" pseudo-mantras. A priest walked up and asked what we were doing. We said, "We're praying."

Large illuminated manuscript of the first verses of
Genesis I drew in high school art class.

"Are you Catholic?" he asked.

"No."

After a long pause, as if in the rhythm of a sitcom, he said, "Strange. Very strange." He walked away and we went back to "Jeeeeeesus."

I went to the church a few times alone. The sense of awe at the panorama of the candlelit Stations of the Cross enveloped me like the evergreen forests down the coast. I started to get an appetite for high church culture, which seemed far beyond most Wineskinners' grasp. It was my quiet, secret passion.

My thirst for "secular" knowledge also intensified. Sort of. For example, I had to "prove" (or disprove) the authenticity of speaking in tongues. So I tried an experiment. I hauled my Craig tape recorder around campus for a week, taping every authentic foreign language speaker I knew, including Roushdi, my friend from Cairo about whom I'd written to my grandparents. I taped other friends who spoke Hindi, Serbo-Croatian, Farsi, and all the standard European languages. I even got a lapsed Jew to recite his old bar-mitzvah texts into the microphone. Then I taped a few of my friends speaking in tongues. The "real" language speakers loved being archived this way. And my tongues-speaking friends loved the thought I might validate their gifts and happily uttered their devout mumbling into my machine.

I listened to all of them in sequence to see if the tongues sounded as convincingly structured as the known languages. I played my six-minute tape over and over. It was tough comparing tongues and "tongues," partly because I knew which was which. I played the tape for friends who didn't know what I'd done and asked them if they could identify the languages. I hoped no one would say, "Hey, that one's not a real language." But linguistic competence, or even curiosity, at Mountain View High was rare. So I got no resolution inside or outside of myself.

I wish I'd kept the tape. But I had no money and had to keep using the same reel for everything, including, this time, James Taylor on the radio.

Despite my left-brain cravings, my life always reverted to right-brain pursuits. Some of those I owe to Satan, who apparently hadn't given up on me since our cribside run in. Satanism was trendy in those days. Since the mid-'60s the San Franciscan esoteric Anton LaVey had gotten lots of airplay in interviews and even had a best-seller with his *Satanic Bible*. You'd see that book carried around now and then at Mountain View. I shunned it, mostly out of fear, since I believed utterly in the prevalence of demons.

You see, Alice championed the Shepherding Movement, two of whose practitioners, Bob Mumford and Derek Prince, dominated the cassette soundtrack to our lives. Prince, in particular, mentored his flock on the need for constant exorcisms. We all had more demons than we could imagine, he said, and it was important to have them cast out of ourselves in Jesus' name as often as possible. Some people did so as regularly as people now get their colons cleansed. When I went up to the altar for my first exorcism—far overdue, some readers might say—it was at a revival service in Pickthorn's church where the visiting preacher had a "demon ministry," travelling around to teach about possession and then cast out devils at the end of the service. I'd been feeling crappy for months, so I went up at the altar call. The preacher knelt beside me and asked if I had a demon.

"Yes."

"Which one?"

I didn't know what he meant—a name? "I don't know," I said.

"Of lust?" he replied.

I nodded—I was a fifteen-year-old guy, so the shoe fit. He grabbed my head and started shaking it as he demanded that Lust leave me in the name of Jesus. I'd finally been Oral Roberts-ed. But, given my healthy endocrine system, that exorcism took about as well as my first baptism.

Through the next two years, I watched many of my friends get exorcised. I even performed a few exorcisms of my own. Late one night, for instance, after yet another revival meeting, a friend and I were strolling in downtown San Jose. A tipsy man walked out of a bar, saw the Bibles in our hands, and started ranting about Jesus. Christianity: what a fraud! My friend and I instinctively started demanding that, in the name of Jesus, the devil come out of this man. He fell on the sidewalk and started convulsing. We got a little scared, knelt down, and started softly praying for him. He soon fell asleep. We strutted away, cockier but shaken.

Unofficial Wineskin doctrine considered alcoholism a kind of demon possession. So our Wineskin House treatment sometimes included laying hands on clients and casting the "demon of alcohol" from them. And I've already mentioned Brad's odor demon. But one exorcism at the Wineskin House went off the rails. A man had been sent by a social worker to the Wineskin House on a Friday afternoon, those grey hours of the week when social workers do their damnedest to clear their desks. This referral, heavy set and in his early forties, with a whiny half-drawling voice, conversed with us breezily until about 8:00 that night. Then, out of the blue, he bowed down on his knees and started praising Satan with a loud voice—a deliberate goading, it seemed, of our frequent, low-voiced "praise the Lord" incantations. Within a minute we started singing gospel songs to drown him out and, we hoped, drive out whatever demon was possessing him. But he kept chanting Satan-praise louder, then boasted that as soon as we went to bed he would kill us all. We prayed and tried to reason with him. Why was he doing this? He told us that we were all wrong. God would not win in the end. Satan would. And this man wanted to be on the winning side. We, of course, denounced this viewpoint as strenuously as we could. But he argued that all the evidence in the world was that Satan was beating God in the cosmic war. To him, the law of entropy was the core of the universe. To us, rebirth, renewal, even resurrection were the laws that overcame entropy. We went back and forth in this weird pseudo-philosophical exchange all night because he was a stranger and we had no reason to disbelieve his threats to kill us. Saturday morning the police came to take him into custody, and we never heard of him again.

During those years, my friends and I not only evicted demons from their temporary "homes," we studied and discussed them. One thing we learned in our studies was that, in Greek, the words for "possessed of a devil" might better be translated as "demonized." And that was the term we started using, long before we ever heard that word in any other context. If someone was possessed, we said they were "demonized."

One of my best friends from the early Wineskin days, Manuel, got demonized, or at least played the role of a LaVey-esque Satanist to the hilt. He and I were close, studied the New Testament together, had a couple sleepovers with gospel chatter into the late hours, and had once gone on a long fast together, four days without food. Then he disappeared for a week. I called him up, and when I reflexively said, "Praise the Lord," he retorted, "I will *not* praise the Lord," then went on to say how destructive our former Jesus freakery was. I don't recall the rest of the conversation beyond the shock of a spiritual knife in my heart. Within weeks we heard tales of Manuel sacrificing a goat in the Santa Cruz mountains, cutting off its ear to carry around as a blessing, and leaving its entrails in another student's locker as a curse. He came and confronted me in art class one day warning me—on the peril of my life—to stop talking to fellow students about Jesus. He was always charismatic, but now he terrified me with that charisma, employed in what I saw as the dark arts.

So, keeping score, I'd now had my life threatened by a Hell's Angel mama, two Satanists, and a juvenile public defender.

One day, I was sitting outside the school art room, where I'd just finished an acrylic painting of a rabbi reading by candlelight. A young Latina in an apparent trance walked up to me and kept putting her fingers near my arms and chest, almost touching me, then retracting them as if she'd gotten a shock. Another friend, Patrick, walked up behind her and said, "She can't touch you. You have the power. You're righteous." He then informed me that both he and she, along with a few other friends, were in a high school coven devoted to white magic. She was now possessed by an evil spirit sent as a curse by the black witch coven on campus, which included Manuel. God's spirit was with me and everybody knew that, Patrick said— her inability to touch me proved it. He asked if I would join with their white coven in a spell to counteract the black coven. He was interrupted by the Latina rapidly uttering the Lord's Prayer backwards. I demurred and we launched into a long discussion of who was on who's side, he making the plea for the solid gold efficacy of white magic and I asserting my power over the occult through the name of Jesus alone. We remained friends, our Latina friend came out of her trance by the next day, and life went on, except for the occasional nod and furtive glance.

The handmaiden of exorcism was healing. I had been hooked on Kathryn Kuhlman radio shows, partly for the healings, which seemed overblown and flimsy, like papier-mâché ocean liners. But I was steeped in magic and illusionism, and she had a weird proto-feminist confidence that landed her between Aimee Semple MacPherson and Alice Allen in my pantheon of B-list goddesses. I'd also listened daily to another Allen on the radio: A. A. Allen. I'd even subscribed to his *Miracle Magazine*—from his headquarters in Miracle Valley, Arizona—until he died of alcohol poisoning in June 1970 in San Francisco. His protégé, Don Stewart, took over the ministry. I renewed my subscription, but Stewart didn't cut it for me. He lacked the overpowering grandiosity of his mentor, and I stopped listening and subscribing in 1971. I even listened to healer Jim Jones on the radio once a week. But he was too scary, often talking as though he were God in his mellifluous baritone voice. Still, his church was in San Francisco, which already gave him street cred for me. He was kind of the anti-Kathryn Kuhlman. She made you smile, he scrunched up your face. And who was I to complain about speaking in God's voice? I and my friends had done it a thousand times.

91

I went to more revival meetings than I can count. They all featured healings. I saw some of the same people get healed more than once of the same thing. These folks were needy, but zealous, I thought. And Jesus said not just to knock and it shall be opened to you, but to keep knocking—at least according to the *Amplified Bible*, which Alice brandished whenever it made a point she needed buttressing. I myself asked for healing just once. Our group prayed for me, laid hands on me, spoke in tongues, and exerted whatever enthusiasm—which came from the Greek for "in God," we'd learned—that they could gin up in my behalf. What occasioned my need for remedy? A broken arm from a stocky, long-haired Latino who slugged me off of the bleachers at school because I laughed at him getting hit by a ball in the pool while playing water polo. Prayers and such may have helped, although I spent the same amount of time in a sling as the doctor had forecast. But prayers absolutely did not heal a friend of mine with a severe stutter. The group laid hands on him, prayed in both tongues and English, and commanded Satan to "loose his tongue," which, as a hybrid of healing and exorcism, still sounded solidly scriptural. But no dice. To explain our failure, we resorted to the cardinal rule in healing, which was to blame the unhealed: they lacked the "faith to be healed."

I got more and more extreme about discipleship, if my two big purges are any proof. First, I decided I needed to forsake my underground comics. Pen technique notwithstanding, they were about as raunchy as anything you could see without proper I.D. in those days. So I slid open the dresser drawer where I kept dozens of them, from *Zap* no. 1 on, tore them up, threw them in a paper grocery sack, and flung it into the big dumpster in the parking lot next to our townhouse. The second purge was taking all my hard rock records— many of which I'd stolen in the '60s—and throwing them into that same dumpster. They included my Hendrix albums. I missed him but didn't want to end up where I was sure he must have landed when he died. The grim sidebar to those two purges was that I tore up Jerri's 8x10 of me on the corner of Haight and Ashbury. Maybe St. Peter will have a negative.

To spread the word on the Wineskin House, we borrowed a printing press from Calvary Gospel Temple. We learned to make plates from typescripts, photos, and drawings, ink the rollers, and crank reams of paper through this old-timey mechanical beast. We not only printed ads for our halfway house, but also fliers for the coffeehouse. We'd stick them up on bulletin boards and telephone poles around the peninsula. I doubt we ever got one continuing patron, let alone donor, from our flyers. But the making of these flyers was a kind of unpaid jobs program for us and, occasionally, for our halfway-house residents. Printing press as therapy.

A balm to my soul, too. I loved books and magazines, so printer's ink ran through my veins. I loved posters, whose imagery had papered the walls of my Rengstorff bedroom. I loved drawing, so the decorated page always felt like scripture to me. My contribution to our new canon? I drew the group's logo for our letterhead, a plump wineskin with a cluster of grapes beside it.

As far as Pastor Rounds cared, we could keep the press as long as we wanted. And since he was boss of the board of deacons that voted on Calvary Gospel policy, we thought we were set for life as publishers.

But in the spring of 1971 Pastor Rounds was diagnosed with late-stage cancer. Cannistraci became the interim pastor during the weeks that we watched Rounds slip in and out of consciousness in his hospital bed. During our last visit, he told us Jesus had appeared to him holding a little lamb. "I knew that lamb was me," he said. After he died, the deacons voted Cannistraci in as the new permanent pastor—at least as "permanent" as pastors get.

Hearing him at the pulpit every Sunday was a letdown. He was boisterous in a way that refuted Rounds's pastoral vibe. He also got more commandeering about how things were to be done in "his" church. One of the more memorable bursts of Cannistraci temperament happened when I was noodling at the organ one day before church and he grabbed my arm, led me to his office, and, without any warning, laid his hands on my head and "ordained" me a "minister of music." The result was no more ability or confidence for me, but a backload of self-consciousness. Oh, and fear of the next outburst.

When Cannistraci found out we had the church's press, he wanted it back for his own publication plans. But we weren't amenable. Pastor Rounds had bequeathed it to us for as long as we needed it, we argued. We got testy phone calls from Cannistraci and had nasty spats in the church hallway with deacons. A deal was a deal, we said, and for a couple of months we tried to find someone that all parties would consider an "apostle," since that's what it would take to settle any dispute in the church, we'd deduced from the Bible. We tossed names back and forth, trying to get some agreement on who would constitute a certified apostle. (Derek Prince was our top choice.) The main problem was, Cannistraci said that he considered himself an apostle. And he'd already made the decision. Checkmate.

After weeks of fighting about the press, and hearing that we were about to be sued for its return, we gave the machine its final run before hauling it back. What did we print? Dozens of copies of a ten-page account of the dispute that, we felt, justified our keeping the press. The Sunday after we printed this quasi-defense brief, we stood on the sidewalk around Calvary Gospel Temple handing copies to anyone who would take one as they walked into church. Only a few did. Inside the chapel, we heard later, Pastor Cannistraci directed the deacons to collect our handouts and then declared to the whole congregation that the Wineskin group was "cut off" from the church. We weren't members anymore, weren't welcome, and, indeed, with or without his excommunication, none of us ever set foot in the church again.

But we'd already concluded that we didn't need a church. We were one. A brotherhood and sisterhood with communal Book of Acts-style consecration and work-sharing, doing good deeds, praising God, studying scripture, praying our guts out, speaking in tongues, prophesying, healing, exorcising, the whole ball of sacred wax. Still, we were restless enough to keep hoping we'd link up with Christians whom we could cross-pollinate with or who at least could give us a taste of some new gospel nectar. When we'd hear about this or that one-off gathering or Jesus-freaky coterie, we'd pay a visit. We'd come home from them mostly with new songs, like the throbbing, power-chord-styled "He's Done So Much for Me I Cannot Tell It All," whose singer-songwriter gave mini-sermons peppered with the phrase "'cause I'll tell ya" as he kept jerking his head to the right to get a seven-inch shock of hair out of his face. Then there was a glorious ad hoc meeting in one preacher's home where we all sang

in tongues for about an hour straight. Some visits to other groups'
meetings were like carnival rides, in which the physics were all familiar, but engineered far outside our everyday world—like our visit
to the "Jesus Only" Apostolic church, whose crowd of mostly white
college-age congregants sat in a circle and sang updates of familiar songs—"Home on the Range," for example, became "Home in
the Church." Lots of tongues, of course, and "praise Gods" rippling
through the crowd.

For a few weeks we went to an enormous, brightly lit arena, whose
worship extravaganzas were run by a guy whose ads I'd seen in the
paper since First Baptist days: Kenny Foreman. In the '60s he had a
crewcut and looked like every suburban right-wing guy I'd avoided
since the Haight hit the headlines. Now, from the middle seating of
his indoor stadium, we saw a tuxedoed pretend porn star with long
wavy jet-black hair who pranced onto the stage to his own theme
song, Bill Gaither's "Because He Lives." He did lots of healing,
off-the-cuff preaching, slaying people in the spirit, all the tricks we
knew well from revivals. Glorious entertainment, but I never liked
spectator sports. Maybe if Kathryn Kuhlman were the show. But
the toupee or whatever badger was on his head was the least of the
glitz-repulsion I felt at this church. To my mind, Wineskinners were
about living rooms and coffee houses with Jesus' spirit permeating
like incense in musty air.

To offset Foreman-ish gospel tawdriness, we held our own private retreats. One was a night and a day in a vacant migrant-picker's
shack in Morgan Hill. It was off-season and one of our financial
patrons, a brusque, hawk-nosed retired professional woman, handed
us the keys. Three drafty rooms, a cracked hard wood floor, rotting
Formica counter tops, a leaky sink, no electricity, and an outhouse in
the backyard. We huddled together in blankets, except for the gui-
tarists, who had to rely on referred body heat. After our usual script
of hours-long singing, praise, and tongues, we slept in sleeping bags
we'd brought—the first time I'd been in one since Egan graduation
eve with Joyce and Madeline. At dawn I got up before anyone else,
walked out to pee in the outhouse, then tried to wash my hair with
a bar of soap in the sink. I learned that that doesn't work, especially

with ice cold water. But my shoulder-length hair was still my crown, and I had to polish it every day.

Another retreat was in the Santa Cruz mountains, where Alice had rented a second-floor hotel room with a record player that I kept cranking up with a Gregorian chant LP I'd bought at St. Vincent de Paul. It was my new crossover music. Classical but Jesusy, reminiscent of the Catholic awe I'd felt in that church across from Mountain View High. My Wineskin friends barely tolerated it and kept switching it off. After a few of those rebuffs, I walked out into the resonant woods to sing in tongues by myself for God knows how long. I came back in, bragged about how great it was, and a couple of friends went out with me and did it themselves—though we all spread out, far from one another's field of vision and hearing. We did everything together, but this we had to keep personal, one-on-one with God.

Then for a few months we aligned with the East Palo Alto church pastored by my friend Renetha Macklin's dad: the New Sweet Home Church of God in Christ. The only looseness of fit for us was our skin. We were all white and they weren't. Gospel singing unites people, though. So, although our skin looked bleached amid this sea of melanin, the congregation welcomed us with broad smiles, constant embraces, and an "Amen" after everything we said or did. As I'd sometimes done at Calvary Gospel, I played the grand piano to accompany the hymns. But, given the Leslie-speakered Hammond organ, an amped-up electric guitar, a drum set, and a congregation singing beyond the top of their lungs, I never heard myself play. I banged the chords as hard as I could, but the hammer-stroked harmonies couldn't fight their way to the top of the aural mountain that filled the church.

In the midst of all this wandering, I wrote a penitent letter to Bruce, a capstone of that relationship in the form of a confession I could check off my purgation list:

Dear Bruce,

Since I have seen or talked to you last, I have come to know the Lord Jesus Christ in a new and powerful way. Through His guiding & dealing with me in my life, He has changed my heart & life which had been messed up with drugs, bad attitudes, & emotional problems. I believe that now the Lord would have me to write this letter to you & make right some former wrongs. Aside from confessing my harsh feelings that I formerly held for you (not anymore) there are some other things.

When we were living together, I stole many things from you—those being: a lot of stamps & "first-day covers" and a lot of change & coins of yours. I regret that I used the money & coins up in spending quite some time ago. However, the stamps & covers (as well as some paper money) I have had packed away. You will find them enclosed.

I hope & pray that you will accept my humble confession and forgive me for the wrongs I've done you. (If you would care to answer I would welcome it—but that's entirely up to you). Thank you very much. I really do now appreciate the training and raising that you gave me and I shall be ever grateful for those things that you taught me. Thank you again—
Sincerely In His Name,
Michael Gray

At about the same time, Mom finally broke up with Stan. She'd been dating other men via Parents Without Partners and Stan knew it. One night she came home with a date and Stan was waiting for her in his car in our complex' parking lot. She kissed her companion goodnight and opened the front door. Stan bolted from his car and followed her inside. They yelled at each other in multiple rooms on both stories of our town house, till he took a silver-sequined mini-skirt he'd given her from the closet and ripped it up in her face.

She stopped "seeing" him, mostly. Every now and then, though, they still went out for a porn flick.

In the cracks between the Wineskin House and Mountain View High my real education started to settle in. Campus was next door to the well-stocked city library. Between classes—or instead of them—I'd walk over, listen to classical records on headsets and check out orchestral pocket scores of the likes of Beethoven and Wagner. Then, after school, on the way home for my pre-Wineskin nap, I'd walk down Castro Street to St. Vincent de Paul and buy sheet music and classical albums for small change. Baroque records like Bach's *Well-Tempered Clavier* played by Wanda Landowska were my favorites. I started learning to read music for guitar and practice Baroque pieces, eventually chiseling away at Bach's lute suite in E-minor, a record of which (played by Julian Bream) I'd bought for a dime. Together with my friend Derek—a much better guitar player—I composed a piece on the lawn next to the school library. "Modified Baroque Guitar Study No. 1" was my first real *composition*, co-written and played on a new nylon string guitar Dad had bought me as part of his bait to get me to join MENSA. He told me that would be a great career move, although he also repeatedly said that he saw my real future in being a square dance caller. "You could make hundreds every night," he said.

Alice knew I was into classical music and so introduced me to Frank, the owner of a small janitorial service who had a grand piano and a theater organ in his cramped apartment. Alice thought we'd hit it off, which we did. I told him about my affection for Baroque music and he introduced me to Romantic pieces like Chopin polonaises, which he could play convincingly. Like me, he played keyboard by ear, although, unlike me, he had perfect pitch and could replicate any piece virtually note perfect. But he had a problem he'd only recently discovered: he learned pieces from records and his BSA turntable ran fast. So he mastered almost every piece a half-step above the original. Thus he could play Beethoven's Moonlight Sonata in its entirety—in D minor. Brilliance coupled with this inadvertent glitch made him a unique beast in the classical music menagerie. To me, transcendentally weird and therefore irresistible.

One day he invited me to an organ recital by the flamboyant Virgil Fox at Palo Alto First Methodist. Frank didn't really like Fox. He preferred E. Power Biggs and similarly dutiful players. But Frank knew I liked Fox because I had listened to him over and over on a record in Dad's *Reader's Digest* box set called *Organ Memories*, which had been my entree into Baroque music in the first place. Frank picked me up in his rust-edged, frayed-interior Chevy Impala. On the way to the concert, he felt he needed to confess something that might make me want to reconsider our night out.

"I'm a bisexual," he said. He started choking up and, with tears in his eyes, told me about how he'd fought his attraction to boys and men his whole life. He'd prayed for healing, but his prayers fell through. If I was uncomfortable, he said, he could take me home. I *was*, but more for the sudden, out-of-context confrontation than from the disclosure itself. Still: this was Virgil Fox. I wouldn't dream of bailing. Afterwards, Frank and I talked a lot about the concert, which had closed with Fox's idiosyncratic take on Bach's Passacaglia and Fugue in C Minor. Frank objected to Fox's liberties, I liked them, especially his ultra-long fermata on the Neapolitan chord near the end of the finale. I had profound fun, if there's such a thing, though I had to figure out what "bisexual" meant besides a watered-down version of what we called "queer." Frank had told Alice about his problem, too. One night we held an exorcism at the Wineskin House to drive out the demon of Frank's homosexuality. I never saw him after that.

By then, I was already imagining my own classical masterpiece. I sang in the Mountain View High choir under Don Nelson. At one concert, we sang Randall Thompson's "Last Words of David." I was so taken with it, I checked out the Mormon Tabernacle Choir's recording of it from the library and decided I wanted to compose a scripture-based piece for our high school choir. I picked Psalm 133, which was, in effect, the stuffier Bible version of the Youngbloods' "Get Together." It was so '60s, this psalm that began: "How good and how pleasant it is for brethren to dwell together in unity." And the psalm was short, only three verses. So I could write three short movements, one verse apiece. I had seen stacks of old orchestral music paper decaying on the music office's shelf since I was a freshman. I walked in one day and said to Mr. Nelson, "If you give me that paper, I'll write something for orchestra on it." His exact response was, "Here, take it and get out of my office." He added that he needed the shelf space and wasn't going to suddenly get stingy about yellowing paper he'd never use.

I got an orchestration book from the library, studied it, then drew barlines on the blank pages I'd gotten from Mr. Nelson and started filling them with notes. Every new piece I listened to or old one I remembered formed the basis for the next few measures of my new work. Faint echoes of Handel—the piece starts with a fugue exposition—one loud echo of the finale to Beethoven's Ninth, and on and on. I prayed and got what I thought was inspiration. I knew that if I could improvise in the voice of Jesus any day at 6:00 a.m., I had the chutzpah to pull off this orchestral work. Just like I'd been a speaking-in-tongues chameleon, I was now a musical chameleon. Or, rather, a sponge: I'd soak it in and squeeze it back out, a little grittier and dirtier, but recognizable by others as new enough for them to think I was a genius. Which I probably was, although I passed on writing a sevenfold amen at the end of *Psalm 133* and settled for a single amen in the last two measures: a whole-note G chord to a whole-note C chord. Four months of writing, from downbeat to double bar, its Baroque shirttails hanging out everywhere. The dedication on the front page was "to my mother and father and most of all to the praise & glory of Almighty God."

When fall semester began, I gave the score to Mr. Nelson, who told my mom it "flabbergasted" him. He pitched it to the other two high schools in the district, and they agreed to perform it at their joint "Spring Fling" concerts in May. Nelson thought I needed to get hipper, though, and told me I should listen to Penderecki's *Threnody for the Victims of Hiroshima*. I checked the record out of the library, listened, and felt as I did after watching *Cosmic Zoom*. Perplexed, happy, scared. Initiated into my own right-brain sequel to *Chillers from Science Fiction* with a dollop of Ligeti's soundtrack music to *2001*.

Nelson had conscripted me to teach two sections of guitar class in the first semester of my senior year. Needing the extra bucks to pay off the VW bus I'd just bought from Mom's new boyfriend, Wally, I eagerly consented. The classes were popular, with around forty students in each section, their curriculum completely mine and improvised to the hilt. I taught chords as well as note-reading. We played folk songs, pop, and a little classical. I was completely untrained as an educator and that's what saved me. Because not knowing better is the ignorance that bliss consists of.

My literate music life was my new public secret life, conducted out in the open at school but shielded from the Wineskin group as much as I could. It was "worldly," which was the ultimate putdown for young Jesus Freaks. When I went to an Andres Segovia concert at De Anza College, I told my Wineskin friends I was sick and couldn't come to the halfway house that night. The concert was divine. But not the right kind of godly. Sacred music vs. gospel music. Those were the two doors in my psyche. Jesus was the hinge that joined them, amazingly ungracefully.

Complicating my double life was my new job. I was now working for Alice. After school each day, I'd drive over to Alice's office in a dingy one-level building to work as an employment counselor for three hours a day just steps away from her. Outside of Alice's cramped cubicle I had a desk from which I phoned businesses, mostly new tech companies and their suppliers throughout Silicon Valley. I'd ask if they had jobs to fill, meet with clients who might fill those jobs, draw up contracts with the clients for what they would pay us if they got the jobs for which we'd set up interviews, then had Alice sign the documents to make them legal. I had to trim my hair, wear a dress shirt, and hone my "personability" skills, because almost everyone I talked to was at least ten years older than I and I needed to look the part of their counselor. Most jobs were in "assembly," installing parts for electronic devices, from video recorders to computer banks. Now and then I'd arrange an interview for a maintenance job or even a higher-level tech job. The clients ranged from bland, well-groomed professionals to a heavily made-up, awkwardly wigged, male-to-female transsexual. I got paid the student minimum wage of $1.45 an hour.

Fall 1972 the Mountain View High community newsletter spotlighted me on its front page.

> Mike, a senior, works for Alice Allen Associates
> agency in Mountain View.

He has been receiving training there for about 4 months as an employment counselor. He interviews applicants for jobs as well as Employers, in the attempt to place the applicant in a job that is best suited for him. Mike says that, "dealing with hundreds of people a week has made me pay closer attention to how I look and act in front of others."

Mike has several interests besides his work. He enjoys music and helps teach the guitar classes with Don Nelson at the high school. He also has written a composition for orchestra and choir entitled "Psalm 133" which may be produced at the annual District Spring concert in May.

Outside of work and music, Mike's energies are directed in Christian work. He has a broad interest in serving people as evidenced by his work with the Wineskin House in Sunnyvale. This rehab house works with people who are in need of help or are looking for a new way of life. Connected with the house is the Wineskin Coffee House which is open Thursday, Friday, and Saturday nights for singing, rapping and for just plain fun. After high school, Mike plans to work but eventually would like to pursue a music career and possibly earn a master's degree in music.

Mrs. Marilyn Gray, his mother, as well as all at Mountain View High School has reason to be proud of this young man. Keep up the good work, Mike!

By the time that newsletter came out, Alice and Jim had bought an eight-unit apartment complex for another, much bigger halfway house three blocks from the Catholic church. Despite rancor and complaints from neighbors, it thrived briefly. We kept up the Sunnyvale house, too, including Sunday outings with Agnews patients, a van full of whom we got permission to bring to the coffeehouse after our hospital visits. We fed them, conversed and sang with them before returning them for lights out. These were some of the rawest and least predictable times, but also among the most beautiful. More than ever, we felt that we were climbing through the Acts of the Apostles.

What we didn't see was that the whole Wineskin structure was about to implode. To put it in Jesus terms, we were already an aging wineskin and the new wine was leaking out. The apartment complex never filled and the Sunnyvale house gradually emptied. Social workers, except the most desperate, had deduced that we weren't equipped to rehabilitate or even monitor our clients well. We couldn't make the mortgage payments, the coffeehouse wasn't worth the rent, and some core group members were migrating away.

Worst of all, Alice had started drinking again. One night she got drunk and drove me home from the Wineskin House because my VW bus was in the shop. I've never been more afraid of being killed than I was during that ride. Maybe alcohol *was* a demon. Despite Alice's typically cheery conversation all the way home, other forces were driving the car. It felt like Jesus and the Devil were fighting over the steering wheel, sometimes barreling straight through stop signs.

Alice's drinking also helped dry up referrals to her employment agency. I had to cover for her at the office—either she didn't show or she did, drunk, and I had to keep clients away from her. In the spring of 1973, halfway through my last semester of high school, I got a call at the agency for a part-time job at Coast Finishing Company in Santa Clara. I didn't make a referral, just interviewed for it myself and got the job. I needed to be somewhere, anywhere, away from Alice and, more than that, make better pay doing grittier work. I was born for this new job, I thought, with spray painters all around and big steel vats and machines dividing the space. It was the reunion of my mom and my dad in a strange way.

The finishing company gave me a small work area with a bench and spools of masking tape. I meticulously taped off tiny sections of machine parts with critical tolerance and facets that needed to be painted. My art chops kicked in for the task and the big boss, Joe, praised my work. After a few months of commuting with my bus up and down the Bayshore Freeway, I got the nerve to ask for a raise to $2 an hour. I got it, along with a promotion to shipping and receiving. My last months of high school I went to prayer meetings at 6:00 a.m. (we still held them or attended the ones at New Sweet Home), spent two contiguous hours of P.E. from 8:00–10:00 a.m. (all I needed to graduate), took a quick shower, then drove to Santa Clara for six hours of work. After that, more Wineskin House duties, then back to bed till the next rerun.

May 17 arrived and the premiere of my choir and orchestra piece, *Psalm 133*. The next day the Los Altos *Town Crier* had a slow enough news day that they ran a story about me on their front page.

Precocious Senior's Psalm To Be Performed Tonight

Beethoven's "Fifth Symphony." Tchaikovsky "1812 Overture,"Handel's "The Messiah" and Hicks' "Psalm 133."

If music lovers don't recognize that last piece, they shouldn't feel ashamed. Or think that their musical prowess is slipping.

For "Psalm 133" has only been performed in public once. That distinction took place Thursday night at Awalt High School in Mountain View when the school's choir joined forces with Mountain View High School group.

In fact the song will receive only its second public audience tonight at the Mountain View High School auditorium, starting at 8. Admission is a $1.50 for adults and $1 for students.

"Psalm 133" is only a single portion of a musical program being performed jointly by the two schools as part of the annual Music Festival. This event is conducted as a fundraising activity in which all proceeds are divided between the two schools and placed in a scholarship fund for music students.

But what makes "Psalm 133" worthy of mention?

Composer Michael Hicks is a 16 year old student at Mountain View High who has never had one iota of formal musical training in his life.

Yet the young senior who had but one semester of music in his first years of high school composed an entire original musical composition all by his lonesome.

Only once did a music teacher at Mountain View check over his score and make a few suggestions. Aside from this, the budding young composer went at it with only the knowledge he had picked up on his own.

In all, Hicks spent between April and July of last year writing his original score. He composed it on both the piano and guitar, two instruments he has taught himself to play over the last 4 years.

"I was fooling around at the piano," Hicks said recently while explaining how he came up with the idea for the piece. But he admitted the inspiration wasn't all that spontaneous.

"I was impressed with 'The Last Words of David' performed at last year's festival," added the young composer, saying it was this particular piece which inspired him to eventually compose his own biblical score.

Though he had been "fooling around" with various pieces for several years, he had remained "unpublished and unperformed," as Don Nelson, a Mountain View High music teacher, put it.

But all that is behind young Hicks now. He has composed his first score, "Psalm 133" and he has had it performed publicly. Now what does a sixteen-year-old do for an encore?

Well, the answer to that question is simple. He enrolls at California State University at San Jose as a music Major and that's exactly what he plans to do after graduating this spring.

Lest one forgot, this Mountain View High student composer hasn't had one day of formal musical training in his life. Nevertheless, he has accomplished something many aspiring young composers wouldn't, or simply couldn't, attempt until they had received instruction.

Beyond the smalltime hype, the piece was a sloppy, energetic success, like a battery-powered puppy with a diamond collar. Though I'd kept its composition and premiere a secret from my Wineskin friends, they heard about it after the fact and asked why I didn't announce it to them—and why I had lied that I was sick those nights.

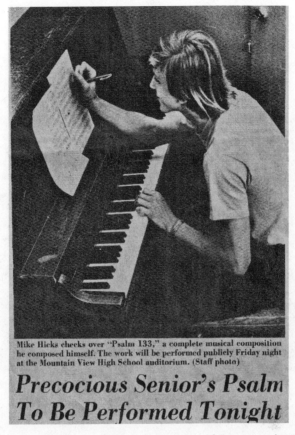

Mike Hicks checks over "Psalm 133," a complete musical composition he composed himself. The work will be performed publicly Friday night at the Mountain View High School auditorium. (Staff photo)

Precocious Senior's Psalm To Be Performed Tonight

Front-page article about me as composer of *Psalm 133* (1973).

I told them I thought they'd think it was too worldly. They were gracious and said I was being silly. But my personal straight and narrow path was forking away from theirs just the same.

On the last day of school my friend Dan and I borrowed another Wollensak tape recorder. But this time, unlike my music room break-in at Egan, I had permission. I was a star of the music room, a paid employee and now a renowned *composer*. Dan and I pretended we were man-on-the-street interviewers and interviewed each other and a few fellow students, then recorded improv covers of Chicago's "Color My World" and James Taylor's "Country Road," with me at the piano and Dan at the drums. "Sail on home to Jesus, won't you

Reading my New Testament at the park just
after high school graduation (1973).

good girls and boys?" I sang, more lustily than ever. This pretend gig
was the prologue to a whole summer of recordings.

The last time I saw Alice, she called me up and wanted to meet
with me privately at the Sunnyvale house. When I got there, she
smelled of beer, but her eyes were aglow with something else. She'd
had a vision. In it, Jesus told her that he'd chosen me to write the
apocalyptic "New Song" spoken of in both Old and New Testaments. My *Psalm 133* had been the audition, she said. I should start
soon, she added. I assured her I would.

I had no intention. But I did follow her lead in one thing. I started
drinking again.

6. THIRD EXODUS

I'd smoked tobacco, weed, and even catnip in the '60s. They mostly gave me a scorched throat and a "high" that ranged from giddiness to paranoia to—nothing. My first taste of alcohol, though, was at that Fillmore West concert, where I drank from the communal bottle of Ripple. It relaxed me in a way no smoke-bound substance ever did. At Dad's house, before my born-again experience, I'd been drinking an ounce here and there from the big bottles of Gallo wine and the smaller bottles of gin, vermouth, and whiskey that his third wife kept in the pantry for cooking and serving to guests. One time I got stone drunk in the middle of the day, detonating lots of laughter from Lil, Dad, and their friend Terry. But I got no censure or prohibition from them, just the conk on the head that a hangover provided. I hated the taste of all these drinks, one worse than the previous. So, aside from the lure of inebriation, I despised drinking. Especially once I'd worked for an alcoholic rehab house.

But when the Wineskin group fell apart, I tried to soften my gloom with the meager inventory of alcohol my mom had stashed in cupboards and the fridge—the inventory that the cops had been so curious about the night I got busted in '69. I mixed and matched small gulps from this or that bottle of hard drink, making my theft harder to detect. I'd down it as fast as possible, washing my mouth out with tap water to erase the bitterness. Fortunately for me, I didn't need much to get drunk.

On the Sunday night after graduation, Mom was out with Wally and I was home alone listening to Dan Hicks and the Hot Licks' latest LP, *Last Train to Hicksville*, which I'd bought for obvious reasons. At each repetition of the line in the chorus of "Payday Blues"—"I think I'll have another drink"—I had another drink. The phone rang. It was Karen, a mutual friend of Dan and me, a saucy long-haired blond who starred in high school musicals and yet could sing Fauré's "Pie Jesu" like a cross between an angel and a diva. She invited me to her house where some friends from her Mormon ward were singing and playing games. I didn't quite understand that "ward" meant congregation and not one of the hospital units I'd visited as a Wineskinner. But it didn't matter much, since I assumed this invitation was a velvet-gloved proselyting ploy. I said I'd think about it, which, along with my pledge to Alice to write the New Song, I tacitly planned not to. I put "Payday Blues" back on and, before I could take my next swallow, I heard a voice in my head—or, rather, felt it in my chest. It said, "If you don't go to Karen's you'll spend the rest of your life wondering what would have happened if you did." It lodged in my brain like the monolith in *2001: A Space Odyssey* lodged on the moon. Then came the mental wrestling: cheery Mormons and me feeling like an outsider, versus solitude and me as the king of my own wine glass at the kitchen table. I finally gave in to the spectral admonition I'd gotten.

By the time I dragged myself to Karen's, everyone else had gone home. She and I talked, even flirted, mostly at my VW bus's door. She was better at the flirting part than I, like Horowitz to Elton John, given my longtime conscription into the dismally chaste army of fundamentalist Christianity. But, with my hand now tentatively resting on her waist, she said, "You're the only person at high school I ever thought was worthy to date." "Worthy"? It was a word as foreign to my vocabulary as sci-fi was to my job at Coast Finishing. I'd soon learn that it was bedrock Mormon lingo. But for now, I was just floored: here was one of the most popular girls I knew wanting to hang out with me like—a girlfriend.

In the weeks that followed, I stopped drinking in exchange for the intoxication of her company. I went to her house whenever I could, day and night. We had music and high school and a handful of friends in common. Even religion, in a fuzzy way.

If I'd thought of Mormonism before high school or Walter Martin's *Kingdom of the Cults*, I don't recall where, aside from eye-rolling at dark-suited teenagers on bikes and my obligatory reverence for the Mormon Tabernacle Choir. Lately, I'd read all sorts of pamphlets and book chapters on Mormonism as a cult. While I loved the religion's Frank Edwards-ish "stranger than fiction" vibe, I had no appetite for the faith.

It was not Karen but another Mormon girl, one I barely knew, who had first fixed her missionary eye on me. We'd been in a class or two together, that was it. But one day in the round-tabled study area of the school library, she sat down next to me and, in her sweetest Southern belle voice, asked me if there was any way I'd let the Mormon missionaries come to my house and teach me about her church. Since my reputation as a Bible-thumper was unrivaled, she must have thought me a good catch. Trying to be peaceable—and undeniably curious about this cult I'd read reams about—I consented.

Within a few days two of those suited teenagers showed up unannounced at our door around four o'clock. I greeted them in my usual after-school bathrobe. Bleary eyed and wrapped in terrycloth, I let this corporate-looking pair of guys two years older than I plop down on the couch and crank up their portable cube-shaped film-strip-cum-cassette player to show *Man's Search for Happiness*, the pint-sized film Mormons had prepared for the New York World's Fair in 1964. I found it weirdly moving, a notch above driver's ed accident films but several notches below *Cosmic Zoom*. Although too brittle and dated for me, it was sweet, like a mini-candy cane you find in the sofa six months after Christmas. The only thing that made me shiver was when the narrator said something like "you have always lived." The idea of a life before Planet Earth was one I'd not considered outside of, say, *Twilight Zone* and Frank Edwards. It frightened me to imagine that my whole life was predicated on amnesia. The only thing that softened the blow of that thought was seeing a crowd of people on the screen in their own bathrobes, drapey white gowns that apparently were the wardrobe-of-choice for dead-but-saved humans. The filmstrip ended, the missionaries tried to get me to commit to yet another baptism, I declined, said thanks and goodbye, then switched on our black and white TV for a rerun of *Bewitched*.

I had no intention of converting to a *cult*. But I remained on the hunt for sacred, edgy, crazily fulfilling weirdness. A couple of weeks before Karen's Sunday night invitation, Dan and I had gone to the Mormon sacrament meeting of the local ward in the imposing chapel next to my old sixth grade school in Los Altos. The meeting was staid and stiff compared to the gospel meetings I'd known. If the Mormon ward that ran this one had had a Sergeant at Arms, though, he'd have arrested Dan and me, because we sat in the overflow area muttering rib-nudging jokes to each other through every talk. Head turning and eye rolling surrounded us. Our humor was about six grades below our age, but we were already on the verge of losing our high school moorings, anyway.

Now, with missionaries ignored and a meeting mocked, I was suddenly hanging out—and sometimes making out—with a Mormon girl, extrovert to my introversion, a legendary kisser, and with a family whose roots sank deep in the faith, at least, as it was planted and harvested in the Bay Area. Even better for the torquing of my religious awareness, Karen's family had bookshelves packed with two things: orthodox Mormon books of history and doctrine alongside the unorthodox, incomparably heady Mormon journal founded seven years earlier a couple of miles away: *Dialogue: A Journal of Mormon Thought*. One of the anti-Mormon tracts I'd picked up off the Wineskin House shelf in 1973, an oblong green 16-pager by a group targeting college students, had critiqued Mormonism in gentler terms than others I'd read. Beyond the change in tone, though, I don't remember anything in the tract except that near the end it said the Mormon Church was becoming more open to scholarship probing its doctrine and history candidly. To wit, the tract mentioned two journals: *Dialogue* and *Courage* (a short-lived cousin of *Dialogue* that came from the Reorganized Church of Jesus Christ of Latter Day Saints, the main alternative to the Utah-based church). As it turned out, Karen's mom had subscribed to *Dialogue* from its first issue.

Even at the Wineskin House I'd thought: "If I want to learn about Jews I wouldn't read Nazi literature, I'd read Jewish literature." The Mormon pamphlets that some missionaries had left at our Sunnyvale door seemed sane and reasonable, even if I was taught to believe that their authors were "deceived." At Karen's house I could finally move beyond cult-exposés and investigate Mormonism on its own terms. I started with *Teachings of the Prophet Joseph Smith*, Smith being the alleged fraudster who'd kicked off this strange new religion. I was amazed how so many of his teachings seemed to solve puzzles my evangelical upbringing had left in its wake. I moved on

110

to LeGrand Richards's *A Marvelous Work and a Wonder*, James Talmage's *Articles of Faith*, Bruce McConkie's *Mormon Doctrine*, and Joseph Fielding Smith's *Answers to Gospel Questions*, which became my Rosetta stone as I tried to untangle and unravel Mormon creeds, notions, and new biblical interpretations. At the same time, I began studying Mormon extra-biblical canon: the Doctrine and Covenants and, eventually, the Book of Mormon—the hardest sell for me, because I knew the Bible intimately and disliked the Book of Mormon's anachronisms and textual "lifting." I read all the tracts I could get, my favorite of which was called *Which Church Is Right?*, by Elder Mark E. Petersen. Almost clairvoyantly, it seemed to address that vexing question we'd had at Calvary Gospel Temple: who's an apostle? The tract made a convincing case for this church having a direct line of apostolic authority via the resurrected apostles Peter, James, and John. That answer worked for me, essentially trumping the hand wringing on the subject we'd mounted with Cannistraci, although requiring an almost frightening leap of faith with respect to ancient apostles as back-from-the-dead authority conveyors. I loved everything I was reading, raised my eyebrows over some of it, attached every sentence to my growing love for Karen, but mainly took intellectual solace in those issues of *Dialogue*, which I browsed and read for months amidst orthodox books and pamphlets.

Because what I read in *Dialogue* was what drew me to Joseph Smith, not as church-maker but as creed-buster, radical, visionary, enigma. I saw him as something of a religious street-tough, a rough-and-ready would-be intellectual who liked to duel with establishment types.

Although I was traversing what they now call a "faith crisis," I never would have used such a phrase. I was just growing, moving from one room of the house of intellect to the next. And that "intellect" part was what plagued me about the evangelical tribes I'd lived in for years. When I was a Jesus Freak, true to our brand, we said "Jesus" over and over—sometimes every other sentence, it seemed—for hours at a time. Quaintly incantational, but with little effect except as a pillowcase to smother rational thought. No person was a better Christian, I came to realize, for saying the name. Much of my gradual conversion to Mormonism sprang from subtracting all that

111

Jesusization and adding a broader vision of the cosmos, internal and external, that this pseudo-cult offered.

I learned later that some Mormons—okay, most Mormons— thought *Dialogue* was "fringey." I never saw it that way, nor could I, because it was so much of what Mormonism meant to me on the circular staircase I'd walked from the lowbrow religiosity of my past to a higher floor—literally a higher "story"—in which, at last, I could celebrate the mind. Because, however shopworn this Doctrine and Covenants phrase feels in the hands of lifelong Mormons, "The glory of God is intelligence."

Still, if the church has anyone to thank—or blame—for me sign- ing up with it, that person would be … Cat Stevens. He was a god in my rock pantheon, one I'd been introduced to by a co-worker at Coast Finishing, who gave me a 7" reel-to-reel tape of Stevens's al- bum *Catch Bull at Four*. I quickly figured out how to play most of its songs on piano or guitar. One afternoon I was at Karen's playing her upright piano and singing the opening song of that album's B-side, "Sitting." Its last lines went: "Life is like a maze of doors and they all open from the side you're on / Keep on pushing hard, boy, try as you may, you're going to wind up where you started from." I played the last chord of the song and she asked me, "So, do you believe that?"

"Believe what?"

"What you just sang. About ending up where you started from."

And that's how we started talking about the Mormon doctrine of pre-Earth life, that idea that had unnerved me in the mission- aries' filmstrip. I now decided, based on the charm of my inquirer and the lure of the doctrine, that I needed to take the full repertoire of missionary lessons and get an official in-person tour of Mormon beliefs. Karen set up some twice-a-week lessons, not with teenage missionaries but with a breezy, high dopamine, neo-unorthodox dentist who only knew the church's older missionary lessons, not the current touchy-feely ones. Those older lessons used para-legal argu- mentation to back Bible believers into traps that made concluding anything other than the Mormon line untenable. I knew the Bible so well that, most times he was leading to a point and said, "Now turn to [scripture X]," I had already turned to it. It was as if I'd co-written the script. If he had unleashed the newer discussions on me, which always resorted to "how do you feel about that?" I'd have bristled. I needed to be gently Bible-bashed into compliance, which those older lessons did. After many nights of these dialogues, we reached the end. My dentist missionary was so open-minded he concluded by saying that, if I liked what I was hearing, I should be sure to explore other "Mormon" denominations, like the Reorganized Church or even the Church of the Firstborn. But I was all in on this one.

It didn't hurt that I loved Karen, her parents, and her siblings, with whom I beatifically loitered after the missionary lessons. Funny, laid back, conciliatory, generous, this family. And, maybe most important, sprung from both folky and classical arts. Almost all of them were musicians (one of Karen's brothers was every bit the singer she was). But I was so marinaded in transactional thinking that my prayers about joining their church kept hitting a stony ceiling. I must be making up my happy feelings about this new faith, I said to God, just because I loved Karen and her genetic entourage so much. How could the ultra-familiar desire for love and the ultra-strange web of doctrine both be true? Given my life thus far, even two good things coinciding was too improbable to accept. Then, one night, a warm thought came to me: it's okay for one thing to be right and not depend on another being wrong. That may not seem profound, but it hit me like Newton's apple.

I needed to join this church. Karen's dad could baptize me. The only problem: since I was still a minor, I'd need my parents' permission. Including Dad's.

He'd have none of it. He handed me a book from his mobile home shelf called *Heresies Exposed*, which had a chapter on Mormonism that began by calling the faith not just a cult but a "black-hand cult," whatever that was. Dad didn't know that I'd already read that book—what else was I supposed to do during these enforced visits to his trailer besides sleep in late, rummage through his shelves, and watch TV? Between finding Bach, Debussy, and Gershwin records in the closet next to the Cynthia Myers Playboy Playmate puzzle, I'd read or at least browsed most of the books about trains, poker, and religion on the shelves at the foot of the bed where I slept. How reasonably and deliberately I made my choice of church, though, didn't matter to Dad. He wasn't budging. "I don't need to read the Book of Mormon to know it's not true," became his stock line.

Amidst my Mormon study binge and courtly pursuit of Karen, two things happened that further shook my world: the draft ended and I got a stereo reel-to-reel tape recorder.

The axe hanging over everything guys did and thought in high school was the need to either serve in the military or find some escape. I'd marched against the war, praised draft-card burners, envied people who left for Canada rather than get spun into the ropes of war, but mostly tried to decide what I'd do when I turned eighteen in May 1974: become a "CO" (conscientious objector), try to get into college for a student deferment, or, as I thought most likely, get a 4-F ranking at my physical for my pancake-flat feet. The creation of the draft lottery had helped me and others feel less vulnerable: what had been a cultural rototiller was now a roulette wheel. But still a pure gamble over who would live or die in the jungle after the sweet colloquy of high school. Then, in an instant, poof. On June 30, 1973, a week after my graduation, Nixon and Congress ended the draft. And the jail door to young men of our generation flung open.

For graduation Mom gave me a Sony reel-to-reel sound-on-sound stereo tape recorder. It was commercial grade, not pro, but far ahead of the tiny-reeled portable Craig I'd been toting around since the Mike Gray years. This machine let me record with other people on a separate channel from mine or even record vocal harmonies with myself via overdubbing. With this Sony tape deck in our hands, Dan and I could move beyond the one-off live Wollensak tracks we recorded on the last day of school.

We spent the summer writing and recording new songs under the rubric "Daniel, Michael, and the Down-to-Earth Heaven-Sent Angel Band." Born again pop. I joined Dan on a few covers and quasi-covers—he tended to "adopt" songs into his own idiom, adding and subtracting lyrics, substituting chords, and similar maneuvers. But his were all songs *new to me*, and that was all that mattered. I wrote and sang all my own originals, sometimes recording them with myself, sometimes with Dan, sometimes using both methods. The songs were essentially dishes cooked up with ingredients from Cat Stevens, James Taylor, and Elton John, my then Holy Trinity of singer-songwriters. The Hicks originals during these sessions were (in order):

— "Goodbye," a farewell song
— "A Song in My Heart," from Wineskin days
— "And the Breeze Take Today," a "let's sail away"-type song straight from the pop annals of the '70s, written for Karen
— "I've Still Got a Song to Sing (Do You Still Sing Along?)," jaunty pop to no one in particular
— "Here," a meditation on how I loved where I was at this time
— "A Christmas Song," sung from the perspective of someone in Bethlehem on the night in question, who notices these weird goings on: (chorus) "On this night, the rarest occasion / In time and creation / He came / The Son of God, the Son of God / Weren't we all waiting for him?"
— "Sweet Child of God," my most overtly Cat Stevens-ish love song to Karen, in which I sang three-part harmony with myself about a pre-earth-life and incipient-afterlife with her: (chorus) "Sweet child of God, we've got so much to know / Take my words and let them go / And if they dance into your dreams / It's only as your own heart redeems / God gave and together we grow"
— "Calm Beyond the Storm," about my mildly tempestuous youth now giving way to—something

That fall I started at Foothill College. From the first day, Foothill indoctrinated me further in the semi-radical Gonella nation where I'd flourished at Egan. My college freshman English reader was its new Bible. *The Rhetoric of Yes* had just been published as a sequel to *The Rhetoric of No*, whose name—reflecting the themes of protest that filled it—vexed some teachers and administrators. The softbound *Rhetoric of No* had a black cover, the new one a cheerier red. But the contents remained both pithy and pugnacious. It opened with excerpts from Eldridge Cleaver's *Soul on Ice*. Then Eiseley, Yevtushenko, D. H. Lawrence, Hesse, Germaine Greer, Rollo May, D. T. Suzuki, Cesar Chavez, Philip Roth, Ho Chi Minh, William Blake, Chief Seattle, William Kunstler, Philip Berrigan, Camus, Wolfe, Vonnegut, Joyce, Alan Watts, and on and on, from Anne Sexton's "In Celebration of My Uterus" to Henry Miller's "Reflections on

Writing." A banquet of progressive writing set out for me and my schoolmates. And we read and read and read. And I got it, got it, got it. It was like high-dose vitamins being injected into my skull. More new scripture was opening its chapters in me.

In the first two quarters, I also enrolled in music theory, Afro-American music, voice lessons, health, and swimming. Part of the entrance exam into first-quarter music theory was to "write a line of music from a piece you know." I wrote the opening line of my first art song for Karen—in Hebrew—which I thought was pretty cheeky. I got in. The most potent elements of my new schooling, though, were probably the two choirs I joined: the main choir and the madrigals. The repertoire was a constant guided tour through compositional styles, techniques, and even texts. The gentle modernism of the twentieth century, especially that of Ives, Orff, Kirke Mechem, and Donald O. Johnston, became an open sesame for me via the choirs.

Incredibly, the church I wanted to join actually considered all this *part of* the gospel of Jesus Christ. *All* truth "circumscribed into one great whole" framed Mormonism's underlying creed. So, at school as much as at church, I was accumulating heaven. I still felt the undertow of guilt my Wineskin years had deposited in me. But if you can surf on an undertow, that's what I was doing.

I kept bringing up the church during visits with Dad and he kept refusing to give me permission for Mormon baptism. On Thanksgiving I finally I told him I'd be eighteen soon enough and wouldn't need his permission. So, if he was sure I'd flee the church once I got into it and thus learned how horrible it really was—his go-to argument—why not give me permission now and get it over with? He grudgingly agreed and signed the permission letter I'd written up for him, though only if he covered up its text while signing.

I got baptized a member of the Church of Jesus Christ of Latter-day Saints on December 8, 1973. I was seventeen and a half years old.

As you might guess, I wanted to stake a claim in my new ward's music. So, even before I was baptized, I offered to sing solos in sacrament meeting. To ingratiate me and vary their programs, ward leaders complied. The first solo I did was John Fischer's "Light," the one I'd sung with piano at that high school talent show. The young

Baptism day in the Church of Jesus Christ of
Latter-day Saints, December 8, 1973.

adults of the ward liked it; the old adults tolerated it with some
head-patting—I was still in the "guest" mode. The second solo ruf-
fled more feathers. It was my own Christmas song "On This Night,"
written for the reel-to-reel tape I'd made with Dan. I heard rum-
blings after I'd played it that it was too "pop" for church. The harshest
critic was the ward organist, who weeks later played Bach's Toccata
and Fugue in D Minor as a special number right after the sacrament.
Its noisy flash ticked off the bishop, who said, on the sly, "That will
never happen again." So Bach took the heat off of me, which seemed
fair play since, as you've read, I'd studied up on so much of his music
via bisexuals and thrift stores.

Soon I rewrote the hymn "Secret Prayer" in the style of folky
music I'd known as a Jesus Freak. Our Los Altos ward young adult
group sang it in sacrament meeting. We got upbraided by some

stodgy old folks, some with bigtime callings. We were also praised by a few hipper listeners, including the filmmaker Kieth Merrill, who was in our ward. He loved it and wanted me to "make it better known." But I was on to other things.

When January 1974 arrived, I'd begun a five-month blitzkrieg of "legit" composition: five more modern art songs for Karen, all but one performed in recitals at Foothill; "The Owl," performed in concert by the madrigals; "O Let the Solid Ground," performed by Foothill's main choir; an arrangement of the hymn "Sweet Is the Work"; two more choral pieces (settings of texts from Psalm 25); and a piece for the Mountain View High choir, which they performed in a competition at the San Jose Civic Auditorium. Halfway through that performance, some singers lost their way, inadvertently mutating my gentle dissonances into widening clusters of pitch, passionately sung. Although I'd loved Penderecki's *Threnody*, I was horrified at this inadvertent sequel. The judges—who didn't have the score—praised the choir for its expertise in rendering, they thought, a boldly experimental work.

I discovered the supreme fusion of music, religion, and transcendent weirdness in Leonard Bernstein's new work *Mass*. I saw it first on PBS in 1973 and then live with Karen at UC Berkeley in 1974. I'd read critiques—it's too eclectic, too gaudy, too narcissistic, sloppy, derivative, etc. So I threw it in my prejudicial hopper with *Jesus Christ Superstar*, *Godspell*, etc. But when I saw it, the traits that critics hated in the work were the ones that caught me up in it. I identified with the enchanted-then-disenchanted celebrant, resonated to the cheesy drama, and was tantalized by the intrinsic Bernsteinian cleverness. I cherished the romantic impulse that fueled Bernstein as a composer, lecturer, writer, conductor, the first three of which roles I longed to inhabit.

All through the front end of 1974, I drifted like a loose paper bag into Mormon culture, trying to fold myself into it and vice versa. Although I hadn't grown up in the church's Primary program for kids, the Aaronic Priesthood for boys, or its male youth auxiliary, the Boy Scouts of America—which we counterculturalists always thought was a relic and possibly a fraud—I was quickly ordained as a priest, the typical station for a male my age. My first official task was to read aloud the prayer over the sacrament water. I had no aural history with the written-out prayer beyond hearing it the previous few months. So it wasn't threadbare to me, as it must have been to my teenage colleagues. When I read it into the microphone at the sacrament altar, I cradled every word of it like a robin's egg. After sacrament meeting, Bill, the tall, Italianate executive secretary of the ward, pulled me aside and told me my reading sounded like the voice of an angel. He added that he'd compared notes with others—including his wife, Ann—and they all agreed. They didn't realize that I was a revivalist convert with my own brand of *sotto voce* vocalizing and a touch of the microphone manipulation I'd learned from Rounds, Cannistraci, Kuhlman, and a dozen more.

Although a priest, I got to attend priesthood meetings with the elders quorum, since I had already graduated high school, which made me, in church terms, an adult. The elders quorum president, athletic, easygoing businessman Curt, took me under his wing. He made me feel I was not just a novelty, or even a boy apprentice, but a jewel in the local crown. I lapped up the quorum lessons, which included statements like this from one nerdish, bespectacled teacher: "Pride is the pretense of omniscience." That was the sort of phrase-making you could get in this new church of mine, I thought, a taste of newer wine than the Jesus bag I'd been drinking from. At the same time, my comments in class blinkered like Christmas light bulbs, since I was the foreign agent to these elders as much as they were to me.

The only burr in my Mormon saddle was the incessant use of the King James Bible, which I'd been shielded from since I was a kid. Although it was archaic and puny by modern scholarly standards, Mormons needed it to be the translation-of-choice because the Book of Mormon and the Doctrine and Covenants were both in Joseph Smith's jangly faux-King James English, which, to him and his peers, was clearly the most efficient way to convey sanctity. If the church switched to modern English translations of the Bible, the new-old scripture that came from Joseph Smith's mouth might see its stock drop precipitously. Better to keep bonsai trees in the shadow of their larger ancestors than that of modern skyscrapers. Still, I did love learning from the King James the source code for so many phrases that, as it turned out, had been alluded to for centuries in literature I admired. "Through a glass darkly." "Thorn in the flesh." "Physician, heal thyself." "The spirit is willing, but the flesh is weak." The dark side of the King James was having to pick through so much of its bramble. The bright side—beyond legitimizing Mormonism's other scriptures' diction—was that it opened a door to a treasure house of English idioms.

Mormonism also had a vast secondary literature of its own, one I'd sampled from Karen's shelves and now hastened to devour. In those days, many Mormon Church buildings had their own bookstores run by the "seventies" quorums. Our ward bookstore's inventory was in a double-doored closet near the rear exit of the chapel. After meetings I'd amble over to it and browse. The first two books I bought straddled both the old-time unsanded Mormonism and the new-school poofily coiffed brands of the faith: *Discourses of Brigham Young* and Paul Dunn's *Ten Most Wanted Men*. I adored the clever, terse outbursts of Young, combed out a bit in this anthology, but still heavy on rarefied doctrine. Yet I and my friends craved Dunn's folksy behaviorism. And, more to the point, I wanted to be a man Karen would *most want*—literally shorn, combed up, better dressed, and more middle-class refined. These two poles of the church had helped draw me in: arcane doctrine to satisfy my appetite for esoterica coupled with an IBM-dress-code style of respectability that was beyond my former grasp.

More books followed, many bought not at church but at an independent Mormon bookstore down the peninsula. When I'd saved up the $75.00 for it, I even bought a complete set of the legendary twenty-six-volume anthology of nineteenth-century speeches by Mormon apostles, et al., the *Journal of Discourses*. That collection drew me into a spicy underground of doctrine couched in vigorous but hipshot oratory.

The *Journal* initiated me further into the argumentative, scruffy street-tough mouthiness of Mormon apologists like the Pratt brothers in the mid-nineteenth century and their eventual follow-ups, including the smooth, well-groomed, but cajoling B. H. Roberts in the mid-twentieth. I tried my own hand at these styles, mostly in a few letter exchanges between me and Mom's parents, who were unprepared for my detailed comebacks to their offhand critiques of the church, which I'd already absorbed fully during my Wineskin days. In my letters, I reasoned to the hilt, using the Bible as my sword, just like my Mormon heroes. I shudder to go back and read them now. Let's just say I brought a gun to a butter-knife fight.

As if to fortify member's doctrinal arsenals, the church sponsored traveling "Know Your Religion" week-long seminars around the country with appealing teachers and scholars. I attended the one in Menlo Park and salivated over the classes by Reed Durham, who delved into what I didn't know were controversial, even taboo, subjects in LDS history and doctrine, including the lost Ten Tribes, the White Horse prophecy, seer stones, the Kinderhook Plates, and more. He did so with grace, charisma, humor, and, above all, tremendous knowledge. I thought that was how it was done—or supposed to be done—in my new church: a new orthodoxy on the outskirts of received wisdom.

In March 1974, Mom bid on a sturdy but musty one-bedroom late-1940s house in the low-rent district of Los Altos, a block away from Egan. The house had gone up for auction after the widow of the man who built it died. It turned out that Mom's offer of $36,000 was the only bid. By the end of April, we packed up our townhouse and moved in. My new bedroom was the office next to the driveway, attached to the house but with its own door to the outside world. Between mom's increasing trysts with boyfriends and my overstuffed schedule, we often went multiple days without seeing each other.

For the rest of 1974 through the middle of 1975, my daily life cycled through five pursuits: work, school, composing, Karen, and the church. With the old job at Coast Finishing now under my belt, I landed a new one as a plating line-worker at a printed circuit board company, Symtron, in one of the boxy industrial parks next to the Bayshore Freeway. My job: loading wafer-thin boards, from wallet-width to platter-sized, onto racks that I'd dip into successive waist-high vats of chemicals and rinse-water. I did four eight-hour shifts a week, 4:00 p.m. to midnight, Monday through Thursday. During these swing-shifts I hung with a gang of far-from-Mormon friends that sang and joked with me amid my reading of the *Journal of Discourses* while I waited the requisite durations to move racks from one vat to the next. I read—and marked up—every page of the *Journal's* first eight volumes during these swing shifts. Meanwhile, from 8:00 a.m. to 2:00 p.m. each day, I sat in classes, did homework, and hung with a completely different set of friends—essentially Karen and her circle. On weekends she and I sometimes went to parties, she the social butterfly, me the isolationist who usually sat at the piano and played Cat Stevens songs, especially his plea for mercy called "Trouble."

That fall I took the first piano lessons of my life. For about six months, I practiced Mozart and Bach. But I lacked the zeal and attention span to perfect my playing of others' works. Instead, I composed a terse oboe-piano duo and a three-movement choral work inspired by a dream of yet another girl I had a crush on: Sonja. I literally dreamed she was singing settings of Hebrew scriptures with a choir behind her. I told her about the dream, and she, a devout Christian, said she'd be delighted to solo in such a work. I started looking up favorite psalm passages in Hebrew, transliterating them and plunking out tunes, chords, and counterpoint on Mom's battered piano in the living room. Although an obvious sequel to my first "big" work, *Psalm 133*, this new one, *Hebraic Psalm Settings*, imitated three twentieth-century Americanist heroes I'd recently saturated my mind with: Bernstein, of course, as well as Copland and Barber. Foothill's choral director, Roger Letson, programmed the piece, including the startlingly difficult fugato section of the last movement, which he begged me to cut, but accepted my pledge that I wouldn't. So, in the first academic quarter of 1975, an actual dream of mine, for the first time, literally came true.

By spring I had migrated toward instrumental music, culminating in a string quartet called *An American Essay: 1876*, which tried to evoke the jubilation of the American Centennial as we looked ahead to the Bicentennial, for which artists of all stripes had been invited to pay tribute. This quartet, my oboe-piano duo, and another new song ("Horses") all premiered on a June 5 recital. The department chairman walked up to me afterward, raved about my work, and insisted I go to a finer school to study composition. He went on and on about Lou Harrison at Mom's alma mater, San Jose State. I'd never heard of Harrison but was assured he was famous. I drove to the college one afternoon, but he wasn't there. So I met with avant-garde electronic composer Allen Strange, none of whose music I knew or probably would have liked at the time. I showed him a few scores of mine and he was very kind about my prospects, although, in retrospect, I'm sure what I was writing was as dead as a doornail to him.

Two weeks after that June recital I passed an essential part of a Mormon's spiritual audition: a "patriarchal blessing." Spoken by the stake patriarch in something between a trance and a pro forma structure, such a blessing declared the Israelitish lineage of its recipient and foretold events and accomplishments that would come to the recipient if he or she proved "faithful." It was a quasi-Möbius strip formula that, in my case, elicited a dash of skepticism, since it meant that (a) if a prediction came true, the person had been faithful, or (b) if it hadn't come true, that person hadn't been faithful *but* with the ubiquitous Mormon escape clause that things that did not come to pass "in this life" would do so "in the next" (i.e., after death).

My blessing said I'd descended from the tribe of Ephraim—by far the most common Mormon tribe, I'd heard—and that I had been held in reserve to come to Earth "at this particular time in its history," another common sentiment of the day. I had prophetic ability, he said: the gift "to discern with clarity and distinctiveness the path which lies ahead." I also "comprehend" and "have begun to incorporate in [my] life the beauties of the virtues which the Lord extolled in the Sermon on the Mount." "In due time" I would "be called to positions of responsibility far beyond [my] present comprehension," which could have been almost anything, given the level of my comprehension of Mormondom at the time. The standard promises of marriage and posterity followed, along with the proviso that, yes, all these blessings depended on how well I behaved. I couldn't have been happier with the blessing's positivity.

When the patriarch finished, he volunteered that he recalled none of the words he'd spoken but only a general impression: "You seek righteousness! And what could be better than that?" In reply, I ventured my most burning question: Should I marry Karen?

"I'm not a fortune teller," was his retort. "Do you love her?"

"Yes."

"Then why don't you marry her?" That seemed almost too simple, but I grasped the advice tightly.

Reading Edward Tullidge's *Women of Mormondom* on the porch, 1975.

Our ward's Young Adult thrill-ride was the Sunday school class taught by the storied Ann, vivacious wife of executive secretary Bill. She had lots of mysterious doctrine at the ready, coated with her personal charisma and the latest fad in Mormonism, that idea that "this generation" had been "held in reserve" in the preexistence for the pre-Millennial Earth's last stand. It dovetailed with my blessing, of course, as well as with the forty-ish Ann's love for—and attempts to resemble—teenagers and twenty-somethings. She loved "the youth." She gathered them around like a hen gathers her chicks. That was especially true for "troubled" teens, with family problems or sinful pasts. To those she gave extra attention. If one needed church acceptance, she would offer it. Hence, if ever there were a cult of personality in local Mormonism, Ann led it. Her class swelled with visitors, including a short parade of young men who almost never said anything, but often seemed to be lodging at her house for weeks on end. She spoke highly of them in tones that unnerved her more matronly peers. But not us. Any rumors you'd hear about impropriety with these young men were validation of her persecutability, a longstanding credential in Christendom generally and Mormondom specifically.

But this was, it turned out, the scaffolding for a big con, of which I started as a mark and soon became an accessory.

Understand what Ann had that allured teenagers like me. First, money. She lived in that "mansion on the hill" in the Hank Williams song of that name, which I'd sung so often with Fred at the Wineskin House. She smacked of old-school glamor, with her buoyant slightly retro hairdo and sparkly high-end jewelry. She also had enough of an hourglass shape under her shroud of age to attract the male gaze, however squinty. She drove a shiny recent-vintage Lincoln sedan. She was well-bred and well-connected, descendant of one member of the First Presidency and distant cousin to the current prophet. She'd also honed her speaking craft. The drama, the pauses, the pacing, the quivering lower lip—like Kathryn Kuhlman without the slurred speech. She even knew how to work a microphone when she was at a podium.

More salient to bargain-basement archivists like me, she had the rare books and photocopies that, pre-internet, drew lovers of esoterica to her side. The tall file drawers in the closet of her den were packed with unpublished Brigham Young speeches. She had bookshelves of rarities that bespoke her love of the lurid, hidden side of frontier religion that drew some of us to it. The best book on Mormonism to her? Fanny Stenhouse's *Tell It All*. Not something she'd say to everyone. But if she said it to you, you were an insider.

Above all, the word on the street, whispered to the initiated—but only when they were "ready for it"—was that she had seen Jesus. He'd visited her living room and made promises to her. In Mormon parlance, she had gotten the "Second Comforter," a Joseph Smith slice-and-dice of John 16's promise to send "another comforter," which Smith said was the resurrected Jesus himself visiting a disciple to promise them eternal life, "exaltation," the highest reward in the hereafter.

I had always longed to get a taste of the upper crust. I was a middle-rung suburban egghead son of a railroad switchman. I was the thrift-store son of a single-mom commercial artist. I bought all my clothes and music at St. Vincent de Paul. I lived in a creaky house on the edge of a semi-rural sidewalk-free neighborhood where cheap properties ran along sketchily paved roads between mortgage defaults and bank auctions. Now a rich woman was having me spend hours at a time in her mansion, sometimes with a friend or two, sometimes on my own. She'd brook no mediocrity, at least, as she defined it. No problem with that in my little mind with the big IQ.

By now I loved Mormon history. I'd lapped up those volumes of *Journal of Discourses*, the once-mainstream oratory that was now doctrinal legend, much of it outright rejected by modern Mormon leaders. Now Ann was offering me the key to the backrooms of its archives. Sure, anyone who took the effort could buy stuff from, say, the Modern Microfilm store in Salt Lake City, where Xeroxed repros of strange documents, published and unpublished, were stock in trade. But this woman got the hyper-rare artifacts, like unpublished revelations and apostolic talks too incendiary even for the *Journal of Discourses*, allegedly purloined by a ringer in the Church Historical Department.

A lot of those documents had to do with polygamy. Now, I'd been marinaded in the idea of free love, if not in the practice. Spading up American middle-class marital conventions was not only part of my Bay Area environs, but a marquee of Mormonism itself. And what helped solidify my attraction to polygamy was the secretive nature of its origins and early practice.

I'd now moved from "He's Done So Much for Me I Cannot Tell It All" to—*Tell It All*.

Because, as you understand by now, the underground was where I must have been destined to live. The tedium of the mere aboveground life I walked every day, from the cookie-cutter suburbs of my childhood to the butt-spanking discipline of my (so far) two fathers, grated on me. The lion's share of my discontent grew from the hifalutin opinion of myself that my IQ testing and "gifted" schooling had bred in me and that now my patriarchal blessing seemed to confirm.

As I lay out the con, you must remember this: I'd just come out of a mini-cult with a halfway house for men run by a woman in her forties. Now I was slipping into a new cult with an imaginary halfway house for damaged young men run by a woman in her forties. So my splotchy future was not only imminent but probably inevitable.

7. THE CON

The centerpiece of this con was the main rite of passage for young Mormon men: a mission. In the 1950s, President McKay had coined a motto: "Every member a missionary." That is, if you're a Mormon, people are watching you, you are proselyting all the time, for better or worse. But McKay's successor Spencer Kimball flipped the idea from descriptive to prescriptive: every young man should go on a two-year full-time mission, preferably as soon as he reached nineteen. I had hoped to skip that requirement and head straight to the temple's altar for a marriage to Karen. I was new in the faith, had checked with the stake patriarch, and felt exempt from what most Mormon boys now had to do before getting married in the temple. But President Kimball was adamant and that had turned missions into a full-blown commandment. I was obedient enough, but maybe more important, I was pragmatic. My eyes were on the prize and the prize was Karen. Now, the mission was the ticket. So I bought the ticket and took the ride.

I went through the usual worthiness interviews with ward bishop and stake president, questions about chastity, tithing, health code, and more. I passed the interviews, we filled out forms, and soon a letter from Kimball arrived in my mailbox, an autopen-signed typed letter calling me to the church's Germany Munich Mission. I now needed my "endowment," the baseline temple ritual. It was a main component of one's fitness for missionary work—not to mention eternal marriage. I went through a second round of worthiness interviews and got my "temple recommend," a small rectangle card signed by the interviewers, allowing me to enter the Oakland Temple—which I'd stared at from my dad's kitchen window for years during summer "visitations."

When I went to the temple, I discovered that big chunks of the ceremony were on film. For all my temple preparation lessons and bishopric chats, no one had told me I was going to be sitting in a room watching a movie. I did expect plenty of exotica: all-seeing eyes, beehives in relief, illustrated walls, celebrants wearing strange garb, maybe even Sophoclean masks. I got some of that, but frankly not enough for my tastes. I also heard many arcane phrases I'd heard before, since Ann and Bill liked to use them with a nod and a wink in everyday conversation, even when a non-initiate like me was around. What made my first visit to the temple so unusual, though, was that, right before the ceremony, the projector's bulb burnt out.

I walked into a spare, immaculate room feeling cheated right off the bat because there were no paintings on the walls, none of those spiffy murals in church temple-prep materials. (I learned later that they were only in a handful of older temples.) Like the rest of the forty or so other men, I was dressed in white, literally head to toe, including white socks and slippers. We sat purse-lipped, men on one side of the room, women on the other, in cushioned theater-style seats under bright lights, listening to the film's *soundtrack* with no visuals. It mimicked a radio drama, a genre I'd studied and listened to recordings of for years. I got to envision all the characters in my head, based on their voices. The devil, for example—a major player in the ceremony's narrative of Adam and Eve, et al.—I saw in my mind's eye as a pudgy, ski-jump-nosed, squinty eyed ruffian wearing a broad-brim hat—something like Nixon as an Amish farmer. Only on a second trip to the temple, with the bulb now replaced and the house lights down, did I see all the actors in the film, including the suave, handsome devil with a neatly trimmed beard and swoon-worthy Sean Connery-ish looks. I liked the actors in my head better.

Ann took glee in my mission call and temple initiation, although it soon became clear that that was because both made me more worthy of *her*. I was her latest human jewelry and this appraisal meant something. I brushed up on my German and hugged Karen more tightly for the remaining weeks, while keeping up my off-the-books studies with Ann in her den and living room, her husband dutiful as a watchdog in keeping out of her space when she had a new acolyte around. It was then and there I told Ann about my cribside encounter with the devil. To her it was a greater validation than the mission call or temple endowment. The devil had been trying to thwart me from the beginning, she said, because my entrance onto the planet was so eventful. I was one of the "young lions" in Isaiah 5:29: "Their roaring shall be like a lion, they shall roar like young lions: yea, they shall roar, and lay hold of the prey, and shall carry it away safe, and none shall deliver it." I didn't quite know what it meant, but gladly accepted the certification.

In our one-on-one tutoring sessions, Ann dripped disclosure after disclosure of what she had believed about herself for a long time, "revealed" aspects of her role in the hierarchy of heaven. She told me that other men had been "sealed" to her (married for eternity, with both spiritual and physical privileges in the mix), all young men, including Eric, the latest young male lodger in her house, whom we all knew as a frequent guest in her Sunday school classes. God had personally performed a "sealing" to Eric and other men in a warm-chested but invisible "ordinance" in her den, coincidentally on the exact spot where we sat. Her bed. This den, she explained, was now her bedroom, separated from Bill, as she prepared for her final sealing to Jesus himself. She was, she said, the actual "Bride of Christ" discussed in the Book of Revelation.

After showing me a sermon by Brigham Young saying that God authorized any man of "higher priesthood" to take the wife of someone with lesser priesthood, she hinted that God might want me sealed to her as well, on the premise that my spiritual proximity to Jesus gave *me* an authority that trumped Bill's. I was both flattered and repulsed—she was twice my age and I was in love with Karen. But I was susceptible to praise and spiritual stature and wanted so much to embrace any Jesusy counterculture that would embrace me back. One late afternoon, as we sat on her bed in the den, she gazed at me a long time in what amounted to a final hypnotic suggestion, and voila! She kept asking me what I was feeling till I said I felt that the Almighty had just sealed me to her for eternity. Eternity began right now, she convinced me. Hence, so did our marriage. In every sense.

After a while, I went back home, dazed by what had just happened. I slept badly, ecstatic as a kid at Christmas, yet stunned as a bull in the slaughterhouse. By this point in my life, I was pretty steely, roughed up by the blows of an off-track upbringing. But I had just effectively cut the lines to every harbor I'd known except Ann's.

While Mom had locked my copy of *The Graduate* up in the hutch, Ann had now locked me into her own rewrite. Think of her as Mrs. Robinson with a temple recommend and a script for seduction cribbed from old Mormon patriarchs but gender-flipped. Was she predatory? Of course. Was I an easy mark? She detected that and she was right. She was a missionary for her own "holy" nymphomania and I was her naive but complicit convert.

On October 12, 1975, I gave my mission farewell talk in sacrament meeting. At my request, Karen, who loved Ann fiercely but knew nothing of my new "sealing," sang an obscure lament on Joseph Smith's assassination, John Taylor's "O Give Me Back My Prophet Dear." Smith, who hid his secret polygamy from the public, was still my talisman, a fact on which Ann played exquisitely. Paradoxically, I had an obsession about doing things by the book, but only if the book was the New Testament and I could wring my own predilections out of it. I say that to set up the trappings of my farewell talk, which I gave without notes. As Jesus had taught, I had to "take no thought" before speaking but let the Spirit "give [me] utterance." Fortunately, I recorded it on cassette.

> Thank you very much for singing that. I love to hear that song, because it was written by John Taylor, a man who knew the Prophet perhaps like few other men. And it tells the agony that he felt when one whom he knew in the bonds of eternal brotherhood was taken from his side.
>
> This kind of love is the love I feel for many of you. Not all. But I hope to for all. These bonds of love and brotherhood and sisterhood are the sublime truths and principles that all the prophets have loved to dwell upon. Every head of every dispensation has loved and delighted in the theme of love of the gods and the love of men. And I delight in it, too. It is the great, grand theme that is at the core and center of all that we talk about and sing about. It is the center of the life of Christ. It *is* Christ in its fulness. My words to describe the feelings that I have are mockery to the depth of it.
>
> The Apostle Paul said, "We have not received the spirit of fear unto bondage, but we have received the spirit of adoption, whereby we cry, Abba, Father." That word "Abba," I guess, could best be translated "Dad" or "Daddy." When the Spirit begins to give you these feelings, that you

can say "Dad" and know that you're speaking to God, there is no greater joy. There is no greater happiness. There is no greater thrill. And to my soul there is nothing else.

Likewise, the feelings of brother to brother. It's so hard to love each other, because we're so inclined to look at what we do instead of who we are. God is able to love us all because he knows us all. He knows us by experience. Because he is light and truth. He comprehends us. He doesn't compare us. But he loves us each for what we are and not for what we do. Thank God for it. Because I know that if he were to love us for what we do, we'd lose out on his love.

Were I to give all my time and all my life and all my spirit and all I possess and every good gift that I have, it would never be enough. It would never come near touching the depth of his love for me. And I know it's true for everyone here.

I would say the same of the tender feelings of love that I've experienced with brothers and friends and those who have turned their love towards me. I feel to thank them for their love. Joseph Smith said, "When a person manifests the least kindness to me or love to me, what power it has over my mind." And it does.

Jonathan loved David. And the scripture says that he loved David as his own soul. When David was in trouble and he had to flee for his life, Jonathan said, "Whatsoever thing thy soul desireth, I will even give it to thee." This is the purity and beauty of the kind of love that I'm speaking of, the love which comes from Christ, which is centered in him. We can't muster it, we can't strain for it, we can't strive for it, because it's a gift. And maybe if I can be an instrument to bring our hearts to the depth of this gift, we would all fall on our knees and pray that we might be a vessel of that love.

We often hear it said—and it's true—that "we show our love by our service." I'm going to take that and maybe put it on another plane for a minute. Paul, again, said, "If I give all my goods to the poor and give my body to be burned and I have not love, it profiteth me nothing." This is the kind of love he's speaking of: the love wherein our "service" is shown by our love. To you that teach, you that are overseers of young people and older people: this love is really the key, isn't it, to all our service? And if we have not that love, it profiteth nothing. And so, I want that love. I want the Lord Jesus Christ to bless me. And I want your prayers as I go on this mission. Because I'm going to serve him.

I'm thankful for this calling. I can't express it. But if I have not love, it profiteth me nothing. I want that love. Many of you have extended it to me and you've been a vessel of love to me. And hopefully I've been to some of you.

As I leave, I want to bear you my testimony of the gospel. I know that the church is true. I know that Jesus Christ lives—and I know it more qualitatively every day. I know that he loves us. I know to some degree his love for us. I want to know more.

I bear you these things in this testimony because they're dearer to me than life itself. And I'm sure of them. They're tangible to me. Many of you I perhaps will not see again; probably most of you I will. But I expect on the morning of the first resurrection to strike hands with many of you and to embrace you. In the name of Jesus Christ, amen.

Any decent armchair psychologist who has read to this point can sift through the clues in that rhetoric. And the inside baseball of the talk was clear to the handful of Ann initiates in the room, not to mention Ann herself, now primed to start a splurge of mail to her new secret "husband" as he went on his mission.

Meanwhile, Gladys wrote Mom to console her about the "big task" it would be to have an open house to fete me for my Mormon friends. "Don't let the Mormons get a hold of you + try to get you to join them. Some of their teachings seem so impossible. Stay with your Bible and the faith of the Christian Church." But the warning was moot. I had no intention of converting Mom. I thought I'd risen above the Mormon rabble into something more esoteric, more truly divine than almost anyone could understand. At the open house I beamed with the fluorescence of a true believer. I'd sucked that radiance up from living in hippie California, being a Jesus Freak, a Wineskinner, a Mormon, and now a Whatever-This-Was.

I packed my bags for the big move to the "mission home" in Salt Lake City, followed by a seven-week installation at the Language Training Mission (LTM), a motley collection of rooms and buildings around Brigham Young University in Provo where missionaries leaving for foreign lands got language-drilled and doctrine-drenched. Before boarding the train to Salt Lake, I wrote to Mom's dad to pull back from my ferocious polemics. Sort of. "Whenever I am able to read one of your letters, I always know it will be well thought out and have some good points to make. I wholeheartedly agree with your sentiments concerning the futility of religious debate. I hope and am fairly sure that you understand that my last letter was not written in the spirit of contention, but rather to set forth in a more understandable manner several of the doctrines of the church. In this I hope I succeeded." Then I went on for three more pages to reason through a few points that he'd made and that I disputed. I ended with thanks "for your thoughtful letter and your kind words. I, too, hope and pray that our hearts will always be open to the light and wisdom of heaven to instruct us in all truth." I was channeling Joseph Smith lingo. I thought it welded me into the chain of Mormon prophetry. But it was also smoothing over the cement I had poured into my spiritual basement to cover the skeletons I was importing.

I arrived at the Union Pacific station in Salt Lake just after daybreak on October 25, 1975, wearing a dress suit and carrying an extra suit on a hanger over my shoulder. In the other hand was my big suitcase, which carried not only my clothes and toiletries but a maudlin short story I'd handwritten on the train concerning Abraham's sacrifice (which was really an allegory about me and the life/lives I was sacrificing). I wandered around State Street and Main, stopping to rest now and then, looking in the storefronts, trying to get a sense of this as the remnants of the Mormon Promised Land. And there *was* something special about it, buried in the history I'd come to revere and the banquet of secret covenants laid out in its storied temple. I walked around for over two hours before check-in time at the mission home. When that time arrived, I walked in and handed my belongings over before they gave me and the dozens of other missionaries a standard welcome and pep talk. Then they put us all in a line we had to walk through to get tapped on the shoulder if our hair was too long. My hair was the shortest it had been in almost a decade, so I thought I was safe. Nope. The tap. I got sent to another line to wait for the in-house barber to shear me like a pre-Beatles grade-schooler. Because, as I was learning, this was not the grizzly pioneer enterprise that had justly seduced me but more of a steak made of corporate beef basted with just enough sauce from the old weird church to claim it was the same dish. Still, I was ready to mutate, since I was already living a double life. I and the other missionaries who'd been assigned to foreign-language missions were hustled onto a bus headed forty miles south to Provo, Utah.

Arriving there, we crowded into an auditorium in the Knight Mangum Building on BYU campus. The president of the LTM gave us one more pep talk, more militaristic than the earlier one, and those of us headed to Germany walked down to Amanda Knight Hall a few blocks away. Once a girl's college dorm in BYU's early days, the hall had earned the salty nickname "a-man-a-night-hall" in the 1920s. It had long since been emptied and then resurrected as a lodge for missionaries. Within a couple of days the building's occupants were only allowed to speak German. What ensued was lot of gesturing, grunting, bad accents, and whispering in English.

Our daily schedule was:

6:00	Arise
6:15–7:30	Breakfast
7:30–9:00	Class [mostly language skills]
9:00–10:00	Retention [study and memorization of class content]
10:00–12:00	Class
12:00–1:00	Lunch
1:00–2:00	Class
2:00–3:00	Retention
3:00–4:00	Class
4:00–5:00	Gospel study [reading scriptures and approved church books]
5:00–7:00	Dinner
7:00–8:30	Class
8:30–9:45	Retention
9:45–10:30	Personal preparation [shower, brushing teeth, etc.]
10:30	Retire

I'd had a year of German in high school, and I was schooled enough in language structures and methods from record sets, dictionaries, and speaking-in-tongues "research" that I rose through the language-learning ranks easily. A few teachers said they thought I must have lived in Germany at some point in my life. Within a week and a half I was assigned to tutor other missionaries in the language.

During scripture study time I inscribed miscellaneous doctrinal musings in spiral bound notebooks, comparing scriptures in parallel columns, speculating on temple symbolism, deducing celestial time frames, and anything else that felt hidden enough and worthy enough for my noble calling with Ann. The sections of the notebook were, in order:

— Intelligence, Spirit, and the Mind of Man
— Perfection, Godliness, and Becoming Like Christ in the New Testament
— Pre-existent and Pre-mortal Themes in the New Testament
— References in the New Testament, Doctrine and Covenants, Teachings of the Prophet Joseph Smith, etc., Regarding Tabernacle, Moses, Zion, etc. [these pertained a lot to Ann, who identified me as the "man like unto Moses" in scripture and herself as "Zion"]
— Notes on the Book of Acts [my personal primer for missionary work]
— Various teachings on the Fatherhood of God and Related Themes
— Short Declarations of Paul Concerning God, Christ, and Their Relationship to Each Other, etc.
— Tabernacle and the Mount of Transfiguration
— Christ as Jehovah in the Bible, Book of Mormon, and Doctrine and Covenants

Ann wrote to me every single day. Some days, two letters. Getting that much mail made me the envy of most other missionaries. But the letters sank my heart in a magma of guilt and befuddlement. The guilt part: these letters, dripping with old-school romance from her—i.e., my mom's—generation, never heartened me as she intended them to. The befuddlement part: they had a sort of code that made me wonder what actual new schemes she was undertaking among my old friends in Los Altos and Mountain View. I felt glad to be away from her and scared to be away from her. I answered her letters perfunctorily each week, usually with the paper in my lap at the barbershop during our weekly trim, hoping the barbers wouldn't read any of it.

I burrowed hard into the refuge of the LTM. I adored the severe language classes, chanting conjugations, packing vocabulary into my head, and showing off my dead-on pronunciation. More than those, I savored the classes with Marcus Von Wellnitz, who showed us intersections between our temple ordinances and Catholic ritual. He was a mini-Hugh Nibley and I was a Nibley fan. I also loved our branch president, a noted baritone who taught us German songs, among which was my favorite verbal sanctuary: "Die Gedanken Sind Frei." The meaning of its words in English consoled me.

> Thoughts are free, who can guess them?
> They fly by like nocturnal shadows.
> No person can know them, no hunter can shoot them
> With powder and lead: Thoughts are free!

Outside of songs the branch president taught us and hymns that we sang in church—held on the outskirts of the Amanda Knight cafeteria—we were forbidden to listen to or play any other music.

I didn't love my roommates, except by fiat. We were four nineteen-year-old strangers crammed into a snugly built Victorian room with a steeply sloped ceiling. But to be fair, we never spent time in our rooms doing much of anything but sleeping. Now and then I had a flashlight under my covers to leaf through photos of Karen.

When we were shipped out to Munich on December 16, my suitcase was packed and I was mentally braced. But I couldn't get on the bus to the airport with the others because I had lost my plane ticket. I looked everywhere all day, said goodbye to my comrades, and met with Murdock Travel, which managed all of the church's travel activities, to re-route me solo on a chain of connecting flights that zig-zagged the country, then landed me in Amsterdam before changing planes for a flight to Munich. Somewhere along the way, the airlines lost my luggage. I arrived in Munich utterly alone with nothing but the clothes I wore, scared as a dog being held above a wood-chipper. When someone from the mission arrived and picked me up, I headed to my first meeting with the mission president, then took a bus to meet my new companion. He—and now I—lived in an apartment two flights up in what had been a chocolate factory in Hof. On the bottom floor was a small grocery store from which we bought fresh fruit and yogurt for breakfast each morning. Our landlady, a giggly, frizzy-haired, pint-size woman with a goiter, lived in an apartment next to ours. It had a nice high-polish ebony upright piano she'd let me play on whenever I wanted to. Which I did, using the excuse that I had to practice for our church meetings, where I was installed as the new pump organ player. The Sunday LDS

Elder Hicks playing and singing at our landlady's
piano, Hof, West Germany, 1976.

meeting room was scrawny, the closest thing I'd seen to a storefront
Pentecostal church in five years.

Hof was mostly Lutheran, at least in upbringing, with small pockets of Jehovah's Witnesses, Seventh Day Adventists, and members
of the New Apostolic Church. We did lots of "tracting," going door
to door with or without bikes, trying to get in anyone's house for a
missionary lesson. Our standard door approach, my genial companion taught me, was to say that we were American students taking a
survey about the ancient inhabitants of America. The dominant re-
sponses were (1) "Those were the Indians, no?" and (2) "Why would
you come to Germany to take such a survey?" Far less common were
pre-doorslam comebacks along the lines of "We had enough of
Americans in the war." I don't recall us ever getting in a door to talk
about Mormonism with someone we'd tracted. But there were a few
longstanding contacts that we visited weekly.

How long these people had gotten visits from missionaries wasn't clear. But they were friendly, tolerant, and enjoyed talking with American teenagers. One was a professor who, because we could rattle off Joseph Smith's fairly erudite testimony in German, used hifalutin technical language with us. I felt like I was in deep water, gasping for intellectual air whenever we were with him. Another contact was a lovely, articulate twenty-three-year-old woman who lived with a ten-year-old that anyone would assume was her little brother. He was her son. She wanted so much to go to America, and we seemed a lifeline—my companion even talked about trying to adopt her. (Marriage was out of the question, because he was already engaged.) And there was a hippie couple who liked to practice English with us. It was at their house where I first saw the movie *Blow-Up*—uncensored—on TV in the background as we talked about Joseph Smith.

In one of my weekly letters to the mission president, I pled with him to let us serve "without purse or scrip" (relying on the kindness of strangers for food and lodging). That was the New Testament way, I tried to convince the president. But no dice. He didn't even acknowledge the inquiry. I'd have been good at it, I think. Gospel hobo. I'd hitchhiked so much and hung out with enough flower children and Agnews inmates to be that clever.

At the same time, I showed off my singing and guitar playing whenever I could get my hands on an instrument. People who heard me—like our *Blow-Up* friends—urged me to do a concert at the Hof town hall, which always looked for local acts to play in their weekly soirees. My companion thought this would be great PR to help get us in doors to teach our faith. When we shopped the idea to our mission president, the response was unequivocal: after just six weeks in Hof I was transferred to another area on the opposite side of the mission. Bühlertal. Whether the prospect of a pop concert gig provoked the transfer, I can't say. But I just did.

Before I left Hof, my lost luggage finally arrived. I'd already bought replacements for all the white shirts and temple garments ("Mormon underwear"). Now I had more white shirts and twice as many garments as I needed.

Or maybe not.

Ann continued to write me each day of the nearly three months

I lived in Germany, first in Hof and now in Bühlertal. Her letters and now lovey-dovey cassettes got more and more obsessive and surreal. I tried to downplay them in my mind and dutifully write back, vaguely pledging devotion to the vision of a life to come that she had planned for me and her other disciples. The last cassette was an hour-long ramble that straddled love letter, diary entry, and mind-blitzed manifesto in which she talked in hushed tones about her breasts being my source of food for eternity as well as the source of life for the 144,000 redeemed high priests in the Book of Revelation—and more. As usual, I had to listen through an earplug on the sly. But I couldn't get through the whole thing. The note wrapped around it said to be sure to destroy it when I finished listening. Since I didn't finish the listening, I didn't do the destroying.

A month into my stay in Bühlertal, I got a letter from Karen telling me that she was now dating one of Ann's sons and getting serious with him. I worried she was now going to marry him instead of me and all this was being directed by Ann, who wanted me all for herself—partly because the other young men she'd "married" had by now abandoned her. I found a pay phone and dumped all the coins I had into it as I tried to talk my improv version of sense into Karen long distance through the cloud of this new turn of events. She was evasive but soon made it clear: she wanted me to be with Ann and she would marry Ann's son. This was God's will, revealed, of course, to Ann and parroted by Karen. When my coins ran out and the phone went dead, I knew I had to get out of Germany and back to the Bay Area to fish or cut bait. However this evolved, I had to do all I could to ensure I'd get Karen as the reward for being Ann's divine fantasy boy-toy.

Unlike most missionaries, I had a bedroom of my own, separate from my companion's, in our Bühlertal apartment. I loved that, since I had been an only child and wanted as much time in solitude as I could drain out of a mission. (Cue surreptitious cassette listening.) The night of my phone call to Karen, I went to bed at 10:00, the same time as Elder H (my companion), but set the alarm to wake me up at midnight. After Elder H and I had prayed together and said goodnight, I locked the door and, rather than strip down to my garments, stayed in my slacks and put on a casual shirt, then started the warm-up for my breakaway.

I cut the lining in the pockets of my overcoat—as I'd learned how to do in my shoplifting days—and slid everything into them that I thought I might need for a long walk out of Germany: candy, small boxes of cereal, a bag of crackers, a knife and spoon, another shirt, all of my letters, and *that* cassette. I was finally going without purse or scrip, all the way to America. I tied my shirts and garments—the complete double portion of them I now had—into a long rope that I wound and knotted around a pipe that ran along the ceiling over the only window in the room, a sideways sliding pane that overlooked a weedy field three floors down.

When my alarm went off, I got up, slid open the window, threw the rope of garments out, and started down. Weighted down as I was, I couldn't help but bang into the metal wall on the balcony one floor down. Afraid I'd be detected, I let go and dropped into the field, then started to run as fast as I could in the dark through vacant lots. After maybe a quarter mile, I went down into the lower porch of a split-level home, caught my breath, and prayed that the owners wouldn't find me there, hoist me out, and call the police—or worse. After about ten minutes, I climbed out and kept walking.

My thought was to find the autobahn and hitchhike to France, blend in as well as I could with my high school French, then go to an American Embassy, where I'd heard they had to help stranded Americans get back to America. I walked aimlessly for hours, with virtually no sense of direction and precious few streetlights, but with an occasional huge stone crucifix on a street corner. (Unlike Hof, Bühlertal was Catholic country.) Eventually I did find the autobahn, tried to hitchhike it with only an isolated car now and then shooting by at over a hundred miles an hour in the middle of the night. After a half-hour of this, I walked back to where I knew the train station was to see if I could at least get a train out of my mission boundaries. As I crossed one unpaved road, a young man hastily pedaled a bike down the road about twenty yards to my left in a different direction.

My companion.

I kept walking, staying in shadows or behind bushes as much as I could, and finally made it to the train station. I watched for Elder H, assuming he'd head there, as I was doing, and try to catch me. I stalked around unused train cars on the backlot of the station. He never showed. But when I went up to the ticket booth, it was, as I'd feared, empty, closed till morning. So I went back to walking.

The next two days are a blur. I know I unintentionally walked in circles a lot, wasting miles of strength, my packed overcoat weighing me down and banging against my legs. I caught a train to Mainz and tried to con a travel agent into booking me a flight on credit I didn't have. That night I made it to a hostel where I spent a few coins to stay the night in a tight bunkroom of snoring wayfarers. When morning arrived, I caught a train to Frankfurt and walked to the American Embassy where I demanded the attending bureaucrat get me a flight back home. He kept asking me questions about why I was there, where I'd been staying, and so on. The best I could come up with was the same fib we missionaries had been instructed to tell people at their doorsteps when we tracted: I was an American student taking a survey about German people's knowledge of *"die Ureinwohner Americas"*—the ancient inhabitants of America. He eyed me hard and I was worried he knew I was a Mormon missionary. Which is why he wouldn't give me more than fifteen minutes of his time and not one *pfennig* of help.

I finally did the one thing I had sworn to myself I wouldn't. I called my anti-Mormon Dad to see if he'd front me a plane ticket home. He did, almost licking his chops at what he believed was a fulfillment of his prophecy that I'd quit the church. When I went to the Frankfurt airport to check in, the lady at the desk oddly said she had to go look up something. She came back in a few minutes, then gave me the boarding pass. I got on the flight, starving more for sleep than for food—I'd been eating out of my overcoat stash—and slipped in and out of sleep and headaches all nine hours on the grim, bumpy flight to New York, where I'd have to switch planes for my flight to San Francisco. When I got to La Guardia and deplaned, before I got on my connecting flight, I literally got on my knees and kissed the pavement.

On the flight to San Francisco, I got more alert as fear set in colder and sharper, aided by the in-flight movie, the paranoid Redford thriller *Three Days of the Condor*. After four hours, the plane finally touched down, I walked the ramp from the plane to the gate and there, beaming at me, was … my old bishop. And, like the tumblers of a lock falling in my head, I started to realize that everyone all along the way had known more or less where I was all the time, tracked me right down to the ticket counter, but never accosted me, just let me do my thing and see if I'd go back to my mission post on my own.

The quiet ride home with the bishop was sullen and cheery at once. I felt loved but nauseated and wanted nothing more than to see Karen. Which I did, but not until Ann and her other disciples formed a tight circle of comfort and singlemindedness around me. I quickly became, in their eyes—including Karen's and even my own—a renegade guru, who'd take up again with Ann, making trips up and down the coast in her Lincoln, staying in hotels or at the home of two adoring friends who knew little about what was really going on with this nineteen-year-old who went everywhere on the sly with a middle-aged woman. Except that they were sharing a bed.

Why did I slip so easily back into this circle? The simple answer: they were family. While I had blood ties to my mom, the embrace and honor that make family feel like a makeshift heaven were more with Ann and her disciples than with anyone else. Besides, I still believed that God had married Ann and me. That thought held me in the grip of duty if not joy.

In the midst of this secret life, the church made a heavy-handed push to get me to return to Germany. They reached me at Mom's house in Los Altos and flew me to Salt Lake City to chat with Elder Hartman Rector, one of the presidents of the church's "Seventy," who oversaw missions and missionaries. I was steeled and resolute as I could be that I would (a) not return to Germany and (b) not say why. Rector was genial at first, but gradually took me through a parade of rhetorical traps—much like missionaries did with potential converts—showing me why if I didn't return to finish my mission I would be left eternally astray and severed from my divine destiny. I'd even "marry the wrong girl and have the wrong children," which sounded both creepy and hysterical to me. He kept badgering me, and I kept digging in my heels: I would not go back to Germany. Exasperated, I finally said, "Why would you want me to go back on a mission just because of the pressure you're putting on me?"

"Don't you think the Savior had a lot of pressure put on him by the Father to perform the Atonement?"

That response both surprised and peeved me. "I absolutely do not. Jesus gave himself willingly of his own volition out of love for his people."

Rector didn't back down. But I'd had enough, cheerily bore my testimony of the gospel, and then brusquely ended our conversation. As I walked out of his office, he seemed shaken and incredulous.

Within the week, the Munich mission president wrote me a letter conveying "my sad duty to release you from missionary service at your own request." He told me I'd been a good companion, spoke the language very well, and so forth. I was "talented," even "gifted." "These facts made me put great hope in you as a future leader in this mission. ... We all liked you and were looking forward to your return." But I was steadfast, thinking my defiance some sort of valiancy in God/Jesus/Ann's inner circle.

In April the mission president sent a second letter accounting for the sale of my bike to cover my leftover bills. But to get my luggage back, I'd have to send $158.00 more. Mom loaned me the money, which I promised to pay back. In a few weeks my suitcase arrived, complete with the enormous rope of shirts and garments still tied together.

By then, everyone in Ann's inner circle thought me the closest person on earth to Jesus. Ann assured them that I was the one sent to prepare her for her imminent tryst with the Son of God, who would father with her the *new* Messiah, the millennial "David." With this on the agenda, she persuaded me to sell all I had. Why? Because we were going away into the "wilderness."

Ann had said for months that all references to "Zion" in scripture secretly referred to her. That was her heavenly name. But more recently she said that she was the woman in Revelation 12 who was driven into the wilderness but would come back with a baby. (I know, that's a little out of the order in the scripture, but we were all flying by the seat of our pants.) With me home from my mission, she was ready to leave for that "wilderness," the location and meaning of which was "To Be Announced." She said we needed cash, because her Bill-based credit card was now frozen. And I needed discipline, she said. So, while I'd been saving all my early issues of *Rolling Stone* since 1968, I'd have to sell the whole heavy box of them. I found a dealer who gave me $50 for it. With that sale and a few others, soon all I had left of my personal belongings was a guitar, some clothes, a few records on Mom's shelf, and the piece of luggage from Germany, complete with the still-tied garments, which I'd kept as both a souvenir and as evidence of my attempted heroism.

For weeks Ann had visited her actual home with Bill only rarely. During one visit, I was with her and Bill came at me with a chair held above his head to swing down and kill me. I raised my arm to the square and rebuked him in the name of Jesus—a trick I'd learned in my Wineskin days. He set the chair down. And that was it for Ann. So, as a waystation en route to "the wilderness," she left Bill's house for good to hostel herself in secret with me (part-time) and two other disciples (full-time) at their apartment. As weeks rolled on, Bill got more and more alarmed. When he'd try to question the three of us about her whereabouts, we lied, in the tradition, as we saw it, of Joseph Smith lying about his polygamy. Lying for the Lord, we believed, was not only an art but a privilege. Each denial was one more ticket punched into the future kingdom we thought Ann was inaugurating.

For now, the "wilderness" was mostly us sitting around the apartment boasting about our proximity to God, watching late night confections like *Mary Hartman, Mary Hartman*, and listening to rock on the radio, fantasizing that our favorite songs were all about *us*. The Doobie Brothers' "Takin' It to the Streets," for instance, celebrated our revolutionary, guerilla-style hyper-gospel. Barry Manilow's "It's a Miracle" was about Ann having Jesus' baby. Ann even had a cassette of Jake Holmes's *So Very Far to Go* album, every track of which she analyzed like scripture that, of course, was about her and her exalted station. (The title track, in particular, described her journey toward hooking up with Jesus, being crowned queen of heaven and earth, etc.) I never quite bought the idea that God had inspired Holmes to write all this about her. But like a sheepishly dutiful husband, I supported her musings, especially since, as she said over and over, I was more like her Big-Name Husband than anyone else on Earth.

Ann's early coquettishness and charm began to harden into transactional patterns. If anyone said anything approving of her in a clever way or in a way that rhymed with her thoughts about, well, anything, then the Lord was speaking through that person. If anyone said anything that smacked of criticism or even mild disagreement with her, that person was being "programmed" by one of the four devils (in descending order of power): Leviathan, Beelzebub, Lucifer, and Satan. She'd gotten that cast list, she told me, from LaVey's *Satanic Bible*, which had lots of truth about "the enemy" that we all needed to learn. The idea of *programming* as computer-like mind control, of course, had migrated from pop culture into our own pop cult. It was cute in a way, as Ann tried to sound hip and up to date, which was her—and our—chronic post-LaVey Silicon Valley rhetorical quest.

I could list more eccentricities, but I'll bring up just one more, because it played into the erosion of the Ann cult more than anything else: the idea of her being "hit" by demons. Being "hit" meant that she would go into convulsions in which her eyes would roll back and her limbs shake. It was almost exactly like what we called being "slain in the spirit" during my Pentecostal days. But in Ann's case, we quickly learned the routine: whoever was around when she was "hit" had to lay hands on any part of her body until the convulsion subsided. She would then require lots of affection, spoken and tactile, during a brief recovery period. No messages or threats from the dark side were whispered to her during her convulsive state. She was just being targeted and attacked, she said—usually when one of us said something remotely critical, made a suggestion, or offered gratuitous counsel. It was a weird, full-body narcissism, fed by acolytes like me, and exacerbated, perhaps, by her steady diet of peanut butter and marshmallow sandwiches. We'd become disciples by her flattery of us. Now she required ten times more in return.

One night, as we sat on her bed at those two disciples' apartment, Ann started crying at the awkwardness of having sex with Jesus. How humbled she'd be. And how jarring, because, she sobbed, "I've never even seen him." What? I was thunderstruck. It was as if she'd just shredded her diploma. I asked her about what people had always said about her and what she'd let them believe. She said that she'd only strongly felt his presence in the room. It was very strong. Super strong. But the problem with that explanation was that almost every born-again Christian I'd ever known—including me—could claim that. And did. At the moment of this admission, I felt both better and worse. Better because she was not so special, after all. Worse, because she was not so special, after all.

As the days wore on, she added to her list of future marriages. It would not be just her husband, then the young "husbands" before me, then me, then Jesus, but also all her sons, and on and on, eventually reaching all 144,000 high priests in Revelation, whom she'd already said she'd be feeding with milk from her breasts. By this point, I was feeling the last-days-of-the-Wineskin vibe. Now, as before, it was as though I'd ridden the *Pirates of the Caribbean* ride's first calm water tour, then whoosh after whoosh came, each steeper than the one before. Then the last glide to the exit.

One night in mid-June, Ann and I, for all intents and purposes, divorced. It was early evening and I had gotten a phone call from our stake president. I went to his office, he asked me lots of questions, I lied on Ann's and my behalf, then returned to her bedside. Because of my having left her to see the president, she was wrapped up in the covers after having been "hit" again. She wasn't sure by which devil, she said. Maybe all of them. Then she spoke angrily about the stake president, how evil he was to pursue her and me. I pushed back, saying that he was a good guy and was doing his best to deal with all this. She said that Leviathan was now in control of me. Feeling a little put out that she wasn't thanking me for lying for her, I let it slip how I looked forward to the time when Karen and I could be together. Ann, I more than implied, was Leah and Karen was the Rachel I'd labor for years to obtain. She scowled and snapped back, "Oh, I know what you want. I know exactly what you want." She told me I'd never be with Karen, Karen was far too *unworthy* of me, and I needed to focus more on the blanket-wrapped demon-targeted woman lying in front of me. I hastily excused myself, saying I was going home. But I drove back to the stake president's office.

He was still there, although his clerk and executive secretary had both left and he was packing his briefcase to leave, too. I stood at his open office door and said, "I want you to ask me the same questions you asked me before."

He paused, then said, "Let me just ask you one." I won't repeat it. But it concerned what Henry Miller said "holds the world together," as Miller—and now I—had "learned from bitter experience."

146

I said that, yes, I had done that with Ann. I and other insiders were convinced that she and I were married. And with that I turned the key in the ignition of the cult's drive off the cliff.

The president and I talked a little more that night and a lot more the next day. I stayed away from the other disciples, although Ann's live-in protectors called me to find out what I was doing. I told them. They tried persuading me to go back and tell the president I'd lied the *second* time I talked with him. But I was done. I had to get out, just as I'd known I had to get out of Germany. Or had to get out of the Wineskin. Or had to get out of every other previous life that didn't work. Beyond that, I had to bring this whole thing down, like Samson at the pillars—or, as I fancied myself in those times, like John Dean bringing down Nixon.

In the next few days the ecclesiastical wheels quickly turned and a massive stake high council disciplinary court was scheduled to be held on June 27—the anniversary of Joseph Smith's assassination. I found out from my friend Doug—an Ann devotee who'd come, reluctantly, to accept my account of what was going on in secret—that Ann's mainstays planned to tell the high council I was obviously mentally ill and had fabricated all this. Just look at how crazily I'd left Germany, they'd say. I was clearly off my rocker. Hearing that, the door to my Ann archive swung open: all the letters she'd sent me on my mission, Karen's lately brainwashed ones, and, most importantly, the cassette I'd declined to destroy, which in Ann's own voice laid out more chilling details than I could have paraphrased. I gave everything to the president, some of it highlighted in yellow marker, and told him exactly how my testimony before the high council was likely to be attacked. As he thanked me, then drove away, I felt like Christian in *Pilgrim's Progress* having my backload unstrapped and carried away.

At the church trial, I asked for excommunication, because, as I told the high council, I wanted a fresh start with this church. Because Mormonism, which I loved, had been boobytrapped for me just by my attendance at Sunday school. When I got home that evening and waited for the council's verdict, I sat by Mom's stereo console for hours listening to records. An LP of motets by Josquin

Des Prez was the one I played most. As I read the texts' translations, the one for "O Virgo Virginum," caught my eye:

O virgin of virgins
How could this have happened?

Just after 9 o'clock, the call came that I'd been excommunicated. The letter would arrive a couple of days later.

They also excommunicated the two disciples who'd been housing Ann, whose own trial was the following Sunday—the American Bicentennial. To no one's surprise, she didn't show up and they exed her in absentia.

One condition of my readmission to the church via rebaptism was to make "restitution," a term usually applied to monetary value. But how do you restitute treachery? One way, to my mind, was to convert my mission defection into admonitions to missionaries on their way to the field. I wrote letters to them urging their obedience to the gospel and to mission rules. I can't imagine their puzzled looks at reading my letters, since our acquaintance was as bare as a brand new bathtub. A more direct way to restitute, I thought, was to write up a manifesto of sorts. So Doug and I worked up a document called "Twenty Items," a sidelong trope on Luther's 95 Theses. We brainstormed, drafted, typed a final version, Xeroxed it, and mailed it to a handful of Ann co-conspirators and hangers-on.

By turns angry, sardonic, flowery, and self-righteous, we laid out the case—or at least *a* case—against Ann. We cited her doctrinal and rhetorical problems, some of them fussy (her notions about predestination, her dates for the Second Coming), others more essential (her rewriting of scriptures, her failed prophecies). We also outlined some of the rhetorical patch-and-fill techniques she used to keep disciples from leaving. We catalogued indiscretions, mostly dealing with her contempt for the downtrodden and lower classes—my old Wineskin clientele—making light of what some of us felt sacred (besides her), mocking chastity of any sort, and even her claim that "Jesus is more like me [Ann] than you have ever imagined." Then there were the gritty pathologies, from being "hit" by devils—although she claimed she could never be possessed, as she said her

148

followers intermittently were—to her "sealings" to an infinitude of men in the deifying of her nymphomania.

It was overkill. But those were the days of overkill. And the document had no results, except a complaint from the bishop about the tactic and a couple of venomous letters in reply. One couple denied knowing anything about any of this, even though they had furnished a mattress on the floor for Ann and me to share at their house.

The one friendly reply was from the teenage "husband" immediately before me, Eric. He slammed Ann lightheartedly and updated me on his new life. He revealed earlier murmurings among Ann's ex-disciples, complaints about her losing her grip on reality and about her doctrinal and behavioral decay. He also confirmed that Bill had supported Ann's mischief for years, including Eric's live-in liaison and fake sealing to her. But the main thrust of the letter was that he was moving on with a real newlywed spouse and an impending temple sealing.

Three months later he committed suicide.

As the cult sputtered out, Karen and I rode a wave of exhilaration into what seemed like a return to the "us" we'd bathed in before the debacle. But our jubilance waned. The bad seeds Ann had sowed in us kept sprouting. And, besides, both of us needed to start planting and harvesting new fields. Karen got into BYU and migrated to Provo in August. And I began to feel like "Amazing Grace" in reverse: I once could see, but now was blind.

Before Karen left town, my bishop's first counselor heard I needed work and recommended me to Jim Bodell, the contractor on our new stake center, for which footings were just starting to be dug. I joined his crew as a laborer, digging, compacting soil, handing tools to carpenters, pulling measuring tape, and doing other assorted tasks fit for a barely skilled worker. I had lots of energy and needed my brain to empty as much of the preceding two years as possible. Long, strenuous days among affable co-workers ensued, along with mounds of Jim's unique mix of positivity and piety. This new brand of labor, added to the employment counseling, tape masking, and shipping/receiving gigs already on my résumé, forecast a blue-collar future that perfectly mirrored my working-class upbringing and current address.

Nevertheless, a month after Karen started at BYU, I applied to get admitted there, too, partly to be near her and partly to flee this local Disasterville to a clean Mormon academy of the learned. BYU admitted non-LDS students, I told myself, so why not me? In my letter of application, though, I had to explain my circumstances, since I had to check "LDS" or "non-LDS" on the application form. I thought my relationship with the church till then actually lifted me a bit over, say, a Baptist. I also thought that to tug their heart strings, teasing out the spirit of mercy, forgiveness, etc., was the Christian way to negotiate. So, with my bishop and stake president's encouragement, here's what I wrote, using the diction and tone I'd gleaned from my reaping of old-school Mormon prose:

Gentlemen:

By way of explanation of my present standing in relation to the Church of Jesus Christ of Latter-day Saints, may I offer the following remarks:

On June 27, 1976, I was excommunicated from the Church, having been until that time a member in good standing since my baptism on December 8, 1973. The grounds for my excommunication stemmed from my association with a small apostate faction led by a former Sunday School teacher of mine. I served several months on a mission for the Church (Oct. 1975–Feb. 1976) but due to the confusion of sentiments then existing in my heart (my involvement with this group had begun prior to my mission), I left the field, returned home, and obtained an early release. In due time, as the details of this faction's apostate views and practices became known to the local authorities, the determination was made that a court of the High Council should be held in order to review the various charges being made in the matter. Prior to that trial, I stepped forward to confess my own involvement, having now become fully cognizant of the falsity of the group's claims as well as the true character of its leader. It was fairly certain, however, that excommunication would be my just lot, and so it was.

Though I was, for a time, led astray from the truth, my heart is with the Church. I know with all the fervency of my soul that the Gospel of Jesus Christ is true and that the men called and sustained to bear authority over the Church are God's representatives to administer salvation unto the same. I am seeking to so order my life that I may soon regain the fellowship of the Saints and stand worthy of membership in the Church and kingdom of God, with all its attendant blessings.

In doing so, my Stake President, my Bishop, and myself are in accord that attendance at BYU would be immensely helpful in enabling me to attain the educational ideals and spiritual goals I have set before me.

Thank you for your consideration.

Sincerely,

Michael Hicks

Unaccountably optimistic, I had no idea that non-members differed as much from ex-members as the moon from a black hole. The admissions committee's terse reply said that "In checking your file, we find that we will be unable to process your application for consideration until your membership in the Church of Jesus Christ of Latter-day Saints has been cleared by a Bishop's Court. At that time, we will need a statement from your bishop and stake president indicating the outcome of the court." My heartfelt, carefully wrought words were a waste, I thought, except as a bankshot to a form letter.

BYU's casual denial, though, turned out to aid my unfolding social and intellectual redemption. At BYU, to constantly have to explain why I couldn't, say, go to priesthood meeting or brag about my mission would have been as intolerable as rats nipping at my toes. But, more important, I needed the breadth of learning that a stringent church-school orthodoxy could never provide. I'd grown up with the idea of "mind-expansion" as the highest ideal. I didn't want it in hallucinogens, though. I needed to be rebaptized in the ocean of western civilization.

That happened in two unforeseeable ways. First, I unaccountably started spending time with the loveliest and most cultivated woman I'd ever met. I say "unaccountably" because, well, I was a rank neophyte from the other side of my own father's railroad tracks. She was brought up in an educated, monied Boston home. I was a snaggletoothed quasi-cute boy, while she was a raving beauty, a few years my senior. I met her after she played the Brahms A-major Intermezzo on the piano at a Sunday evening fireside in our chapel. I was so moved by the piece, which I'd not heard, and by her robust pianism, that I overcame my shyness (and shame) to walk up and talk to her after the meeting. Soon I wrote a poem about her performance, gave it to her, and asked her to have a picnic with me. I don't remember where or even much about the next few months in her company beyond the sense of honor I felt, a much-needed removal to another world—along with the delectable weight of intimidation, as I tried to be something I could never be, a nineteenth-century Byron-type of poet-adorer, with twin stripes of chivalry and religiosity. I never felt myself her match. Because I wasn't. Still, I also wasn't the typical twenty-year-old—she said so—and, new in town, she savored that much about me. We talked art, shared music and theater and I was profoundly smitten. She was … I don't know. Consult the pertinent songs that have been written on the subject since the 1400s and you'll get the scenario.

There was one drawback. She worked for Bill. What might he have said to her about me? It would have been legit, though she and I never talked about it. Yet that leaden cloud always hung over my head. In December she left town to go back east. On her way out, I composed a gushing, neo-Romantic piano piece for her, "A Winter's Aire," a kind of answer to the fireside Brahms that occasioned our meeting. I played it in recital at Foothill and she played it at a fireside in Boston. And while this relationship could never be a finale, it was a magnificent intermezzo in my life.

The second step in my spiritual resuscitation came in a commission to compose a new work for two pianos. I'd composed exactly nothing the whole year of 1976, except for "Winter's Aire" and two gospel pop songs: "My Will" and "The Father of Me," both with lyrics by the poet Gloria Tester, a friend of Karen's family. I turned the first set of lyrics, which began with the line "I will sing of my will to be free," into a bopping Paul McCartney-ish number, uptempo with strummy guitar. It disappointed Gloria, but invigorated me. The second, which began "He is the quiet of rest coming on," was a more Gordon Light-foot-style ballad, with finger picked guitar in Mixolydian mode and a melody that slowly rose up that scale. Gloria much preferred it to "My Will." But these songs were two for three in 1976—no more pop and nothing at all "serious" except "Winter's Aire."

My former second-year music theory teacher and madrigals con-ductor, Linda Mankin, heard I was working a construction job and she summoned me to her house. She insisted I drop the shovel and start cultivating my mind again. She offered me a contract. If I wrote a three-movement two-piano sonata for her and her duet partner,

Judith Mitchell, she'd pay me $150 and premier the work in concert. But *only* if I re-enrolled at Foothill. We both signed the contract, and I registered for the school quarter that started in January.

While I never told Mom about the dunghill I'd waded through that year, her mom had her own take on my sudden mission exit. "What a musical genius Mike is!" she wrote. "He may be famous someday. I think his love for music was what drove him home from Germany. He was hungry for it and yearned to be working on it, don't you think so?" I thought, "Nice try, Grandmother." Nevertheless, when 1977 opened, I entered one of the more astonishing years of my life, wandering back into the church through the alleyways of my back-up religion: Art.

8. FOURTH EXODUS

Two things to know about churches. First, they are repositories of some of the best—or, let's say, most self-sacrificial—feelings people have. Second, they are siphons of time and verve. Being kicked out of church did gut some of my sociality. That was only fair because, if the term "excommunication" has any meaning, it's that the excommunicant can no longer *communicate* with others as he'd done before. But pinching off the churchy siphon allowed the inner barrel of creativity to fill quickly—and overspill. So the first full year of being cut off restrained me, yes, but, more important, it *retrained* me to be the person I was built to be. In 1977 I did more drawing, composing, writing, and performing than in my previous twenty years combined. Was it any good? Some drummed-up humility would flog me into saying, "No, it was mostly junk." But actually it was mostly good. Not in the way God said "good" about his/her successive days of creating new cosmic genres. But my creations were, at least, *not bad*. Grief, alienation, schooling, and freshly unscheduled time all combined to spout out dozens of visual artworks, pop songs, mid-century modern recital solos and choral pieces, brooding short stories, terse rhyming quatrains, almost weekly coffee-house appearances, wedding gigs, and even a string of community theatre performances—all in 1977, the best worst year of my life.

Before touring you through those months, though, let me open up the splotchy petri dish of Mormon excommunication. Nowadays the punishment is seldom enacted on anyone but thought-criminals and married gays. I've known money-lusting fraudsters who were incarcerated in the federal pen for years but remained members in good standing. While excommunication was a sentence far easier to receive in the 1970s than now, I was especially vulnerable. I was just a kid when I was thrown out, a child both in duration of membership and overall boyishness. Plus, my tithing receipts were negligible. All told, I was easier to discard. I was the "bad boy," but not the safer kind of bad boy, i.e., well-connected, monied, and from a stalwart lineage.

That vulnerability bequeathed me three distinct perils of '70s-style Mormon excommunication. First, people didn't sit by me in church anymore. Many times I'd go into the chapel early, sit in the middle of a row, as every row in the chapel—and its overflow area—would sometimes fill up before anyone sat on the row I was in. That's one way of communicating the otherwise incommunicable to the excommunicated.

Second, people lied about me. I'd hear about people who claimed to have spotted me with Ann here and there after my excommunication and, they'd add, that's why no one should consider allowing me back in the church. But I'd never seen Ann, even from a distance, since that night I left her to confess. In dreams, to be sure, I saw her for at least ten more years. Whenever I did, it was in blatant revenge scenarios. In each one she got smaller until in one she was a bug I stepped on. And that was it. No more Ann cameos in my dreams. But I was vexed by the blind-leading-themselves who claimed I was with her on the loose after June 1976.

The third peril was the peculiar "repentance process" bureaucracy that permeated my quest for reinstatement. One task my bishop required, for example, was for me to listen to and index all of the religious spoken word cassettes he owned. Lots of Paul Dunn, a few general conference talks and BYU Devotionals, plus this or that lecture from Education Weeks—though none by Reed Durham. It was tedious, although, to be fair, an uplifting education-by-inventory. Still, I had to meet and confess my sins or account for myself in various ways to him several times a month for months on end. I knew I couldn't be rebaptized into the church for at least a year from being exed. Priesthood leaders at all levels knew it, too. They felt I had to be scrubbed as hard as possible before I could get back into the baptismal font. I felt as though I'd become the welcome mat to a labyrinth of exile from the Church of Jesus Christ of Latter-day Saints.

Notwithstanding my vulnerability as an outré excommunicant, I was as faithful as a St. Bernard. I took part in every way I could, attending sacrament meetings and Sunday school classes, while exerting an almost ferocious devotion to the Mormonism I'd converted to. My pro-Mormon polemicism intensified. I became even more a true Defender of the Faith in the intellectual(ized) tradition of the Pratt brothers, B. H. Roberts, John Widtsoe, James Talmage, and the like. I wrote treatises, both curt and voluminous, to friends who swung their anti-Mormon blades in my direction. One friend wrote me a five-page double-spaced tract on what he deemed authentic Christian beliefs. I wrote back a twelve-page Mormonism-soaked quasi-legal brief. I suppose it was what Elder Bruce McConkie called a gospel hobby, but it suited me fine as a branch of my private church. God knows I was born to take the path of most resistance. And that's what I held in common with the Mormon pioneers themselves.

As for things I was still allowed to do in church, there was music. I always sang tenor or baritone in the choirs of both wards that met in our building. I organized and arranged music for ad hoc youth groups that sang in sacrament meetings. I led young adult groups in singing at a local rest home—a sequel to my Wineskinner Agnews gig. Music is one thing that's divinely mandated for Mormons yet requires no "authority" to enact.

Well, almost.

When I asked our ward choir director to sing my arrangement of the hymn "Sweet Is the Work," she stalled me. I'd keep bringing it up—were we going to sing it or not?—but she always put me off without explanation. Behind the scenes, though, she had met with the ward music chairman—the bishop's wife—to try and keep me from doing anything public in ward music. When a new choir director was called to replace her, he wanted to program an original piece of mine, "As the Hart Panteth," with text from Psalm 42. It was about to be performed by the Foothill College choir, and he thought it would be sweet to have it *premiered* by our ward choir. But the music chairman told him that singing both it and my hymn arrangement were forbidden because of my ex-member status. Soon a singer for a special number in sacrament meeting told me the orders were that I could not accompany her in church. The music chairman finally laid down the law to me and others on the record: Michael Hicks (a) was not eligible to have work of his sung or played in any meeting, (b) was told "explicitly" of that constraint as a condition of his excommunication, and (c) was "presumptuous" to submit anything for performance or accept a request to play the piano in a church meeting.

The edict sparked a plaintive five-page handwritten letter from me to the bishop, one I worried might set me back in my quest for rebaptism. A few excerpts show my Mormonistic reasoning and tone back then.

After relating the basic facts, I began my defense:

> In all candor, as to whether my music is appropriate to a sacrament meeting or not has puzzled me somewhat. It is a concept which I do have certain difficulties fully comprehending, as the music of other composers has been, to my understanding, approved or disapproved on the basis of intrinsic merit and the spiritual sentiments it expresses, and not generally on the church standing of its respective author. In the case of the piece submitted to the ward choir [the arrangement of "Sweet Is the Work"], written over two years ago, while I was a member in good standing, it became difficult to discern wherein a piece that carried with it a spiritual beauty worthy of the attention of all saints (as [ward music leaders] noted upon first hearing it) could have so summarily and decidedly have lost that beauty upon my excommunication. If such were the case, I must conclude that all the good works, all the testimonies born, and all the lessons taught while I was yet in the church were of none effect. ... Precedents to the contrary abound: W. W. Phelps's pre-excommunication hymns remained, Oliver Cowdery's writings were still quoted from the pulpit, Orson Pratt's tracts freely distributed—though I dare not presume to number myself among such men in terms of greatness, still, excommunication has been the lot of all. Their works remained, however, in use by the saints, because they had worth, despite the difficulties their respective sources encountered.

After relating at length the times when the bishop had authorized my post-excommunication musical events, I wrote:

> It has never been explicitly nor implicitly set forth to me by yourself nor the stake president that compositions I have written are to be banned from the Church, as performances of them would be no more

an active participation, on my part, in the program of a service, I would think, than would be a reading of the Passion story a participation of Judas and the mob, and I hope I am not considered among the likes of such. Had these things been told me, I would have been obedient to them, to be sure. But I was not told them, else would not have squandered such a great amount of time, effort, and especially hope and anticipation, precious commodities as they are to me.

In fine, I would beg that several points be at least noted, if not considered:

1. As to the music I submitted to the ward choir, I have been promised continued consideration repeatedly, no word to the contrary forthcoming—and all this encouraging a false hope, when, in fact, a decision had already been made. Do I err in wishing to be dealt with more squarely and openly than this?

2. As to the manner in which I was informed of these proceedings, viz., through statements made to a third party, should I not feel that propriety demanded a full discussion of the situation with me personally, before with another, especially when my good faith and respect for Priesthood dictation is thus called into question?

Throughout, I pledged loyalty to the constraints placed on me by church leaders. But I closed this way, with my old-school Mormon cadences bubbling up:

Perhaps the matters herein seem all but weighty, "much ado about nothing," as it is said. But please know, from a sincere heart, that when one has failed in the task of life with the enormity of transgression mine has been, the soul is wounded, the feelings stripped bare, and the heartbreak abiding in me beyond all you know, nor ever ought to. Things which appear trivial to the sturdy and weather-worn soldier of God can be massive "stumbling blocks" and "stones of offense" to one whose miniscule efforts to incur the favor of the Almighty with little support from brethren, kindred, comrades, and neighbors, are all he has left to cling to. If, at times, these modest endeavors are rebuffed by the counsels of God, lo, all is well. But when requests for aid in carrying out these endeavors in a manner pleasing to our Father are ignored or waylaid and then my judgment, based on the best light and counsel available to me, called into such severe question, surely I find myself in a position that offers little consolation or hope.

Thank you for your consideration in reading this. I close with the hope that the words of John Milton shall prove true, "They also serve who only stand and wait."

The bishop, to my surprise, thanked me, praised my letter, and even said, "Letters like that will help get you back in the church." But he still held firm on the no-Hicks-music policy.

Come January, per my contract with Linda Mankin, I was back at Foothill taking German, Social and Political Philosophy, English Literature, Creative Writing, and Public Speaking. I managed to parlay my Mormonism into the classes where possible. For instance, I recited the story of Joseph Smith's first vision as a talk for German class, and they thought I knew more vocabulary than anyone there, even though I just recited a missionary script I'd spouted off many times. I talked about Joseph Smith as a prophet and religious genius in my Public Speaking course. For Creative Writing I wrote stories that were purgations of Ann cult behavior or stewings about church alienation. Almost every branch of my schoolwork grew out of my pining for the home-brewed blend of Protestantism and Mormonism that had become my creed, despite being estranged from their churches.

I was swimming in a lake of creative and ad hoc educational projects that, because our temple ceremony taught that "all truth is circumscribed into one great whole," I could credit as religious devotion. I read Mark Twain and William Blake alongside Donna Hill's new biography of Joseph Smith. I kept planning—or, at least, telling people I was planning—to write a book on the history of high councils, that genre of punitiveness-cum-prospective-redemption in my recent life. (By August, I'd quit the project with only a file full of references from the *History of the Church* to show for it.) I kept working on my two-piano sonata, which was "about" life among Mormon pioneers. The Foothill choir performed my ward-blacklisted "As the Hart Panteth." And, still bridling to get into BYU, I sent a sheaf of compositions to music professor Merrill Bradshaw at BYU on the advice of a friend that if the music department offered me a scholarship, the university would *have to* admit me.

I'd venerated Bradshaw, even before I joined the church, after hearing an LP at Karen's, *Music for Worship*, which included some of his piano compositions. Now, here he was, one of my heroes in Mormon music composition, reviewing my own scores and recordings. He wrote me back a terse but hopeful letter, saying that, "In checking through applications, we understand there are some sort of problems on your application for admission. As soon as your admission is cleared, we are prepared to send through recommendations that you receive some scholarship assistance. Please accept our congratulations on your fine achievements to date. We hope to be able to work with you next year."

In April 1977, worthy neither for BYU nor for playing piano in church, I was appointed by Foothill College's LDS Institute director to be president of their "Latter-day Saint Student Service Association." Some local Mormons complained about it to the Institute director, arguing that LDSSA had no business being headed by a non-Mormon, let alone an ex-Mormon. But, in fact, our stake president had authorized it, and that tamped down the protests. My duties in the job were meager, amounting to taking roll and calling on students for prayers in our off-hours religion classes at Foothill. But the title meant something to me—as it did to Foothill's larger Christian fellowship group. Hearing that I was an excommunicant from the church, the Christian fellowship group invited me to speak to them *as an ex-Mormon*. I knew what they were expecting. They didn't get it. I offered them the arguments I'd honed in my polemical letters from the past three years. No red meat for these lion cubs.

I started to feel that my new Mormon/non-Mormon double life—a funhouse mirror version of the double life I'd led with Ann—somehow realigned me with an underground vibe that first drew me to Mormonism from the counterculture in which I'd been bred. I was back to alienation-via-strangeness as the substance of my religious identity. For half my spiritual life that year, I leaned on *Sacred Harp* singing with a few Protestant friends, observing Holy Week studiously, and watching the multi-part premiere of Zeffirelli's *Jesus of Nazareth* on television. For the other half, I did as much "official" Mormon service as possible, from playing Amulek in a Sunday school playlet to having, for the first time ever, the Young Adult "family home evening" at my house.

As zealous as I'd ever be, in May I wrote a three-page single-spaced letter to the bishop requesting to be readmitted into the church. In it I recounted *pro forma* the history of Ann's cult, my part in it, my renunciation of it, and all the things I'd been doing to stay as active as possible in the church from which I'd been excised. In the final paragraph, I alluded to Jesus' parable of the Prodigal Son: "I seek no fatted calf, no robe, nor ring—my one heart's request is to be restored to the household of faith. The husks I have left with the swine."

When I handed the letter to the bishop, he smiled and said, "Don't get your hopes up."

Ten days earlier, I had laid down in free verse the terms of my current religious existence in a trope on Edgar Allan Poe that I shared with a few friends:

Sometimes I feel like a raven, Lord,
Amidst a brood of snowy doves.
My feathered cloak is black, but doves glisten
Like shells upon the Red sea shores,
Flickering in moonlight, swept by vaguer tides,
And I, like coal of charred driftwood,
Stand darkly by their side.

They say that I am like a raven, Lord:
"He sows not, neither reaps," they coo.
And they have nests and barns of spacious store
In which to heap their grain. But crows like me,
They say, have robbed and scoured their bins—
The reapings of their crops.

They stare at me and see a raven, Lord:
Once sent forth from the ark, I flit
Above the steeping judgment waters and seek,
While they gaze from the wooden sill
And wait for land to appear.

They are the doves and scorn the black raven:
They are the signs of holy ghosts
And I only a sign of paradox:
Draped as if in mourning, my feathers
Somehow more brightly shine.

Yea, am I so? I, a raven, Lord?
It is well. For, caged, the doves are sold
And lay, their breasts split wide upon the altars,
While ravens fan along the Cherith brooks
And feed Elijah there.

It was my little manifesto of the sacredness of the ostracism I was
suffering and yet, in my own idiom, celebrating.

I wrote more formal, far longer, and drearily pretentious poems
around this time, all rhyming and leaning on faux Elizabethan diction. One was "A Song of David," a fourteen-quatrain ballad on
David's encounter with Goliath. Another was an eighteen-quatrain
Christmas poem called "O Holy Night." Orbiting around my own
cultish history was a nine-verse elegy entitled "On a Fallen Queen."
Each five-line rhyming verse was preceded by the incantation "O
Woman of Shame!" (the epithet chosen for Ann in this poem). Each
verse ended with a different rhyme for "shame." The last verse gives
the flavor—or aftertaste—of the whole:

O Woman of Shame!
Thou who didst ever promise "soon
the Miracle," know this, thy ruin
Shall swifter come than vision or sign;
Thou shalt yet with the demons dine—
And they shall toast thy name!

Next, I wrote a forty-seven-quatrain post-Ann confession and
plea to Jesus and even a 271-line rhyming ode to Joseph Smith.
Other moderate-length but relentlessly gushy and affected poems
surrounded these, some to friends, some to, I suppose, myself-as-
willing-reader, other prospective readers being scarce indeed.

I realized I was now in my own "wilderness," the metaphorical
destination once so prized by Ann. That led to a huge batch of short
poems in a more Emily Dickinson vein. Some of this quixotic verse
came out as transcendence, some as rebuke or even defiance. I was
sure the wilderness through which I was mapping a path gave me
some sort of insight, even privilege, à la the Prodigal Son. On June
4, for instance, I wrote this:

I walk within a living cage,
A seething mortal cell
Barred up in iron foliage,
my soul chained to the wall.

Prisoner comrades keep the watch,
Polish the black-iron rods,
And bolt with care the dungeon latch
That holds me from the Gods.

What awe may whisper near the gate
When, at the last Amen,
Jesus shall lead me softly out
And they not enter in.

And as the one-year anniversary of my excommunication approached I wrote this nod to both the light and dark sides of my personal moon:

I am a year cut off
But muses mark the time:
The calendar's the meter,
And Sabbaths are the rhyme;

Meetings, alliteration—
The metaphor is grand:
The year become a verse
Penned by the Gracious Hand.

But each forgetful ear
And condescending look
Blots out the poetry
And closes up the book.

Despite the judgment of many older folks in the ward, my young adult comrades—many of whom had been taught by Ann in Sunday school—stayed thick as thieves with me. They seemed innately more filled with compassion, however tinged with pity. If and when anyone sat by me in church, it was them. And sometimes I felt sorrier for some of them than for myself. I think of one sister who gathered us at her house for a home evening one Monday night. On the table in her family room was a thick book of Michelangelo prints. I picked it up, leafed through, and discovered that her parents had run a black laundry marker through every female breast and every male and female crotch. I felt sick. I never looked at that sister without sorrow from then on. To me, this defacement of art was a brand of apostasy rivaling almost anything in the hyper-Mormon fantasy cultism I'd been through.

As for boy-girl social life, I'd tried to scrub the debris of the Ann cult out of my head, which was hard, since I still lived at the same address and attended church in the same chapel. I'd long had my sights on a temple marriage, so I shied away from cozying up to non-Mormon girls. Although I'd actually never been on a date like I'd seen on TV or heard about in high school, on the advice of my bishop I asked girls to go with me to parks or movies. Most knew my unchurched situation. A couple of new move-ins to the neighborhood didn't (at least, not from me). We had fun, they got charity points and I scratched my head at the artificiality of this ritual. I was completely ungainly at the task. My idea of a good time involved talking in depth about movies after seeing them, talking about concerts after going to them, talking about books we'd both read, or talking about music we'd played for each other. None of those things happened, although I tried to make them. I did play dates tapes of offbeat records I liked, which left them mostly shaking their heads. Or, more weirdly, I read girls long short stories, especially John Collier's "Are You Too Late or Was I Too Early?" and Philip Roth's "Conversion of the Jews," about Jewish boys debating whether Mary could have had a baby without intercourse. For the girls I thought were religiously hip enough or susceptible to becoming so, I read passages from Sam Taylor's *Nightfall at Nauvoo* or the paragraph about Joseph Smith's first vision in Vardis Fisher's *Children of God*. We had nice enough times, but I always felt like the ward service project.

I preferred solitude, anyway. Not just for reading and writing. All that summer I did more drawing than ever, some commissioned, some as gifts, and all using no. 2 lead pencils and Pilot very-fine-point felt tips and Flair pens. All told, in 1977 I did four drawings of scenes from the Holy Land, seven portraits of Mormon church leaders (from Joseph Smith to David O. McKay), four drawings of Jesus (two of them with Mary), and five more miscellaneous portraits:

Sherlock Holmes, Gustav Mahler, Alexander Graham Bell, a friend's wife, and another friend's grandparents. Was I heading for a life in art, music, or poetry? Yes. These were all the sacraments of beauty that old-time religion had pushed away and new-time religion had embraced but could never take away, despite pulling strings with the Almighty to cut me off from the less extraordinary sacraments.

Come fall, I was back in school, broadening not only my mind but my magical musical tour. Because my VW bus had blown its engine, I had to junk it and bus to and from home and these various stops:

— a local Presbyterian nursery school, where I led singing with kids
— a local private school to help kids learn how to work the TAP (Temporal Acuity Products) machines one of my Foothill professors had co-created
— the new Community School of Music and Art in Mountain View, a co-op where I taught piano and guitar largely to Vietnamese refugees
— classes and practice-room monitoring at Foothill
— back home for private guitar lessons
— back to the Owl's Nest—Foothill's coffee house—either to sing and play or to listen to whomever I, the new music-booker there, had hired

Waiting for buses to arrive, I read novels, politics, religion, essays on art, music, and literature, and, maybe more than anything, Strunk and White's *Elements of Style*, which I nearly memorized chapter and verse as though it were the New Testament. As for money, I didn't make much, but didn't require much, except to buy books and records. I lived with my mom and carefully manipulated non-VW bus transfers.

One job I turned down, though, spaded up my life. After a three-hour Foothill College jazz-rock festival called "Celebration of Spring," in which I co-starred, my friend Lawrence shopped me around to local restaurants and bars as a singer-songwriter. In August he finally landed me a month-long gig at the Winery in Palo Alto. My Mormon friends got over the name of the place—singer-songwriters played bars, everyone knew that. But the gig was for the entry-level nights of Sunday and Monday, and my friends worried that if I started working Sundays—a Mormon "Sabbath" violation—I'd drift away from the faith. I pushed back, but they convinced me, so I turned the offer down. Lawrence was furious that I'd wasted his time, and the Winery boss replied in the "he'll never work in this town again" vein. But it was the moment I irrevocably turned my back on a B-list gigging career in pursuit of heavenly gold.

On September 1, I filled out the official application form for re-baptism into the church—my fourth baptism in fifteen-ish years. The application required a letter of recommendation from the party I'd wronged, now interpreted as Bill. I was taken aback, since Bill had sanctioned—and of which Ann had shown me handwritten evidence—her pursuit of all the young bonus "husbands." To some extent, he was part of The Con. I owed him, though, no doubt. So we met at his business office for a reconciliatory talk. It was cordial. We showed each other our mental scars and pledged to move on, which he'd begun to do via divorcing Ann and remarrying. He wrote a letter of recommendation for me, and we never spoke again.

That same week, out of the blue, Mom's mom sent me a half-sheet of stationery on which she'd written this passage from *Julius Caesar*, with no commentary other than saying she thought I should consider it:

> There is a tide in the affairs of men,
> Which, taken at the flood, leads on to fortune;
> Omitted, all the voyage of their life
> Is bound in shallows and in miseries

I did consider it, a lot, and even copied it into my journal on September 13. The night after doing so, my life was indelibly rewritten. Again.

When my former boss's daughter Pam Bodell graduated from BYU that summer, she drove to Los Altos and moved in with her parents. On Wednesday night, September 14, she came to our young adult family home evening and asked if anyone knew where she could get piano lessons. I quickly volunteered. Given my packed schedule, though, I could only give her lessons at 6:00 p.m. Fridays at my house. (Hidden agenda alert.) Lessons ensued and, per my obviously ulterior motives, we hung out afterward. I showed her books, played her records, told her stories, all my usual private extroversion, as a way of luring this beautiful woman into my shuttered world. Trying to get a jump on the scandal train, I told her right off about my "situation." She said her dad had already told her about it, but he liked me and, most important in his book, I was a good worker. She was coming off a bad breakup at BYU and thought we should see how this mutual flirtation evolved.

I kept up my meeting attendance and quasi-activity in the church, often with Pam nearby. I even gave an off-the-books 90-minute Sunday night fireside at the home of Pam's parents' bishop, who rejected the stringent proscriptions of my bishop. The topic? "Toward a Mormon Music." I had mimeographed handouts, musical examples on cassette, and lots to say, including where and how I thought the church should crystalize its sacred music traditions. The few people that came seemed pleased, even if only for giving an extra-mile penitent a shot. Which was fine with me. I needed the audience, even if—or especially if—it was slightly rogue.

In October, a couple more people came forward claiming recent "sightings" of me with Ann and insisted I not be let back in the church. Fortunately, no church authorities believed them, although they grilled me about the claims. That same month, Karen finally "Dear Johned" me officially. Her letter explaining her love for another man was reasoned and, sadly, reasonable. My personality was "too complex," she wrote, for us to spend our lives together. "I need simplicity. You need every puzzle piece."

The month spiraled down from there. On October 23 our ward held its annual conference. But I couldn't bear yet another one: "Today was ward conference. I am not a member of the ward and so conferred with myself." Two days later, the calendar blew smoke in my face. My journal: "Today marks two years since I entered the mission home in Salt Lake. I'm not home yet." Finally, a letter arrived from *Sunstone* magazine, that heady independent journal to which I'd sent some of the verses I'd been writing. They sent them back saying they weren't "Mormon" enough. Excommunicated by my own poetry.

But I had a Mormon ace up my sleeve. Months earlier I had auditioned for a part in a play for a new church-member-owned venue, the Santa Clara Arena Theatre. The play, by the up-and-coming

Playing Oliver Cowdery in the witness box during a performance
of *And Some Cried Fraud!*, Santa Clara Arena Theatre, 1977.
(Attorneys played by Cecil Webb and Lin Stangl.)

Mormon thespian Thom Duncan, was called *And Some Cried Fraud!*,
a dramatized version of Jack West's *Trial of the Stick of Joseph*. It pre-
sented a moot-court-style scrutiny of the truthfulness of the Book
of Mormon's origins, which included calling the book's three main
"witnesses" to the stand. After several rounds of auditions, I got the
meatiest non-lawyer part: Oliver Cowdery, who gets badgered by
the prosecuting attorney and, in a shouting match with her, forces
the court into recess—intermission—then resumes, more calmly,
when the lights come back up.

The play ran every Monday, Tuesday, and Wednesday from September 27–October 20. So here I was, the most active non-Mormon
Mormon around, adding theater to my résumé by dramatizing the
testimony of one of the church's founding leaders. Attendance was
mild, though grew over the show's run—and included a couple of
members of our stake high council.

Two weeks after the show closed, the high council reconvened to
consider my application for readmission. I took the floor in front of the

three members of the stake presidency, the stake clerk, the stake executive secretary, and twelve high councilors. After recounting briefly my renunciation of the Ann cult in favor of the church proper, I said:

> As you know, there have been many things this past year that I have not been able to do—many restrictions placed upon me. I have not been able to attend priesthood meetings, I have not been permitted to speak in meetings. But there have been many things that I have been able to do to serve the Lord and stay close to the church. I have consistently availed myself of all these opportunities and counted it always a privilege to be "in" the church as much as I can be. I am likewise grateful for the help and encouragement that has been given me, much of it by members of this council.
>
> Justice has been done. It is now my plea that mercy be effected in my behalf, in allowing me to again enter the waters of baptism and make anew the covenants that I once made with the Lord, and in which I faltered.

I then bore testimony that Jesus lives and the church has his authority, from President Spencer Kimball to this high council itself. I took a long pause. Many of the men's eyes glistened. The stake president nodded slowly. After a few seconds, I spoke again, more softly.

> Again, I want to say that I am very grateful for the help and encouragement of my friends on the council with whom I am privileged to associate in our ward and otherwise, and for the help of many other friends. By them the burden has been lightened. That is all I have to say.

The president asked the council if there were any questions. Silence. "No questions?" More silence. "Then, Mike, let me ask you three questions. One, you mentioned that you know that President Kimball is a prophet. Will you sustain him and the other authorities of the church, both general and local?"

"I will and do."

"Have you repented fully and totally of the activities that initially led to your excommunication and do you feel that the Lord has accepted your efforts and is ready to receive you into his church?

"Yes."

"Finally, are you prepared to keep all the covenants you will make with the Lord?"

"Yes."

"Thank you, Mike. Now, if you will give us a few minutes and step outside, we will get back to you in a moment."

I stood up, stepped into the hallway, and closed the locked door behind me. After a few minutes, the executive secretary opened it, stepped out, and, grinning broadly, said, "It is my privilege to inform you that the council has approved your rebaptism into the church." He explained that all the paperwork would go to President Kimball, who had to approve my rebaptism personally. "We don't know how long this will take. But the council has recommended that it be done speedily."

By December, Pam and I were spending more and more time together. We went to the Charles Dickens Fair in San Francisco, dressed in Victorian clothes and strolling around with friends as carolers who sang American shape-note hymns and fuging tunes. We went to the local *Messiah* sing, where we sang parts in the 1,000-plus member chorus. Amid such outings Pam was teaching me how to dance: Latin Hustle, Western Swing, Two-Step, and Foxtrot. I was nervous about those lessons, not just because I was uncoordinated— cf. my "fishy" four-square days—but because I was using Pam to get to yet another girl. I wrote in my journal that, although Pam and I were "growing close" and "holding hands," I believed there was a "discrepancy in our emotions." I worried that she was "in love" with me and not I with her. I needed more "magnetic attraction and sense of wonder." I went on in nerdy, formal-voiced musings on the "perpetual problem between the male and female of the species" and ended with prayers "for God to watch over the matters of the heart, especially, during this somewhat precarious moment in my eternal existence." And so, milking Pam's love for me with the dance lessons, I planned to ask another girl—Beverly, one of Karen's roommates at BYU—to the New Year's Eve dance.

Beverly soon came home to our area, but she declined my invitation to the dance—I was too late. And so, well-practiced as her dance partner, I asked Pam on the rebound. As Christmas approached, our nocturnal TV-watching at her parents' home and vintage radio-show tape-listening at mine—everything from *CBS Mystery Hour* to *Amos and Andy*—carried on later and later, till on December 22 we ventured our first kiss. When New Year's Eve arrived, we showed off our moves on the dance floor and appeared to be a rock-solid couple. Beverly and her date showed up just before midnight, I blanched, and Pam and I left quickly.

The next day, Sunday, January 1, 1978, I wrote this three-quatrain verse trying both to console myself and rattle the bars of the cosmic forgiveness-bureaucracy in which I was locked:

There is no sextant to our souls,
Though some assume the lens,
With license of certified scrolls
And notary amens.

But when all Israel shall adjourn
To mutual chagrin,
Who then with scope will dare discern
Comparatively sin?

Transparent there, like tourmaline,
Shall all be manifest:
Then shall we see as we are seen
And wonder at the rest.

A week later, Pam and I—who'd now read each other's patriarchal blessings, a huge step between Mormons—auditioned together for another new play at the Santa Clara Arena Theatre: *Mission Call,* by Marie Myer, slated to run Monday, Tuesday, and Wednesday nights from March 6–29. I channeled a trunkful of past hurts as I read the death scene from the script at the audition. I got the lead. Pam was cast as my sister. I described the show in a letter to my friend Carrie, another emigrant to BYU:

This play is a tear-jerker, not much west of a soap opera, but with some potent scenes toward the end, and a good Spirit throughout. I have a number of "meaty" scenes that are exciting to play; I get angry in one, cry in another, there's a love scene, and a death scene. The story concerns a young man called on a mission in 1950. He has waited long and hard for his call and has a devil of a time finally getting out to the field (postponed sailing dates, etc.). At last he gets to the field, Tahiti, only to be sent home several weeks later for an "operation." He turns out to have cancer and the final scenes deal with his resolve, and that of his family and girlfriend, to his death.

I was finally going back on a mission, pretend-style. I drank up the irony of it every day.

As I waited for President Kimball's approval of my re-entry into the church, I wrote this pair of quatrains—more of the self-exorcism I'd trained myself in:

They act as if God were no more than a clock
With little brass gears behind a white face
And luminous numbers to shine in the dark
And measure repentance and keep it in place.

They acknowledge his Hand in all things but it sweeps
Only according to a cogwheel's track—
Irrevocable, its precision but keeps
Forgiveness from tolling to welcome me back.

With theater rehearsals about to start, on February 2, 1978, my two-piano *Sonata in Three Tableaux* premiered. It sported three movements meant to evoke moments in early Mormon history. The first was "Kingdom of the Saints," a birdseye flyover of what I imagined Nauvoo, Illinois—the "City of Joseph"—to be like, both majestic and bustling. The second movement, "Thomas Kane Visits the Empty City," referred to a well-known sympathizer of the Saints as he described the now deserted city portrayed in the first movement. The last movement, "Jubilation," was a burbling evocation of Mormons entering, inhabiting, and cultivating the Salt Lake Valley. It included variations on the 1884 sacrament hymn "How Great the Wisdom and the Love." It was a crowd-pleaser, with a standing ovation and my bowing in the belief I'd practiced what I'd preached in that fireside about Mormon music.

My daily schedule, Mondays through Thursdays, had settled into leaving the house at 6:45 a.m. and getting home late in the evening. School and teaching in the daytime, rehearsals at night, and, in the interstitial spaces, more writing and drawing—drafting short stories and doggerel, carefully penciling portraits of characters from Joseph Smith to my mom's dad to Karen herself. The portrait, I confessed to my journal, was "labored over with the most sincere affection," partly for her longevity in my heart and, more tellingly, because she was the open sesame to my entry into this new faith, with its profound mix of effervescence and disaster in my life. Everything that meant anything to me now—including my blossoming love for Pam—had emerged from Karen, her family, their generosity, and their bookshelves. So a final portrait seemed as inevitable to me as stone tablets on Sinai.

Come March, I was nailing my role as Will in *Mission Call*. One person even said after a performance, "You were far too realistic." But not everyone agreed. One audience member asked me if I was LDS. I said yes, and he replied, "I can tell." But he was staring at my collarbone. And that was a problem. Because I wore a white shirt through the whole show, and it was clear I didn't have that distinctive huge neck opening that Mormon temple undergarments had. In fact, I was wearing a white shirt over a bare torso.

One night, as I was in my dressing room putting my street clothes on, one of the directors started speaking through the door to me.

"We notice you're not wearing your garments. We were wondering why."

So through the dressing room door I disclosed my excommunicant status. He seemed shocked but was kind about it. We quickly agreed on a solution: I got some T-shirts with the distinctive inverted-U neckline that Mormon garments had and wore one every night. Impersonating a temple-endowed Mormon—which I was yet wasn't—became my new hobby.

Just then Spencer Kimball finally thumbs-upped my readmission. He sent a letter to my stake president, and, the Sunday after my first three performances of *Mission Call*, the president interviewed me yet again for rebaptism. He paced through the usual worthiness questions, added ones to reconfirm I'd forsaken Ann and her circle, then signed the form. He also let it slip that the apostles had eighteen *years* of complaints on file about Ann, her doctrinal adventures and probable college-age boy-seduction. Now, amid interviews, forms, and recommendations, I'd needed eighteen months getting back into the church. I tallied it up: one month of Hicksian exile for every year of complaints about her. Quite the exchange rate.

On March 18, 1978, we held the baptism at the very stake center I'd help build with Jim Bodell's construction crew. I wrote Carrie to tell her about it:

We hadn't really spread the word so much, but about forty people were there, and it was good to see all of them. The first hindrance I found in keeping a spiritual tone to it all was when, ten minutes before we were supposed to start, I realized I had forgotten the extra pair of dry underwear I needed. My friend Doug and I scampered off for home—we made it back a little after 6:00 (when it should have started) to a whole crowd of people that had been wondering, "Where is the guy, anyway?" We hurried back into the dressing room, where I was reminded again that I am but a stringbean—all the clothes they had were impossible to either get on or keep on. Finally, I settled for a short jumpsuit whose legs came only to just above my knees. I came out and saw the smiling crowd, then sat down. We sang "We Thank Thee, O God, for a Prophet" and our Elder's quorum President gave an excellent talk on the Prodigal Son. Then the baptism. We had to do it twice: my left hand and wrist didn't quite make it all the way under the first time. I remarked that we could do it three or four more times as far as I was concerned, to nothing but good effect.

When we came back out, they had the confirmation, performed by Doug. The blessing told me to labor diligently for my ancestors who were behind the veil, as they had labored diligently for me. Then, he said, "It is right that we prophesy and say that you will leave your mark on the cultural heritage of the Church and of the Kingdom."

Who came to the event? The bishop and some of his family, his counselor who'd gotten me the stake center construction job, Pam and her family, Karen's parents—including her dad, who'd baptized me a Mormon the first time—and assorted friends, from Young Adult group regulars to *Mission Call*'s director and cast members. In the reception book, where you'd write your relationship to the person being baptized, most everyone wrote "friend." *Mission Call*'s co-director, Liz, wrote "sister." Karen's mom wrote "fan, admirer." Pam was the only person who left it blank. Which was probably her way of staying non-committal, scratching her head with an unclicked ballpoint.

Because the following Sunday was our church's general conference, our regular first-Sunday-of-the-month testimony meeting was moved up a week to March 26. It was also Easter. Resurrection day. And the eighteenth anniversary of my born-again experience in 1970. My Christianity was now an adult. I stood up, walked to the pulpit and, before a congregation full of expectant eyes, said this:

F. Scott Fitzgerald once wrote, "It is always 3 a.m. in the long dark night of the soul." I know by experience that when one departs from the gospel, when the thread is cut that binds one to the Priesthood of God, one is brought to that moment: 3 a.m. If you have ever been awake and alone at that hour, you know that there is something peculiarly lonely and still about it—the darkest hour of the night. But if there is one thing I have learned in the past two years, it is that if you have friends—true friends—friends who know God and know how to love as Jesus loved and loves, then 3 a.m. might as well be noonday in spring. It might as well be Easter. There is light, there is hope, there is love, there is life.

We, lambs as we are, get a little rambunctious sometimes. We go out looking for a little greener pasture, a little cooler shade, a little fresher grass. But I have learned there is no greener pasture than where the Savior walks, no cooler shade than at his right hand, no fresher grass than in the path where he walks.

I then went on to bear a more pro forma testimony: I know this and that (the Atonement is real, the church is true, Spencer Kimball is a prophet, and so on). I walked back to my seat in a full pew, now with no gaps between me and my fellow saints.

The reference to Fitzgerald represented the kind of double—or, actually, polygonal—life that had drawn me to the church in the first place, the possibility that sacred and secular stood in the same river—and both had baptismal certificates. My months off the rolls had driven me to the bliss of friendships, including the friendship of words that seemed to invite me home for supper. Jesus, yes, but the whole house of mirrors in which his image is both endlessly replicated and lost in mystery.

The last night of *Mission Call* we had a small cast party, but I don't remember anything about it. Why would I? I was Will Neilson's latest convert. I wrote to my friend John, another of our circle who'd emigrated to BYU:

> I'm just getting used to my wings, trying to remember to take the sacrament [which had been forbidden], sustain people [which had been forbidden], trying to realize that I *am* worthy now, despite feeling much the same irascible self. I do feel the Spirit, though, in very definite ways, and feel much better about the big, grey universe.

9. DEUTERONOMY

Jesus talked about having "an eye single." One focus. For better or worse, mine was on getting into BYU. I saw it as the Valhalla of mid-century Mormon demigods of the mind. I had the bishop and stake presidents send letters authorizing my admittance into what was known in Mormon vernacular as "the Lord's University." And then, as I'd become a virtuoso at doing, I waited.

While I was waiting, the bishop offered me another taste of irony. Asking me to "prepare kids for baptism," he called me to Junior Sunday School to teach seven-year-olds. (Mormon kids are baptized when they turn eight.) I'd been a trunkful of mischief at that age and yet sorely lacked patience for the same luggage in these kids. Still, I pulled up my bootstraps. I prepared simple lessons on religious practices like tithing, of which the bulk of my lesson consisted of me having them repeat over and over "The earth is the Lord's and the fulness thereof," i.e., the rationale for giving "back" to the Lord with money. Teaching fasting was harder, especially since a fellow teacher urged me to always bring a treat for the kids to make the class time palatable. (I never took his advice.) I taught loftier things, too, like the Lord's Supper and even Passover. But overall this calling was dipping me in a steaming boiler of doctrine-for-children that resembled hardly any drop of my own. I remained at the assignment less than three months, not for incompetence—which might have been just—but because, with my time now served, BYU executed the quickest turnaround I'd experienced in years. They welcomed me in with a full-tuition scholarship. I could enroll for the next term, which began the last week of June.

As I prepared to leave town, the church took a huge step in its own repentance. On June 9, 1978, I was singing with a rock band made of Celebration of Spring players for a mid-day concert in the Foothill band room. We took a ten-minute break, and Pam breathlessly ran up to tell me that the church had just dumped its prohibition against Blacks holding the priesthood and performing temple ordinances. With the stroke of his pen, Spencer Kimball lifted the cross from the back of the church. I came back to the band room and started singing the next song on our list, George Benson's "This Masquerade," I fixed my eye on the two Black men at the back of the room. They'd been smiling, giving me spiritual high fives and thumbs ups for the whole concert so far. Now I smiled back and thought, "You have no idea …" Before I began singing, I'd already dedicated the song to them in my mind.

> Are we really happy here
> With this lonely game we play?
> … We're lost in a masquerade

And when I reached the song's final lines, I choked up, but more for myself than for them:

> No matter how hard I try
> To understand the reasons
> that we carry on this way
> We're lost in a masquerade

It was as if the song had been written for this moment both in my life and in that of the church that had finally wrung its hands and welcomed me into the side door. Now it was as though the church had been rebaptized, too.

I'd always been queasy about this misshapen arrow in the church's quiver. It just seemed so much like the Baptist church I'd left as a boy. Mormons had done a decent job of proof-texting the priesthood ban by tying it to Cain and Ham, ploys that resonated with proof-texts for slavery and all the other historic predations on Black people. But its linking to the idea that people born with African roots had been traitors or half-hearted in the pre-Earth war in heaven was, as we used to say, a horse that wouldn't run.

Meanwhile, I'd read Bruce McConkie insisting that the priesthood ban wouldn't be lifted till more or less the end of time. I swallowed hard at that but had spent years "trusting in the Lord" that he'd sort all this out. So I let it sit on the shelf as I built my own cottage in Mormon doctrine-ville. When the announcement came, we went from shaky about the ban to shaken at its reversal. But mostly jolted back into the proto-American sense of fair play we'd boasted about at the Bicentennial two years earlier.

Two weeks after that day, I left for Provo, Utah, or as I called it in my first letter home, "Land of the Bee and Home of the Knave." When I arrived, I got an apartment in a multi-building complex across the street from the ritzier one where Donny and Marie Osmond lived. I don't know about their apartments, but in mine, disco music played around the clock and from every side, one song at a time or sometimes two or three in percussive counterpoint. As it thumped in the ceiling and walls, I felt like my hopes for a kind of educational grandeur was being beaten out of me.

Our apartment complex housed six tenants apiece in each three-bedroom unit. But, because it was summer, off season, I had just two roommates, both of whom I rarely saw. One, Jake, was a long-haired rock guitarist who was out playing gigs most nights. If he was on the road or even just playing Salt Lake, he didn't come back to the apartment. The other roommate, Brent, co-owned a carpet company and flew around the country selling product. One of the few times I saw Jake he told me that Brent had only slept there twice in the previous two months, although I had no idea how he'd know that. So all summer I spent long hours alone in the apartment, either in bed or the bathtub reading a bio-ag textbook, scripture, or *Catcher in the Rye* with muffled disco pummeling my ears.

I paid $60 a month rent, including utilities, and bought my food at Ream's, a strange, Mormon-tabernacle shaped grocery store that advertised its food prices with the asterisked proviso "We only add ten percent to these prices." The store was nearby, so I bought the two staples of my diet there: wheat germ, which my mom had sworn by for years, and spinach, which I hated but instinctively trusted after a boyhood of watching Popeye. I paid for rent and food by working as a custodian at a girls dorm at the school's on-campus "Deseret Towers" from 1:00 p.m. to 5:00 p.m. weekday afternoons. Mostly vacuuming, occasionally cleaning up spills or removing stains, for the minimum wage of $2.65 an hour. It was a nice turn of the tables, I thought: I had lived in a crumbling old girls dorm the last time I lived in Provo and now my job was to keep a new one clean.

Church in California had been spread across the day like mayonnaise. Here it was three hours sandwiched together, starting ridiculously early: 7:30 a.m. Priesthood, 8:30 Sunday school, and 9:30 sacrament meeting. My first Sunday, between priesthood and Sunday school, I got tagged to sing a solo in sacrament meeting—"O My Father," backed by the choir. It wasn't the Lowell Mason version I'd sung as a solo for my Foothill voice class, but the McGranahan version that I hated but everyone else seemed to like. After my solo, a young firebrand gave a talk castigating—I wrote this down—"those apostates who speak so well and try and make you believe that our prophets have not all taught the same things or contradicted one another in certain points." I met him after the meeting. He told me how he could tell how strong in the gospel I was, how he was watching me as he gave his talk and saw I had a "good countenance." We talked a while, and I disclosed that I was one of those eloquent "apostates" about whom he'd spoken. We didn't talk at all after that, even though he lived just three doors down.

And, anyway, within a couple weeks, I started going to church with—Pam. She had moved to her oldest sister's house in Salt Lake and commuted down to Provo to work for the BYU summer program called "Academy for Girls," which her next oldest sister had overseen for years. Pam agreed to pick me up after work on Friday and take me to Salt Lake with her. We'd spend Saturday finding stuff to do up there, go to church Sunday, and come back to Provo together Monday. I slept on the living room floor at her sister's. Pam slept in the guest room. My sleeping in a building where a female also slept, no matter how many walls between us, violated BYU policy. But after the past eighteen months, I was unflapped by ecclesia-bureaucratic caprice anymore.

My first professors at BYU spanned the various teacherly species there. My first religion professor was Eldin Ricks, a stocky, flint-voiced, suit-wearing veteran, whose vision of Mormonism was an overspill of rural Utah, tinged with David O. McKay cosmopolitanism.

There wasn't much intellectual content, but he clearly loved memorization and had a gregarious, anecdotal style. He was a storyteller at heart, as when he told us about polygamist Ervil LeBaron giving a Book of Mormon to Pope Pius XII and demanding at gunpoint that the pontiff read it. Ricks graded generously, too, and since the last thing I needed was severe religiosity-for-academic-credit, I resolved to take as many classes from him as I could. The content of all of them was mostly the same, no matter the ostensible topic.

I had a rougher time with my short story teacher, George Bennion. Lithe, wiry, incisive, well-read as one could hope for, he challenged us and I dug in my heels, argued aesthetics with him as often as I could. I got an A- in the class, a notch lower than I thought I deserved. I explained in a letter home: "The minus signifies my blatant devil's advocacy in class discussion. I kept wrecking the teacher's explanations, writing on the walls of his expository towers. So I got an A- because I was too damn brilliant to give less to, but too cocky to give an A." My sense of mission, like an untucked t-shirt, was always showing. "Hapless, I spend time wandering about, the proverbial crazed artist, my crafts slung like an ax on my shoulder, looking for trees to fell. But I carry, too, a fat bag of seeds."

What I learned the most during that first term at BYU was less how to navigate different ways of teaching but more the conflicting ways one had to think. I wrote to Lawrence in July that the classes were no harder than Foothill's but the problem was "changing mental gears from one class to the next. For example, obviously a certain type of thought pattern and *way of thinking* is required with an Evolutionary Biology lecture that is utterly different from what is needed for a Book of Mormon class. One is thoroughly empirical, the other is rhetorical. I'm not knocking either of them, mind you, it's just rough slamming down your mental clutch all the time."

My best education that term came from the *New York Times Book Review* on the magazine racks at the BYU Bookstore. It was cheap and regular and opened dozens of new doors in my brain each week. It introduced me to so many authors, especially poets, most of them via its review of John Gardner's *On Moral Fiction*. I was so dogged in the quest for "moral" anything—beyond the sexual obsession that dictated that term's use in Mormonism—I just had to buy Gardner's book. I remember little now of his views, but everything about the modern poets he endorsed and quoted. My new trinity of literary inspirations, the ones whose books I hunted down and whose styles I tried to mimic, were Carl Dennis, Anne Sexton, and, more than anyone else, Linda Pastan. None of those three ever came up in any class I took at BYU. Yet the bankshot of the *Times* to Gardner to those three poets reset my intellectual billiard game from then on.

In Salt Lake City, Pam drove me to Mormon sacred sites, from Temple Square to Memory Grove to the Garden Park Ward to Brigham Young's grave. I also made her take me to bookstores with Mormon exotica. Sam Weller's Zion Book Store, of course. Utah Lighthouse Ministry, too, sometimes known by the name of its rare-book Xerox-reproduction imprint "Modern Microfilm," or, even more commonly, by the name of its proprietors: the Tanners. It was a sturdy old house on the west side whose front door on the main floor had a "Yes, We're OPEN" sign behind the screen door. There was another bookstore on State Street five blocks south of Temple Square called "The Reading Room" where I saw a Modern Microfilm copy of Joseph Smith's "Egyptian Alphabet and Grammar" in the window. The store was closed when I tried to go in, but there was an elderly couple inside arranging books on the shelves. I knocked on the window. The woman opened the door, smiling. "Are you an Allred?" she asked.

"No."

"He looks like an Allred, don't you think?" she asked the man. He agreed. I was savvy enough to know that the Allreds were a famous polygamous family with its own offshoot brand of Mormonism. The man started telling me about *their* church, "The Church of Christ, Patriarchal." I stood there for almost a half hour as he explained to his one-man congregation why their church was the correct one, peppering his sales pitch with an array of allegedly irrefutable quotations, resembling the missionary discussion tactics used on me before I joined *our* church. His proselytizing was a pittance, though, for admission to their store after hours. Between the Tanners and the Reading Room, not to mention the upstairs alcove at Sam Weller's, I spent much of my Deseret Towers custodial earnings on Joseph Smith's Egyptian Alphabet and Grammar, the Reed Peck Manuscript, Lucy Mack

Smith's memoir, John Whitmer's history, Bill Hickman's *Brigham's Destroying Angel*, B. H. Roberts's "Year Books," and Lamar Petersen's *Hearts Made Glad*, a survey of Smith's indulgence in light wines and beer. I also got lots of free "literature" from all three stores. Those booklets were a fountain of the mysterious doctrine I'd salivated for since my *Journal of Discourses* days. I was in Mormon studies heaven, or some backdoor mid-level degree of it, anyway.

Pam drove me around Utah County, too. The Provo Tabernacle, for example, where the tour guide was aglow about the recent acceptance of "the Sons of Cain" (his words) into the Mormon priesthood. Or Osmond Studios, where I literally bumped into supermodel Cheryl Tiegs. I wrote home about the place: "The studio is massive, dull, expensive, flashy, false, made of Brick and filled with Babylon. In short, like the Los Altos chapel during a youth dance, only bigger." The Freedom Festival for the Fourth of July—"half-baked," I wrote about it. Lots of other spots, from the Utah State Hospital to Sundance to quirky Mormon-themed eateries like Porter Rockwell's Steak House. I loved being with her on one hand and spouting off about our wanderings on the other.

Our biggest excursion came circuitously from Scott Kenney, founder and co-editor of *Sunstone*, an intellectual/spiritual/cultural savior of mine—and rejecter of my poetry—for the past three years. The magazine was holding an extravaganza, and Pam and I got invited because, as it turned out, Scott's brother was married to Pam's sister. That made us Sunstone family. About seventy people showed up at the McCune Mansion with its mirrored walls, frescoed ceilings, and marble everywhere, with guests including former senator Wallace Bennett, best known to me by his book *Why I Am a Mormon*. The soundtrack for the evening began with a string quartet and ended with a bluegrass band. The centerpiece of the gala was a reading of scenes from a play based on Gladys Farmer's *Elders and Sisters*, written by Orson Scott Card. I was, as we say, edified to see and stand between the same walls with the faces behind pages I revered.

I wasn't really thinking about those celebrities much, though. I was getting ready to ask Pam's dad for permission to marry her.

Just before the Sunstone event in July, I'd written a small testament about romance in my journal. Here it is, in all its self-conscious sentimentality, overwritten in the only way I knew to show gravity, veering from Joseph Smith to Fitzgerald via a Hallmark greeting card:

I have written much in this journal concerning love—the tender emotions I have felt for one, the unbridled passion for another, at times the deceptive lusts that have overtaken me. I have known much love in my life and in this I have been blessed. Many are not so fortunate as I. But the reader will note that the affections I have shown for others have rarely been reciprocal. When it has, other emotions, fierce ones, have fastened themselves like barnacles to the pure emotion of charity: jealousy, envy, intemperance, and so on. I regret these plagues of the spirit, but know that I am mere mortal, passionately so, intensely so; I and my associates often falter through life.

But as the day star, there arises in the life of a man a vision of a pure love, one that is impervious to the blackness of mortal night, for it carries with it the power of endless lives. And it is a reciprocal love, sparked at once by God, then kindled by the best feelings of two children until it burns of its own, never consuming, but giving light to others, flaming, churning, rising—it is eternal. Hearts are, as Paul said, "knit together," in a supernatural fashion. Often the material sorrows of the world and a desire to conquer the mortal realm, then, victorious, to part from it to a better, bind two hearts together.

But enough of philosophy—I love Pamela Bodell, simply and purely. I desire her to be my eternal wife and queen. Her love is strong, full of patience and all the gracious qualities that make womanhood noble. She is beautiful to look at, always happy to be with, and well, I love her and she loves me. There is hope in this and eternal joy. I pray God will always make me worthy of her. I love her.

Seeing how serious Pam and I were getting, Pam's parents talked to our old stake president about me. They asked him about my character: "Is he a good boy?" The president said the past was over and that he considered me, in fact, "a great man." On August 6, I asked Jim Bodell for his consent to marry Pam, she having already consented to me. He said yes, and I gushed all the more in my journal, calling the joy I felt "a chorusing of suns, the cool loveliness of many streams, holidays bursting forth with parades, brightly colored ribbons, tiers of lace, ancient delicate fragrances borne back through every age and on into eternity."

My BYU bishop, though, tried to close the spigot of my joy. Hearing I was engaged, he called me in for an interview. He scolded me for sleeping in the same house as a female as well as for attending church in Salt Lake. He told me to start sleeping only in my apartment and attending only his ward at BYU, with or without Pam. He dropped his heaviest bomb on our plan to marry outside the temple. I told him what our old stake president had said: if I found the "right one," we should marry civilly and get sealed later. This bishop insisted that counsel was wrong and that *he* was my actual priesthood leader now. Hence the old counsel was moot. He added that he had been my old stake president's bishop years earlier, which he said gave his counsel to me bonus authority. I was recalcitrant. This new prelate didn't know me from Adam and the old one knew me in many ways better than my own mom did. The interview ended on bad terms. But since I didn't need a temple recommend from him, I walked away light as a feather.

Besides, I was already settling into "my" (i.e., Pam's, i.e., her sister's) Salt Lake ward in the Sugar House neighborhood. I spoke in sacrament meeting, substitute-taught in youth Sunday school classes, and gradually assumed musical leadership in the ward. I became the ward choir director, conducting the group in music ranging from Mozart to Vaughan-Williams. I played special numbers in sacrament meeting, including a flamboyant piano improvisation on "Come, Come Ye Saints," blatantly imitating the piano effusions of Dino Kartsonakis on Kathryn Kuhlman's broadcasts. I paraded my eclectic musical dilettantism, which embraced Bach and Liberace with both arms.

At the end of August, fall semester began. My weekday schedule was somewhere between a monk's and a farmer's. I arose every morning at 5:00 for personal devotions, study, breakfast, shower, and dressing. I threw on my coat at 6:40 and walked in the chilly air for my 7:00 a.m. five-day-a-week Hebrew class on the northwest side of campus. Monday, Wednesday, and Friday I hustled to Contemporary American Literature class at 8:00, followed by Orchestration at 11:00. Tuesday and Thursday I had a Bible as Literature class at 9:00. I also took a composition lesson once a week with Merrill Bradshaw on

185

variable days. Monday through Fridays I continued janitoring at Deseret Towers from 1:00 p.m. to 5:00 p.m. And on Wednesday nights I had a two-hour New Testament class with Robert Matthews.

My second favorite class was my first one of the day: Hebrew. Rigorous, but nothing as severe as the language immersion of the Language Training Mission I'd already endured. I made stacks of handsomely calligraphed flash cards to boost my vocabulary, but the workout to even get to class invigorated me most, even left me feeling a tad invincible for just making it up the hill in the dark every morning as I softly sang hymns—or a little of my old reliable tongues-singing, duetting, in a way, with God.

My favorite class, though, the one that turned the dribble of John Gardner's book into a gushing fountain, was the American Lit class, taught by the heady, compassionate, freeform yet meticulous Stephen Tanner. I wrote home about him that October: "What other teacher comes to class from time to time breathless, having just written a marvelous essay for the edification of the class—he *reads* to us, in a brilliant review style, from endearment to indictment, all about the literature at hand. The class is always a pleasant depot of thought." A couple of times he brought his guitar to sing folk ballads. I had mine there, too, since I had to practice where and when I could. I sometimes got to jam with him.

The biggest letdown was Matthews's New Testament (Acts through Revelation) class. I had enrolled largely because I knew his landmark scholarly book on what was colloquially known as Joseph Smith's "Inspired Version" of the Bible, more formally known as the "Joseph Smith Translation." I wrote at the time:

> He's not very good, though I can't put my finger on the problem. The class occasionally serves as a forum for the "learned man" of our present distress. Last week, case in point, someone mentioned the "Inspired Version" and seventeen hands went up, returned missionaries and all, anxious to explain to Dr. Matthews the facts concerning the Inspired Version. Their ignorance was overpowering, their boldness exhilaratingly funny. Bro. Matthews did not say much, occasionally made a small correction, to which a dozen new hands would spring up, anxious to signal the instructor's misapprehensions. I almost fell off my seat laughing,

or maybe weeping, at these blustering bulls in the china shop, wholly ignorant of Bro. Matthews' pioneering work and authority.

Other moments were less embarrassing and more comedic. After Matthews finished explaining the Jewish calendar—how Passover, Pentecost, Feast of Tabernacles, and others were calculated—a young returned missionary in the front row, astonished at the complexity of it all, raised his hand and asked with a straight face, "Do the Jews know all that?"

Still, I wrote, "For all the entertainment, the class goes not deep enough for me." Unlike other Mormons in the class, I'd been raised like a lamb on the mother's milk of the New Testament. A few awkward exchanges in this class arose, as when, after Matthews noted that the Book of Acts had been written by Luke, someone asked him how we knew that. He said because the style and prologue explicitly connoted Luke's gospel. Then I asked, trying to get deeper into questions of authorship, dating, and so forth, "How do we know that Luke wrote the Gospel of Luke?" He said, "Because his name's on it!" The class laughed loudly. But not even the teacher got the point of my question, which was a serious one, not a vaudeville straight-man set up. So, in later semesters, it was back to Eldin Ricks whenever possible. That was how to get through my BYU religion requirements in the least number of moves. You know, Dad's "finesse."

I had enrolled in Orchestration hoping to learn how to expand my *Sonata in Three Tableaux* into a quasi-symphonic ballet. Dr. Bradshaw pushed me away from that ambition, though, and toward the aping of more adventurous styles. Thankfully, he also waived the department's rejection of my second-year theory training at Foothill and told me I didn't need to stay in the lower-division composition seminar as a "provisional" major (to which Professor Manookin had consigned me). Indeed, as I wrote home in October:

> Brother Bradshaw is pleased with me and I with him. There are here some silly composers, and in our seminars where new "works" are presented, if I dare open my mouth at all, I give terse critiques. Brother Bradshaw tells me in private, "I'm glad you said that," though he is more delicate in his in-class assessments. I'm not nasty, you understand, just don't shilly-shally around when I think it's gobbledygook.

My janitorial job was the greenhouse for both scholarship and creativity. Four hours of pushing a vacuum cleaner down hallways, scrubbing baseboards, wiping off elevator button plates, etc., freed my mind to write papers, short stories, and even the occasional poem. Music, too. I'd lay sections out in my mind, concoct rhythms, assemble pitch collections, and even invent new "experimental" ideas for compositions. Being forced to do "mindless" labor freed me to do mindful labor. I looked forward every day to that afternoon shift where I could process in my head all I'd been injected with before noon.

I finally felt like a card-carrying apprentice in Mormon arts when two things happened. One was that three drawings of mine appeared in the First Annual Mormon Illustration show in the main gallery of the Harris Fine Arts Center—BYU's arts showcase building—during most of the month of September. The second was word from *Sunstone* in October that they were at last going to publish a submission I'd made to them, a short story called "Man at the Bar." It was an almost squeamishly sentimental story based on my couple of months as a German missionary. But it was a turning point: my first published prose that wasn't a letter to the editor or a quote in the local paper.

Instead of staying in Utah for our wedding, Pam and I decided to have it in the Los Altos stake center I'd helped build with Pam's dad a year and a half earlier. Although most of Pam's friends and family lived in Salt Lake, having our nuptials elsewhere seemed best. The taint of staging a non-temple wedding verged on scarlet, just as my BYU bishop had warned. But we were determined to follow my old stake president's counsel, that is, to tamp down temptation between two vigorous, cuddly Mormons instead of inviting it in the house every day for who-knows-how-long of a wait. Besides, the Los Altos stake center was not really neutral ground. For us, it was sacred ground.

Pam's dad's bishop conducted the ceremony in a half-full chapel the night of December 28. The two of us recited quotes from the Brownings' *Sonnets from the Portuguese* as our vows. A reception followed in the basketball-court—what Mormons call the "cultural hall"—adjacent to the chapel. The court was ringed by thirty

My drawing of Mormon apostle Orson Pratt, featured at
BYU's first annual Mormon Illustration Show, 1978.

Christmas trees, which, three days after Christmas, were on their
way to the dump before we gave them this swan song. The dance
band was a jazz quartet led by my Celebration of Spring cohort,
Rich, to whom I'd dedicated my *American Essay* string quartet three
years earlier. Both my mom and dad were there, along with my
half-brothers, Dad's third wife, Mom's third husband, and an as-
sortment of everything from hippies to high councilors, stoners to
teetotalers, a menagerie of my collective pasts, lovingly nurtured by
Pam and her family in a living proclamation of forgiveness and an
embrace of the Mormon street's proverbial other side.

The first two months of 1979 Pam and I rented a small house
near Pam's sister in Sugar House. Its owners, like birds, migrated
south every winter and agreed to let us live in their house, use their
water, electricity, and even phone for less money than I had paid for

189

my half bedroom in a student apartment in Provo. We crammed our new sloshy, slightly vertigo-inducing waterbed into a room barely big enough to hold it. Because I now lived so far away from BYU, I had to quit my janitor job at the dorms and only commute south to Provo three days a week in the new Subaru Pam had bought right before we got engaged.

When March arrived, we moved into a four-room third-floor apartment on an elm-lined street two blocks south of BYU campus. The majestic Mt. Timpanogos sat at eye-level through the bedroom window facing north. Our Sugar House bishop had urged us to ignore the church's edict against any "artificial" form of birth control until we were really ready to parent children. We followed his counsel for a few months until, having kept plants alive during the interim, we felt we could probably do the same with a child. Pam skipped the pill for a month and instantly became an expectant mom. It was her ZCMI wages keeping us afloat, though—after we'd sold her Subaru and opted not to own either a television or a phone. The laundromat next door had a pay phone, which we used when we had to make a call out. But no one could make a call in, which was an unforeseen delight.

The members of our new ward, the Provo 9th Ward, included my old hero Hugh Nibley, who taught one of three sections of Sunday school. To accommodate hordes of visiting fans, his section was held in the chapel, not a regular classroom. I attended it now and then, but his style was to mutter at the pulpit, virtually never looking up, and remaining as distracted from his acolytes as a mid-level potentate. Addicted to conversing in class, I almost always went with Pam to one of the smaller, Nibley-immune sections where one's mind could breathe easier.

BYU's president, Dallin Oaks, also attended the ward. He spent most of every sacrament meeting leafing through his scriptures, reading silently, then looking up and moving his lips, apparently memorizing scriptures. How did I know that? Because I was the sacrament meeting chorister and sat on the stand looking over the congregation. My conducting of the hymns got lots of compliments, largely because I conducted more like the casual but flamboyant conductors of my former churches and less like the pseudo-mechanical choristers who populated vernacular Mormondom. One more adaptation of worship I was able to subtly inject into a batch of lifetime Latter-day Saints. I still had no priesthood, though, which made church all the more awkward. But it enhanced the case for not having a phone: I couldn't be called to do things that I'd have to declare myself ineligible for.

My real devotional life was at the university. That first semester of 1979 I took a course in women's literature from the legendary Elouise Bell. All semester we read from female essayists, poets, and short story authors, along with Austen's *Pride and Prejudice* (my second journey through the book). While the discussions were free-form, Professor Bell's blend of taciturn expression and dry joviality took some getting used to. She seemed to like me, though, one of the three men in a class of thirty, especially when I used the phrase "lip-chewing thoughtfulness" about Austen, a construct I'd cribbed from a recent *New Yorker* movie review by my female prose idol, Pauline Kael.

I finally enrolled in a required Book of Mormon class. After two class periods in a section for returned missionaries, I quit. I'd come to loathe the blustery one-upmanship of guys—the class was all guys but one—selling their proficiency in that book of scripture that I knew the least and never much liked. I switched to a section *not* for returned missionaries. The gender balance was better, as was the teacher, psychologist Bruce Brown, who framed much of our discussion around human behavior and who also, coincidentally, was addicted to Hugh Nibley. He even said one time: "I'm sorry if it sounds like I'm quoting Nibley all the time. Which reminds me of something Nibley once said ..."

For my music major, I took counterpoint, composition, and second-semester orchestration. The last of these was the best, or at least the most mind-torquing. Taught by David Sargent, it was a jolly but learned indoctrination in the avant-garde and experimentalist traditions of the latter-half of the twentieth century. Beyond the techniques of Ligeti and Penderecki—the musical mystifiers of my adolescence—we went merrily into the most playful sonic explorations. For one class about graphic scores (free from conventional notation), Sargent invited us to bring our own instruments. I brought my old popcorn pan, which I half filled with water, and a wooden spoon to strike it with, then tilt it, so the pitch would slide up and down at will. This united my lifelong craving for weirdness with what I loved about Mormonism's visionary origins and early teachings. I began to see the forging of the future Mormon music as requiring a degree of fantasy at its core. With that idea and an attendant zeal in my heart, I wrote these pieces during the year's first four months:

— *Epitaphium* (alto saxophone with mixed chamber ensemble)
— "And There Shall Come Forth a Rod" (voice and piano)
— *Blues I* (piano, two players—one at the keys, the other at the strings with a Mason jar)
— *Uranos* (mixed chamber ensemble)
— *Epitaphium II* (piano, clarinet, and two radios)
— Variations (oboe and piano)
— *Gigue* (guitar and flute)
— *Sea Piece* (three alto flutes)
— *Humoresque for Emmett Kelly* (choir, piano, three television sets)

Along the way, a few students and I formed a club. We thought we'd call it the "BYU Association of Student Composers," but decided against anything that parochial. So we called it the *National Association of Student Composers*. Because, after all, underpinning Mormonism was the belief that it would someday fill and dominate the world. So why not the nation?

We held the first meeting in a basement apartment on Ash Avenue on the evening of April 9, 1979. We wrote a constitution, elected officers, and planned a first recital of club members' works. Four days later, the president, Stan Zenk, addressed the group in a music theory classroom in the Harris Fine Arts Center. He explained:

> I am convinced that the Lord is behind our enthusiasm and feel that his hand was in the planting of the ideas to form such an organization. ... It can be a tool for sharpening our God-given talents to serve him and mankind, as also it should be a place where charity and service can teach us to consecrate our lives to the building up of the kingdom.

He waxed on, calling for love and cooperation, with musical experimentation as the foundation for establishing "Zion," as Mormons called their version of Utopia. He closed with this thought:

To the Lord and his purposes we dedicate our efforts in making this organization a tool in his hands and subject ourselves and our talents to his shaping influence and plans. May we be worthy so that his spirit may give place and meaning to our efforts and to our art.

We met weekly at first, discussing works in progress, analyzing favorite pieces, and exhorting one another to lead the nation in compositional craft. In the midst of this ferment, I veered further into esotericism. I wrote in my journal that I now found a direct path from my speaking in tongues at the front end of the decade to the sonic avant-garde in which I was now setting up shop. "Both forms [of praise] may be inspired of the Spirit and profound, but to many hearers unintelligible. True praise must find avenues of experimentation [and], as a corollary, all experimentation is a form of praise."

To match my rhetoric, I spent the next two months writing a musical manifesto, a four-movement "theatre piece" called *Relics*, scored for seven performers: soprano, flute, B-flat clarinet, violin, cello, piano, and percussion. All players had to wear translucent Halloween masks that portrayed human faces "smiling blandly but resembling no one in particular." They also had to wear clothing of all types, some "dressy," some casual, but with the soprano wearing a floor-length white dress. A long rectangular table with seven candles on it sat at the front of the stage.

The piece traveled a narrative arc of sorts, from Jesus' nativity to his burial, with each movement evoking a revered Christian relic along the way:

1. The Holy Manger at Saint Mary's
2. The Holy Stairs at Sancta Sanctorum
3. The Nail and Thorns at Santa Cruce
(and, after an interlude that dreamily evoked Bach's *Christ Lag in Todesbanden*)
4. The Holy Shroud of Turin

The musical notation of *Relics* drifted among loose insinuations of pitch and rhythm, interrupted by the occasional "normal" notation. Stylistic scraps drawn from multiple centuries and styles—my nod to the Mormon gospel's "latter-days" eclecticism—permeated the piece's musical canvas. Performers' actions ranged from lighting

193

candles to throwing dice on the floor, not to mention performing on their instruments in exotic, even transgressive, ways. All players spoke fragments of scripture or liturgy, mostly in Latin, sometimes into their instruments, with the soprano vocalizing only during the first movement and the last, a kind of hypnotic induction based on a slow, Gregorian-style chanting of a melodic fragment in B-Lydian mode, as all the players successively leave the stage, though continue the chant offstage. The references in imagery, sound, text, and even lighting, would surround and envelop the audience, I hoped, as though they'd been plunged into a constellation of symbols.

I worked on the piece from the forming of the NASC in April till I finished its inked manuscript on June 12. I showed it to Bradshaw the next day. He called it "profound," and I wrote about his comment in my journal: "I could not ask for more, unless it is an understanding of my ideas on the part of audiences."

The rest of the summer offered more custodial work, cleaning the rooms of co-eds who'd graduated. My tasks became one more sidebar to my formal education. I learned, for example, how much matted hair, carpet stains, and offhand odors it took to create a dazzling pair of roommates for whom the campus was a catwalk. I also learned that seminary teachers have sex, too. During the LDS Church Educational System conference in August, I was vacuuming a fifth-floor dorm room, looked out the window, and, in the building next to mine, which housed seminary and Institute teachers, saw a naked couple doing it in a dorm room two floors down. I assumed they were married. Read: I hoped they were married. But, honestly, I don't think they were married. It gave me my first experience of seeing other people have sex live. Bolstering my "worthiness" quotient, I averted my eyes. After a while.

While janitoring I dreamt up more experimental pieces. July through August I composed:

— The first of a set of piano pieces called *Ländler for Albert Einstein*, growing out of my brief obsession that year with science via the likes of Lewis Thomas, Richard Selzer, and, well, Einstein.

— *Epitaphium IV*, for soprano, tenor, piano, toy piano, percussion, and chorus—continuing this series of morbid pieces, this one surrounding the notion of the sudden death of infants. The piece required the

S-hall flounders in flood

Universe photo by Bill Slater

Michael Hicks, a junior music composition major from Los Altos, Calif., sweeps the water from the flood that occurred Monday afternoon after a pump in the air conditioning system broke down at S Hall, Deseret Towers.

As janitor cleaning up a flood at Brigham Young University, 1979.

stage to be filled with cribs. (For those keeping score, I didn't write *Epitaphium III*, for two sopranos, two B-flat clarinets, bass clarinet, two percussionists, and piano, until September. But it was percolating in my mind as I wrote its sequel.)

— The first two of a solo piano set called *Four Beasts*, each movement of which was to represent a beast drawn from the various beastly quartets mentioned in Ezekiel, Daniel, and the Book of Revelation.

Come fall, I got to retire from my custodial career. The music department hired me on a fifteen-hour-a-week contract to be Tom

195

Durham's teaching assistant in first- and fourth-semester theory classes—four hours a week in classrooms and, allegedly, eleven hours a week preparing for those other four. Added to that windfall, the music publisher Theodore Presser had created a scholarship for budding composers, and I got the BYU version of it: $900 for tuition, and $300 for books, which in my case mostly meant records from the Discount Records store next to the campus's main entrance. That $1,200 was supposed to be matched by BYU, giving me $2,400 total. But, without telling Presser, BYU reneged, giving me only $300 of Presser's money and none of their own. The reason? Because no one at BYU was allowed to receive more financial awards from any source than were given in the Spencer W. Kimball Scholarship, advertised as the highest award on campus—full tuition plus $300. Since I already was on a full tuition academic scholarship, I couldn't get more than 300 of the Presser dollars and none of the matching $1,200 BYU had contracted with Presser. The college pocketed the remainder of Presser's money and held tight to their own, which was technically mine. The episode gave me more sideways education in bedrock Mormon behavior, none of which they teach in religion classes.

My best teachers continued to guide my private evolution. I continued my studies in music theory, counterpoint, and composition. A music history course, though, pricked me into a new ardency for detective work, a logical sequel to the dumpster diving I'd done as a boy in Los Altos. I started browsing the library harder than ever, digging through old periodicals, interlibrary-loaning esoteric British stuff, even plying my long-decayed German to try and read things in their original tongue. I wrote a term paper on the history of glass harmonicas and thought it should be published. My teacher disagreed. (He was right.) But I had a new addiction: solving music-historical puzzles in relative solitude.

By October, Pam was feeling the baby tumbling in her, though she continued working full time at ZCMI, taking enough Bendectin to keep her from vomiting on the merchandise. That same month, I wrote three of my most important works yet.

— *Rain Music* for seven players—a sonorous piece designed to be just above the threshold of hearing, which included radios set on white noise and popcorn seeds dropped in glass bowls with other players drumming their fingers on them.

— *Two and Half Minute Talk*—based on the Mormon tradition of short children's talks in Sunday school bearing that name. This version included tape loops running on multiple reel-to-reel recorders, live reciters, and instrumentalists who imitated them.

— *Lullabye for Rachel*—a setting for tenor and piano of Linda Pastan's poem "Rachel" about the naming of her daughter. If we had a girl, Pam and I had decided to name our daughter that and this song honored that decision. I didn't have a boy's song, so we kind of hoped for a girl.

In these three works I felt I'd fused the nether regions of what I knew of "avant-garde" with the surface features of Mormon church life, from the Sacred Grove of Joseph Smith's first vision to the pulpit in a suburban chapel. At the same time, one could argue that I was writing the soundtrack to the psychodramas I'd lived through in this new, beloved church of spiritually stained glass.

For those of us who craved it, serious "culture" blossomed everywhere, from shelves to stage, even in Provo, Utah. *My* Provo, at least. Besides assigned readings for classes, that fall I read Bonhoeffer's *Cost of Discipleship*, Matthiessen's *Snow Leopard*, Hellman's *Scoundrel Time*, Thomas's *Medusa and the Snail*, and Selzer's *Mortal Lessons*, alongside a steady diet of the *New Yorker*, the *New York Times Book Review*, *Dialogue*, *Sunstone*, and texts from the Nag Hammadi scrolls. Pam and I even got to see Michael Tolaydo's one-man performance of *St. Mark's Gospel* at the Provo Tabernacle. But I read no "Mormon" books and saw no "Mormon" shows, because my understanding of Mormonism continued to be that all truth, in whatever form, boils down—or up—to Mormonism. I wrote passages like these in my journal:

Which is more "beautiful"? The temples of the Greeks as they once stood, complete, or their ruins? Broken and worn away by the strong elements?

Art must consist in connotations—ruins and relics suggest more than fresh things, new things; they suggest both the former glory they possessed and their whole history since—the Sphinx connotes more for a nose broken off.

197

Our notion of proportion, balance, the whole concept of strict classicism, is all wrong for these last days. Our art must reflect the summation of an earthful of cultures risen up and turned to dust again. Our art must stretch back into Eden and stretch forward into New Eden, all the while spanning what's between, borrowing, dabbling, collecting pieces of the past like a child gathering shells by the sea.

On and on, would-be aphorisms plunging like rockslides into my journals, papers, and letters. It was as if I were hitchhiking again, only now through the whole world of culture.

By year's end we'd faithfully attended church, paid tithing, kept the Word of Wisdom, and all the other assorted deeds that define "worthiness" in our faith. I enjoyed church meetings, but, as I wrote home four days before Christmas, "I doubt I have said ten words in a public meeting, other than to pray, [in all the time] I have lived in Provo." Meanwhile, I wrote, "I take refuge in my studies. I have been devoted to my classes with a burning zeal."

That summer, my Los Altos bishop had assured me he had "written" a letter to get my blessings restored. Pam and I teased each other that he never said he'd *sent* it. Sure enough, no letter of the sort reached our new bishop until the first of December—about six months after we'd been told it was written. But our Provo bishop told me he didn't need it. He had proceeded on his own to process my case. Next stop: my stake president, a favorite Mormon literata of mine, Richard Cracroft, chairman of the English department and co-editor of my then-favorite Mormon anthology, *A Believing People*. I wrote home about my session with him:

We met in his school office (he had said to just drop by and see him there). I had spent all morning watching my tongue—I didn't want to make a bad impression by a grammatical slip-up. Unlike the other authorities who have interviewed me, he did *not* say, "I don't want to dredge all this up or go into any great detail …" etc. No, he wanted *great detail*, dates, how many times I ever "did it" with Ann, all names, all facts pertaining, including items I had not dwelt on for at least two years. He wrote down notes with a blue Flair-pen on a sheet of typing paper, as though preparing a brief for a retrial, and not at all as though contemplating forgiving me. But, at the end of the hour, he simply said, "I sense by the Spirit that you have fully repented of all those activities, and that you are ready to have a full restoration of all blessings. And I will send my recommendation to that effect to the brethren." Then, he took a more philosophical tone and wanted to discuss just what it is that gets people mixed up with the Anns of the world. Then we parted.

Three weeks later, I got a note in the mail from Elder Mark E. Petersen. He wanted me to call his office and schedule an appointment. Since we had no home phone, Tom Durham let me place the long distance call from his BYU office. I made the appointment for January 16, 2:00 p.m.

My first live encounter with an apostle and it was to beg for mercy.

10. THE BOOK OF REVELATION

I knew a few things about Elder Petersen. He was the apostle in charge of ferreting out twentieth-century Mormon polygamists. He was the author of the *Church News*'s back page editorials, a weekly quasi-canon-update for many Mormons. He was the author of that tract that helped convert me, *Which Church Is Right?* He'd also written many slim books declaring doctrine and giving advice, shelves full of which sat on one wall of his office in the squat old Church Office Building in the shadow of the newer white skyscraper beside it. Unlike that newer one, this older building had no murals or visitors areas or snapshotty vistas of the city block it sat on. It was all business, the historic site of offices for authorities who were closest to its own age. And Elder Petersen was close to the top of the seniority scorecard.

I was awed by his experience, his authority, and now, entering his office, of his sheer persona. He was old, of course—one couldn't be a senior apostle without a certain antiquity. But he was also big, stern, and weathered. He moved like a lumbering robot who'd done this task how many thousand times before and knew he'd have to keep doing it till the day he died. The interview was routine, scripted, honed. I felt like an enemy he was trying to vanquish unless I could show I'd switched sides. He had almost nothing to say about my particular circumstance or Ann's, but verbally paced through a well-trod corridor of questions one "had to" ask Mormon fundamentalists to squelch them.

He asked if I sustained the authorities of the church. "Yes." Did I sympathize with any other claimants to that authority? "No." He asked a few doctrinal questions, whose import I didn't quite understand. For example, he asked me, "Do you believe that Jesus was married?"

"It had never occurred to me that he wasn't."

"Are you willing to accept that it is the doctrine of this church that Jesus was *not* married?"

"Well, Elder Orson Hyde said that Jesus married Mary Magdalene, Mary of Bethany, *and* Martha."

This angered Elder Petersen. He pounded his fist on his desk and said, loudly, "Orson Hyde didn't know what he was talking about!"

He asked me again if I was willing to accept that Jesus being *unmarried* was "the doctrine of this church."

Frankly, what did I care? My prosperity was on the line over a snippet of history with dubious relevance. "Yes," I told him. A few more standard temple recommend questions, and he signed the form authorizing the restoration of my blessings, invited Pam in, walked over to my chair, laid his hands on my head, and uttered the formal restoration ordinance, word by word.

Beyond the return of my priesthood and eligibility for the temple, two things had just happened. First, two apostles—Petersen and Hyde—had just cancelled each other out in my mind. I was now free to believe whatever I wanted on that point—and maybe other points, too, whenever mutual cancellations took place. Second, I realized that what made Jesus' nuptials such a big deal was that if he *were* married, then he would have had children, and there were people who could claim their descent from Jesus as the source of some special kind of authority. (Which some early Mormon apostles had done, including an ancestor of Ann.) That latter thought suited my instinct for trivia. But the former one helped remold my sense of the humanity of even the most self-assuredly divine humans. It was as if God had slammed his own fist down on the celestial desk and said, "None of you really knows what he's talking about. Next."

Ten days later, Pam and I were in a Salt Lake Temple sealing room. Pam was notably pregnant, and we had to explain ourselves about that. The ordinance was short and to the point. We had a small party uptown when it was over.

But we had no second honeymoon. We had no money. We had no car. And I had my senior composition recital on February 21. The graduation requirement of a senior recital was to mount a live portfolio of one's best—and presumably latest—compositions. I chose, though, to make it a narrative of my compositional quest, from

Handwritten title and first page (of forty) from the last composition written while an undergraduate at BYU— completed on January 26, 1980, the day Pam and I were sealed for time and eternity in the Salt Lake Temple.

Foothill trifles through the pieces that included radios and televisions to my capstone, the premiere of *Relics*. My main anxieties: (1) would the performance of this staged anthology come off spic and span, and (2) what would my in-laws think of the fringier repertoire? The first worry was quelled by the default reliability of musicians, especially ones you've befriended. The players and singers all came, played and sung their hearts out. The second worry's answer was best distilled in the comment of one brother-in-law, who after the stunned silence

Promotional photo for my senior composition recital, February 1980.

that followed *Rain Music I*, said to me, excitedly, "I don't know what that was, but I like it!" When *Relics* ended, with the stage empty except for seven candlesticks burning onstage—the only light in the hall except for the EXIT signs—the wait for a reaction was excruciating and delicious at once. No one was sure what to do. A couple of claps finally sounded, swelling into an avalanche of applause. The lights went on, the crowd stood up, and I bowed deeply.

Three weeks later, two more things came due: my last term paper and our first child. As though fulfilling the prophecy of my song, Rachel arrived on March 14, which was also the due date of my second-semester music history paper. Because of Pam's arduous forty-hour labor and delivery, the teacher gave me a one-day extension to get the paper in. Thus began the first all-nighter of my life since spending the night with Joyce and Madeline on the creek bank in Los Altos. Typing breathlessly on a cheap Brother manual type-writer no bigger than a shoebox, I got the prose down, then glued in the examples, and marked-up photocopied excerpts from the third movement of Luciano Berio's *Sinfonia*, whose spoken refrain "Keep going!" had been my mantra all year. I turned in the paper at the next class meeting, in which I fought to stay awake. Then followed the wakeful nights with our new daughter.

With my restoration of blessings, temple sealing, senior recital, first childbirth, and last term paper all checked off my list, I was ready to officially close the books on the 1970s. Just one more task loomed in front of me: the final exam in my last semester of En-glish. That semester I'd done my first writing-on-demand in "blue books." So far in this class I'd had to write three impromptu essays. The first was on Edward Arlington Robinson's "Richard Cory." The teacher loved it, red-penned superlatives in the margins, "specific and insightful," "excellent depth," and so on. My second essay was a critique of John Holt's "How Teachers Make Children Hate Read-ing." The teacher wrote that I had "a talent for incisive and biting wit." My third essay was on William Cullen Bryant's "To a Water-fowl," on which I ramped up that incisive, biting wit under the title "One Man's Ornithology." I didn't like the poem. I was too steeped in Dickinson's terse flair and all the heady modernist strategies I'd picked up in Stephen Tanner's class. My teacher wrote, "You are very effective in your ability to squelch." But he wished I'd now start to "experiment with some variety in tone and style." A gauntlet laid down like a velvet glove.

The final in-class essay assignment, it turned out, was not to write about someone else's poetry or prose but about a personal experi-ence. Anything that had heft in our lives. By now, I had a repertoire of flickers, glimpses, excursions, every God-awful or God-supreme scene I've been talking about since the first chapter of this book. But here is what I wrote, my own improvised lullaby for Rachel:

When the doctor says, "It's time," you know it isn't quite. But the body waits for no man. The flesh knows nothing, sometimes, of its brothers in incarnation—emotion, thought, the will. It becomes a law unto itself. And when you've waited the requisite months and you've spent all day in the labor room drinking Coke to keep you awake, your hands greasy from take-out chicken, and the doctor comes in and says, "It's time," there is nothing for you but to wipe your hands and get into your paper shower cap and green smock and follow the nurse and the doctor and the mechanical bed with the numbed woman in it into the dim gray air of the delivery room.

It wasn't right, I thought: hospital rooms must be brightly lit, as if aglow with the purity of a sainted Hippocrates. But this one was dim, the bare, receding afternoon light gleaming dully on the glass cabinets and monitor handles and bed chrome. The room was quiet, relieved yet businesslike, the instruments and bottles and props all erect at attention. I looked around and around at the greyness and the greenness, the smocks and the paint, as I counted aloud for my wife, knowing that, for me it wasn't time. I began to—I had to—let my imagination seduce me away from all of this. I let my eyes drop, studying the waxy green linoleum, letting it suggest whatever it would: it seemed, I thought, like an immaculate lawn worn down to the bone, like the floor of the cemetery, the catacombs, the tombs, the souls of the dead of the whole green earth worn away, washed away by the life and sense and innocence that were flooding into this place. Such were my idle, too-literary thoughts—one has to have them—because the reality of blood- and fluid-soaked linens and the lovely woman strapped and propped at the legs, pushing and puffing our child from between them, was too cruel, too harsh a miracle for me to persist in sensibility. I grasped her hand tightly, squeezed it, kept counting for her. But as her drugs had dulled the sharpness of pain into a vague, wearying pressure, I let my own visions and fancy mesmerize away the bluntness of this creation.

When our daughter came, I heard that slipping sound and the flush of liquid on the table—but no cry. I expected that cry, waited for it, because I have seen all the movies and I knew it should come. But there came only a soft gurgle, primordial, a struggling at speech. My wife sighed and the doctor and nurse washed the creamy film from the baby in a small, green porcelain basin by the darkening windows. This, our child, was here in the real world, but I sensed it only vaguely, as "through a glass darkly" from out of the world of shadows, possibilities, guesses, the ghosts of the future. She had emerged from the caverns of the body—yet I was now lost in my own. When they placed her in my arms, wrapped in fresh linen, I looked long into the great half-shut eyes, looking perhaps for a welcome back into reality, a sign of recognition and of acceptance. But it never came. I sensed she and I were each as bewildered as the other at the strange newness of things—she with the opening of her senses, I with the shutting away of mine. We both might have dreamt it all.

Two weeks later, when her mother was asleep and I not yet ready for bed, I took our daughter out of her polished, quilted crib, and carried her into the living room. It was dark, darker than the hour she had entered the world, but as I laid her down on the big pillow by the bookshelf, I could still make out her features: her eyes were clearer now, the skin soft and unwrinkled, the ears now faintly resembling the shape of my own. Somehow—I can't explain why—as I sat beside her in the dying light of that quiet, shuttered room, I felt the frustration of nine and a half months begin to narrow, to sharpen, then diminish into what seemed like pin pricks at the corners of my eyes. The tears were quick, gone in a few moments. But I knew it was real, it was time: I'd cried for the love of my little girl. You see, I'd wondered when I was going to do that.

The hour was up and I laid my blue book on the teacher's desk and walked out of the Jesse Knight Building into the warm Utah air.

I breathed deep and stared up at the Wasatch mountains leaning over the east side of campus. They were at their greenest. Not the stern evergreen of the hills south of San Jose, through which I'd driven a hundred times. And not the fluorescent-lit institutional green of the delivery room I'd written about. They were more of a perky lime Jell-O color that would last a few weeks then fade until they finally reddened in the fall. I couldn't help but think of how beautiful they were—optimistic, even, if beauty can be that. At the same time, I thought of how I couldn't wait to drive away from them.

By then the map of my soul's future had been drawn. I had been denied to three of the five graduate music programs I'd applied for. One of the two that accepted me, University of Texas at Austin, offered a pittance of a scholarship that would barely blunt the blade of tuition. But that school was fifth on my wish list, anyway. The other one that accepted me was my top choice, the exotic intellectual harbor I kept reading about in our Eric Salzman modern music textbook and whose faculty composers I kept listening to on a CRI album I'd bought at Discount Records: University of Illinois at Urbana-Champaign. Cage had been there. Partch had been there. Ben Johnston, Partch's apprentice, was there now. On and on. Serialists, conceptual sound artists, computer musicians, microtonalists, mixed media composers. I had a crush on the eccentric vibe-ology of the place and all the boundary lines it had laid down or rototilled in the landscape of wild Americana.

And I knew, then as now, that that was Mormonism to me, the faith I'd discovered on the side of the road in high school. The one about divine eclecticism. The one about radical social experimentation. The one about "the pursuit of excellence." The improvisational hurtling toward a future that God was unfolding. I was now, as Cat Stevens sang, irrevocably "on the road to Find Out." This new Mormon potion of belief had been, if not injected, at least slow dripped into the "faith of my fathers." But, unlike that old-time religion, this new-time religion was, at last, "good enough for me." And I was quite sure by now, praise the Lord, I was good enough for it.

We packed up the U-Haul and headed for Illinois, the state from which Brigham Young's followers had fled in 1846 to what would become Utah. I was now determined to reclaim it for myself, baptizing my mind in the miraculous avant-weirdness I was born for. It was time. I was ready to leave. The way I was always leaving.

ABOUT THE AUTHOR

Michael Hicks was a Professor of Music at Brigham Young University for thirty-five years. Among the books he has authored are *Mormonism and Music: A History*, *The Mormon Tabernacle Choir: A Biography*, and *Spencer Kimball's Record Collection: Essays on Mormon Music*. He has also contributed to the *Encyclopedia of Popular Music of the World* and the *Oxford Handbook of Mormonism* and has published in many journals, including *Journal of the American Musicological Society* and *Journal of Aesthetic Education*. He is a three-time recipient of the ASCAP-Deems Taylor Award for his writing about music and as editor of the journal *American Music*. He and his wife, Pam, are the parents of four children and have fifteen grandchildren.